Bones in the Basement
Surviving the S.K. Pierce Victorian Mansion

Edwin Gonzalez & Lillian Otero's Story

By

Joni Mayhan

Also by Joni Mayhan:

Lightning Strikes (Angels of Ember Dystopian Trilogy– Book 1)
Ember Rain (Angels of Ember Dystopian Trilogy – Book 2)
Angel Storm (Angels of Ember Dystopian Trilogy – Book 3)
The Soul Collector
Ghostly Defenses – A Sensitive's Guide for Protection
The Spirit Board (Winter Woods – Book 1)
The Labyrinth (Winter Woods – Book 2)

Bones in the Basement. *Copyright 2014 by Joni Mayhan. All rights reserved. No part of this book may be used or reproduced in any manner without written permission from the author.*

This is a true story, however some of the names have been changed or omitted. Any resemblances to actual places, people (living or dead), or incidents that happened that are not listed are purely coincidental. Prior written approval has been obtained from all parties who are mentioned in this book.

Acknowledgements

Like many others, I was mesmerized by the gothic Victorian on the corner of West Broadway and Union Streets. It felt like it was calling to me, wanting me to come take a closer look. Little did I know how impactful it would be to my life, as well as the lives of the people around me.

It's more than a house. You feel it the moment you walk through the door. It has a restless soul and a need to be appreciated. It has a story to tell and I did my best to honor that.

I couldn't have written this without the help from many key players in this saga. Thank you to Edwin Gonzalez and Lillian Otero for sharing your story with me. No one should have to witness the horrors you lived through, but I'm thankful you survived and will continue on to live your lives.

Through the writing of this book, I interviewed many people who were a part of this story. I'd like to thank them for their willingness to share their experiences. Many thanks to the following people: Eleanor Gavazzi, Marian King, Pam Meitzler, Mark Veau, Thomas D'Agastino, Heather Anderson, Michael Cram, Marion Luoma, Tina Aube, Derek Cormier, William Wallace, Sara Christopher, Barb Wright (for editing), Frank Grace and Jason Baker (photographs), Michael Robishaw, Kimberly Huertas, Sandy MacLeod, Jeff Bartley, Lucky Belicamino, Kayle Boyce, Barbara Williams, Andrew Lake, Terri Harlow, Marc Arvilla, Lauren Sheridan, Mike Galante, Peter Lovsco, and Carl Johnson.

The S.K. Pierce Victorian Mansion is falling in quick decline. I don't know what its fate will be, but my hope is that the souls that linger there finally find peace.

For Edwin and Lillian

Photo courtesy of Frank Grace (Trig Photography)

Forward

by

Thomas D'Agostino

In April of 2006, Arlene and I set out on an adventure that would take us through several years of incredible discoveries and occurrences in regard to the world of the paranormal. The adventure came to be known as The Victorian in Gardner, Massachusetts.

To state that the mansion is haunted seems rather under whelming in comparison to the actual amount of activity within its walls. In the course of our investigations and visits to The Victorian in the past eight years, Arlene and I have come to regard the stately 1875 mansion as the most haunted house in New England, if not further.

Had we not had the opportunity to experience the astonishing magnitude of activity that whiles within the mansion, we would have passed most of the stories over as a bit of exaggerated hype or imagination gone wild in a place that truly puts one's senses on immediate alert. The flows of those who still bide time long after their mortal tenure on earth is constant and ever present.

From the very beginning it seemed the ground was doomed to negativity. S.K. Pierce displaced a home in order to construct his across from his factory where he could reportedly watch over his workers. Negative influx gained a foothold over the decades, gathering impetus with each new occupant.

The ghosts of The Victorian know who you are and why you are there. In many cases, they are not pleased with your presence and are not afraid to lash out at you for intruding upon their domain. Whether they are trapped within the walls of The Victorian, unable to break through the barrier of eternal wandering and peace is not known. What is known is that they seemed to have collected in the house where they once tenanted in life and frequently cross the veil between our world and theirs at will. There is a powerful force that resides within The Victorian. It is this force that keeps pounding at the soul of the building and its living occupants. Those who wish to remain but are constantly at bay with those who will always remain.

Thomas D'Agastino
Author of *Haunted Massachusetts*

Chapter 1

The boy stared up at the creepy old house, feeling a lump grow in his throat.

The other kids wanted to break in and play a game of hide-and-seek. He wasn't sure he wanted to. Something about the house troubled him.

When he drove past it with his mother, he always glanced up at the dark windows, feeling like someone was watching him. Nobody had lived in the house for as long as he could remember, but everybody knew about it. It was the haunted Victorian mansion.

He went to school with a girl who used to live next door. She talked about seeing faces at the windows and lights blinking off and on all during the night. She told him that a man once burned to death in the house when he spontaneously combusted, and how his ghost still roamed the shadowed hallways. At the time, he swore he'd never go inside that scary old house, but here he was, all the same.

"Are you coming, Trevor?" one of the kids called.

He glanced around, noticing that he was the only one who hadn't crawled through the basement window yet. He swallowed the lump in his throat, wanting very badly to retreat to the safety of his home and watch an episode of *Scooby Doo* instead, but he couldn't figure how to do it without looking like a chicken.

He gave the house one more cautious glance and then climbed in after his friends.

I'll only stay for a little while. Then I'll tell them I have to go home for something.

They crept in through a basement window. The space was so dark, all he could see was the bobbing light from the flashlight ahead of him. Something brushed the back of his neck and he jolted with a gasp.

The other kids jumped too, but soon laughed as they realized what happened.

"What's the matter, Trevor? Afraid of a little spider's web?"

He took a deep breath to steady his nerves and tried to shake off the feeling that wouldn't leave him. They weren't supposed to be there. He could feel it in every cell of his body.

At the top of the stairs they found a doorway that led to the first floor. Trevor looked around, taking in the wooden floors and the furniture covered by sheets. It was exactly what he thought of when he imagined a haunted house. The only thing missing was the ghosts.

As they tiptoed through the old house, they began hearing strange sounds. At first, the sounds were subtle. They heard the creak of a floorboard in another room, which was followed by the echo of footsteps on the grand staircase.

One of the children started counting, so he scrambled up the grand staircase to the second floor to look for a hiding place.

The first room he came to had red walls. Something about the room made him feel uncomfortable, as if someone hid in the corner watching him. He gave the doorway a wide berth and studied the second room he came to.

It looked like it could have been a kid's bedroom. It was small and square, with two doorways and a strange looking closet. Something about the closet appealed to him. The door was short, as if it was made for a kid. As he stood in front of it, he heard the counting girl reach twenty.

"Ready or not, here I come," she announced.

He opened the closet door and scrambled in.

The darkness nearly closed in on him, so he cracked the door an inch and allowed a ribbon of light inside. He watched several kids run past the doorway, looking for a place to hide, as the counter made her way up the stairs.

"I see you, Jimmy!" she yelled.

Trevor held his breath, praying she didn't look in his direction. If she did, she'd probably find him in a second. It wasn't exactly the greatest hiding spot.

She continued past, and he let out his breath.

I made it.

He listened as the girl walked up the narrow staircase to the third floor, thinking that he'd just stay in the closet until all the other children were found. He heard the sound of more footsteps in the hallway. As he leaned forward to see who it was, something happened that would haunt him for the rest of his life. Hands grabbed onto his shoulders.

"Get out!" a voice whispered in his ear, before giving him a shove forward.

He stumbled out of the closet, a scream lodged deep in his throat.

As he rounded the doorway, he turned back in time to see a transparent boy grinning at him from the depths of the closet he'd just departed. He didn't stop running until he reached his own doorstep.

He wouldn't return to the house until years later, until his aunt Marion took him on a tour.

Edwin Gonzalez and Lillian Otero when they first met

Edwin and Lillian in 2013

Chapter 2

Edwin's stomach twisted into knots as they drove to look at a Victorian mansion in Gardner. He wasn't sure why they were driving so far to look at a house. They already had a house, and he was perfectly happy where they were, but once Lillian caught wind of the mansion, there was no resisting her. Lillian loved Victorians like some women loved fine jewelry.

He glanced at her sitting in the passenger seat, her long black hair pulled into a high, sleek ponytail. She wore heavy silver earrings that swung back and forth as her head bobbed to the beat of the music. Her happiness was nearly contagious. He couldn't help smiling at her, causing some of his uneasiness to slough away.

It was hard to believe they'd been together for over twenty years. They met at the bindery factory where they both worked at the time. He was blown away the first time he saw her walking across the parking lot, her dark hair dancing around her face as she laughed. He was enamored in an instant, something he still felt years later. There was nothing he wouldn't do for her.

Their happily-ever-after led them to an ordinary existence in Dorchester, a Boston neighborhood, where they shared a triple-decker with Lillian's mother and sister. Life was comfortable, if not predictable, with the fixtures of friends and family surrounding them like a safety net. The days passed by with a steady hum, the highs and lows too minimal to notice. Days were spent working at their respective jobs, while weekends were consumed by daytrips to antique stores and to local restaurants, or doing repairs around the house. Everything changed when Lillian's sister showed her a real estate listing for a Victorian mansion. Their lives were promptly fractured into a thousand pieces. Nothing would ever be comfortable or predictable again.

Edwin wasn't sure what to make of Lillian's sudden need to see the house.

It was more than just a passing fancy or a decision made after seeing something alluring and wanting a closer look. It was more of an obsession, a dire need as magnetic as the pull of addiction.

Once she saw the listing, she had to go there. There was no other option.

It troubled Edwin on several levels. Lillian was usually so fastidious. She wasn't reckless or prone to impulse. She had an agenda, and she usually stuck with it. It was one of the things he loved most about her. She was consistent. She made lists and schedules; she thought things out to the last detail before she reacted. He knew what to expect of her, and it gave him a great sense of comfort. Her suggesting they go look at a house sixty miles out of town was very much out of character for her. At first, he blamed it on her passion for Victorians.

Lillian had loved Victorians since she was a little girl. She used to live down the street from a beautiful Victorian. She walked past it every day on her way to school, swearing that one day she'd have a house just like it. The dream stayed with her through her adulthood. He often caught her scrolling through the real estate listings, daydreaming about owning one, but it had never advanced to a point where they actually got in the car to go look at one.

By the way she described it, the house they were driving to sounded similar to the house of her childhood dreams. The Second Empire Victorian mansion was over six-thousand square feet in size, and had twenty-six rooms, including a tower that rose above the house, providing sweeping views of South Gardner. According to the realtor, the house had been vacant for the past two years as the owner tried to find a buyer. Every deal that came through for the house mysteriously fell apart. It was as if the house was waiting for the right owner.

"Are you excited?" Edwin asked, reaching over to hold Lillian's hand.

She turned, her lips curving into a broad smile that lit up her entire face. "I'm beyond excited. Just imagine living in our own Victorian," she said, staring wistfully off into space.

Edwin wished he could be half as excited.

Part of his anxiety was based in reality. Victorians were known to be money pits. An old house would require a lot of upkeep, something he wasn't sure they could handle both physically and financially. He imagined the long hours and the added expenses, and it was enough to make him sigh. The other reason was the uneasy feeling in his gut.

Something just wasn't right about that house.

He knew it from the minute he called the realtor to request a viewing. The woman had been very strange about it. She asked him at least three times if he was sure he wanted to see *that* house.

And then there was the dream.

He'd barely fallen asleep the night before, when he found himself in the middle of the strangest dream.

In the dream, he found himself drifting through the massive front door of a Victorian mansion. It was as though he didn't have feet or legs. He just floated along like a ghost on the wind. He looked up to see a bright chandelier shining above him, the light casting dark whimsical shadows into the corners of the room. To his right, he heard the melodic sound of music.

It was soft and enchanting, the kind of music people listened to at the turn of the century. The house had a glorious feeling to it, as if people were at the highest peak of their lives, thoroughly enjoying all the wealth and splendor it offered them. It was like a vintage snapshot in time, encapsulating the souls who refused to relinquish the moment. He felt himself traveling towards a set of white doors towards the source of the music, unable and unwilling to stop.

The doors swung open as he approached them, and he found himself in the midst of a large social gathering.

People crowded inside the parlor room, dressed in early Victorian finery. Ice cubes clinked in glasses as drinks were served, and the hum of conversation filled the air. Women with bright smiles talked to one another, while dapper men shared confidences over a glass of finely-aged brandy. The room smelled of perfume and pipe smoke, which caught the light as it clouded the air.

No one seemed to notice him as he silently wafted into the room.

He floated among them as if he were invisible.

They smiled and talked to one another, their voices momentarily rising above the lilting sound of the music. As Edwin glided further into the depths, the crowd parted and he became aware of a man sitting in the middle of the room.

Unlike the others, the man was watching him. He was dressed all in black with a debonair mustache that curled upwards at the ends. With his straight carriage and direct gaze, he presented himself as the master of the house. He nodded at Edwin as if welcoming him to the party, a slight knowing smile curving the corners of his lips. And with that, Edwin woke up, feeling disoriented like he just time traveled back from a bygone era.

Lillian squeezed his hand and he glanced back at her, coming back to reality from his daydream. She was still smiling.

"We really need something good to happen to us," she told him.

He sighed again.

It was true. Their dog Casper passed away several months ago, and it was a devastating blow for both of them. Their dogs were like family members, and losing one left a large hole in their lives. Edwin hadn't seen Lillian smile so broadly since Casper's death. Maybe this would be a good thing for them both.

He tried to clear his mind of the nagging feelings so he could enjoy the moment.

Lillian was right. They needed something good to happen to them.

Photographic rendition of Edwin's dream

Bill Wallace in front of the Victorian Mansion   Photo by the author

Chapter 3

Bill Wallace sat across the street from the Victorian, nursing a beer at the South Gardner Hotel. Voices and music buzzed around him, but he hardly noticed. His eyes trained through the milky window as he stared at the golden-yellow mansion on the corner.

Something was changing in that house, and he didn't like it.

Bill looked like a cross between Santa Claus and Albert Einstein. With his full white beard and wild hair, he came across as an eccentric sort at first, but there was an intelligence and warmth in his eyes that made people reconsider their first impression.

He always knew he was different. Routine things didn't interest him. He always found himself drawn to the peculiar side of life, the intricacies and the elements that most people never considered. Life was more than what it seemed. He knew this on an empathic, psychic level. While he never called himself a psychic medium, his talents as an empathic medium were undeniable.

His family was known to have the gift of psychic insight. His father used to spend countless hours trying to surprise Bill's grandmother with a visit, but no matter when they showed up at her house, she was ready for them, often with a meal on the table. Bill's own abilities didn't surface until after he died during triple bypass surgery and was successfully resuscitated. When he woke up, he wasn't the same person.

He could talk to ghosts.

Bill could feel the spirits calling to him as he walked the streets of Gardner. He would look up at the side of the buildings, sometimes seeing an apparition standing there, silently watching him. The Victorian Mansion had been pulling at him for several years.

When most people drove past the house, they looked up at the dark windows and wondered if someone was looking back at them. Bill didn't have to wonder. He knew they were there.

The spirit of a young woman named Mattie had been there since the late 1800's. Petite, with long dark hair that she wore in a bun, she once cared for the Pierce children. Bill saw her as a kind person with a charitable heart, but not someone who tolerated nonsense. Chores were scheduled at specific times, and the children were taught to behave. Even though she was long dead, she remained the protector of the house, keeping it safe from trespassers and ensuring the other resident ghosts behaved themselves.

He became aware of her as he drove past the house on Union Street. He heard the sounds of her in his head, singing a folk song he had never heard before. At the time, he discounted the sound as a consequence from his near-death experience, but after a while he couldn't deny it. She was reaching out to him.

She was calling to him again as he sat across the street, asking for his help.

Unfortunately, Bill had no way of getting inside the house. It had been vacant for two years since the previous owners left. Breaking and entering wasn't something he was willing to do.

"Sorry, Mattie. No can do," he whispered under his breath.

He looked at the house, wondering what was transpiring behind those dark and dingy windows. Whatever it was, it wasn't good.

Bill's relationship with the mansion started in 2000.

He and his friend Mike were sitting on the hood of his car at the pizza shop across the street, waiting for their order. It was late August and the night was thick with humidity and mosquitoes. Mike was talking about the religious training he was undergoing to become a minister, but Bill hardly heard a word he said. All he could do was stare at the house across the street.

He could feel Mattie lingering near a second floor window, watching him.

Bill was pulled from his daydream when a man burst out of the Victorian mansion and started walking towards them. Bill was immediately captivated by the sight.

The tall, dark-haired man was dressed in a long black coat and had a decided air of confidence to him. Bill laughed when he saw him because, for all the world, he reminded him of Gomez

Addams walking out of his creepy haunted house. He was surprised when the man crossed the street and headed towards the pizza shop.

The minute the man approached them, the two made eye contact. Bill, being the jovial type, began humming the theme song to *The Addams Family*. The man seemed taken back for a moment, but recovered after a minute. The two then introduced themselves.

"Mark Veau," the man said, giving Bill a firm handshake. Bill nodded and introduced himself as well, finding himself instantly drawn to Mark's unique character. The fact that he owned such a magnificent house only added to the allure.

"That's a beautiful house," Bill told him, looking over Mark's shoulder at the yellow mansion. It was as though he couldn't look away for long before his gaze was pulled back to those spellbinding windows.

"Would you like to see it?" Mark asked.

Bill nearly lunged for the door. "Very much so," he said, almost forgetting about his friend in his eagerness to see the house.

They came through the door, and Bill felt the outside world melt away. All he could think about was getting upstairs to see Mattie. Mark introduced him to his fiancée Suzanne, but he barely noticed. His gaze was pulled to the staircase.

As they passed the wall to his right, Bill felt a sizzle run up the side of his body. He stopped and looked at his arm. Every hair was standing on end. It was as if the house had an electrical current running right through it. He could feel it buzzing in the air like a pulse.

He found himself walking towards the stairs. He knew it was odd, not waiting for Mark to lead the tour, but there was something about the upstairs that he had to see. It was where Mattie waited. Being so deliciously close was more than he could handle. He needed to see her now.

Even though he never saw the inside the house before, he instinctively knew the layout. He walked up the servant's staircase to the second floor, then made his way down the long hallway.

The space was different than it was in the 1880's when Mattie lived there. The walk-in closet off the master bedroom was once a small sewing room. She liked to sit here and crochet doilies out of bits of string that she found on packages.

The doorway that once connected the room to the second floor landing had been plastered over many years ago, turning it into a closet. Mattie still spent ample amounts of time there, preferring the quietness of the room to the more congested areas of the house. It was where she went to collect her thoughts.

Mattie.

The minute she noticed him, she reached out to him with her mind. She seemed happy to see him, pleased to finally find someone who could communicate with her. She told him many things, the words nearly tumbling out too fast for comprehension. It was as though she'd kept them bottled up for decades and the pressure of releasing them was just too much for her to handle.

"Bill?" Mark said, touching his arm. "Are you okay?"

Bill snapped out of it long enough to explain. "Every time I drive by, she calls to me. She likes it here," he said.

Mark gave him a curious glance. "Are you talking about Mattie Cornwell? The nanny?" he asked.

Bill was surprised that Mark knew about Mattie. "You know about her?"

Mark smiled. "Several weeks after we moved in, our contractor told us the house was haunted and asked if he could bring in his two nieces who were mediums. They told me about her," he said with an incredulous tone. "How do you know about her?"

Bill told Mark about his gift, never worrying that the other man would think he was crazy. There seemed to be an instant understanding between the two of them that the friendship would never be what other people considered normal. Bill was just as colorful as Mark.

"She takes care of the house. She always has," he told Mark. "This house sat empty for over twenty years before you bought it.

Do you ever wonder how this house made it through the years of being abandoned without suffering immense damage?" he asked.

Mark looked at him inquisitively. "What do you mean?"

Bill pointed to the pristine woodwork that framed every window, doorway, floor, and ceiling. "You would think after twenty years of sitting empty with people sneaking in here day and night, someone would have carved their initials into the woodwork, or even burned one of the doors for warmth. Mattie's the reason why they didn't."

Mark nodded and then shared a story of his own. "I've had several psychics tell me the same thing. There's even a police report to prove it. Back in the seventies, Mattie chased two guys out of here," Mark said.

"Really?"

Mark smiled. "Yeah, they were just thugs. They were were up to no good. They broke into the house, thinking they were going to steal something, but they got the crap scared out of them instead. Somebody called the police because one of the guys ended up outside on the ground in a fetal position blubbering about being chased out of the house. Apparently, the cops searched the house and didn't find anyone inside. They told the guy on the sidewalk that he must have imagined it. There was nobody in the house. The guy looked up at them from the sidewalk and stated, 'I said we were chased out of the house. I didn't say it was somebody,'" Mark finished with a smile.

He went on to share what he knew about Mattie Cornwell.

She was born in 1859 in Nova Scotia, Canada. She was twenty-one when she came to work for the Pierce family as a servant in the house. Her primary focus was caring for the Pierce children. She was firm but loving with the children, keeping them mindful of their manners and helping them grow into the influential men they would one day become.

Later research would show that Mattie died at the young age of twenty-five from an acute inflammation of the hip just two years after getting married. Her tragedy would be just one among many at the Victorian mansion. It was as if the house collected them, like some people collected old coins.

Bill opened his mouth to respond, but was suddenly overwhelmed by a tightening in his chest. He slumped back against the wall as the world faded around the edges.

"Are you okay?" Mark asked with concern. "Do you need me to call an ambulance?"

Bill took a few breaths before he answered. Although he felt weak, he was fairly certain he wasn't having another heart attack. It was something else altogether. It was the house. It was getting to him. "No. I'm fine," he finally managed to say. "Just let me catch my breath for a second."

After a few minutes, he began to feel better, but the sensation was momentary. Visions began to flood his mind. He could barely get the words out.

"Mattie doesn't like your dog," he told Mark. "They had dogs at the mansion, but they were never allowed to run loose around the house. It bothers her because the master of the house would have never allowed it."

Mark seemed taken back. "How do you know I have a dog?" he asked.

Bill stared down at the floor. "Because I can see him in the basement. He's a big black fluffy dog," he said. It was as though he could see straight through the floors.

Mark gave him a dubious look. "That's unreal," he said. "You can really see that?"

Bill wasn't finished with his visions. "There's something in the house that Mattie doesn't like. You need to find it and get it out," he said.

He began to describe an area of the basement, an area he had never seen. "It's in a room with a fieldstone foundation near a set of stairs. It's flat. It might be a document, or a piece of paper, but you'll know it when you see it."

After Bill left, Mark and his wife searched the basement until they found the item Bill had described. It was a canning jar with Nazi swastikas drawn on the label. It was tucked into a bookcase along the backside of the wall behind the servant's staircase. The moment Mark moved the jar across the threshold of the property, a sudden gust of wind caught the label and whisked it away. They never found out who drew the swastikas on the label or why Mattie was so offended by them, but it seemed to appease her nonetheless.

Unfortunately, Mark and Suzanne's marriage only lasted until 2006. When they divorced, the house went back on the market. It took two years before they accepted a solid bid, years that left Bill on the outside looking in again.

Something in the house was changing.

A plan was set into motion and nothing would stop it until it reached the end.

"The Grand Staircase" Photo by Frank Grace (Trig Photography)

The Second Floor Landing   Photo by Frank Grace (Trig Photography)

Chapter 4

Thirty miles away in Worcester, Mark Veau was at work as a disc jockey at WORC radio.

The realtor called him earlier in the day to let him know they were showing the house. Mark had mixed feelings about selling the Victorian. The house was in his blood and despite everything, he was having a hard time letting it go.

Mark and his wife Suzanne originally purchased the house in 2000. The house was in rough shape when they took ownership of it. Nobody in his right mind would have purchased it.

After the Pierce family died out, the house went to a man named Jay Stemmerman, who lived there off and on during the next twenty years before abandoning the house altogether. The results were predictable. The house was falling apart.

The floor in the master bedroom had partially collapsed, and the front bay window was so badly deteriorated, it was hanging on by rotten splinters. Both porches needed replacing and the house hadn't been painted in over thirty years. They spent six years painstakingly renovating the house, but it all ended in 2006, along with his marriage. He hated leaving, but he wasn't left with any choices. The house was far more than he could handle on his own.

He sat back in his chair, feeling the loss with a heavy heart.

Living in the house was like living on a movie set. So much was going on there. It was more than just a house. It was if the house had a palpable pulse.

It revealed itself to them slowly, starting when their contractor came to him after working on the house for a few days.

"You should get this house checked out," he told Mark." When you and Suzanne are at work during the day and I'm here by myself, there is some stuff going on in this house you should know about."

The contractor offered to bring his nieces over, who were both mediums. They walked around the house and confirmed his suspicions.

The house was haunted. There was no doubt.

The mediums connected with Mattie Cornwall the nanny, and a little boy, as well as a man who had breathing problems. Many psychics over the years would confirm the presence of these three spirits again and again.

While Mark had always welcomed people in for tours, he began inviting paranormal teams into the house for investigations, as well. Investigators made contact with the man on the second floor, someone he identified through public records as Eino Saari, the man who burned to death in 1963. They learned of Eino's passion for liquor and his quick temper. They even captured his voice on a digital recorder saying the Portuguese word for cheers. The more they explored the hauntings, the deeper the mystery evolved. Mark wasn't sure anyone would ever figure it all out.

He was barely beginning to scratch the surface before he was forced to sell.

Chapter 5

Edwin's anxiety grew stronger as they got closer to Gardner.

He wasn't sure if he was ready for something this monumental to happen. Change wasn't something he was comfortable with. He liked their life in Dorchester. They had a nice place to live, and it was close to all their friends and family. As the miles fell behind him, he wondered why they would consider living so far away from everything that was familiar to them.

Edwin grew up in Dorchester, the largest neighborhood in Boston. With a population of over 130,000, it was more than just a big city. Its historical roots were monumental, being home to the early Puritan settlers before becoming a retreat for the Boston elite. In recent times, Dorchester, along with nearby Roxbury and Mattapan, claimed the highest crime rates in the Boston area. Growing up there took a special kind of person. If you weren't that kind of person, you either quickly became one or you sank like concrete in a pond.

Fear was something Edwin's family learned to live with. Their house was broken into so many times they lost count. They would return home from work and school to find everything of value missing. Through all this, he learned to safeguard what was his and fight for it if necessary. It changed who he was. Instead of being the carefree boy he started out as, he became fearful of having his possessions taken from him and learned how to fight to keep them.

He wasn't sure what to make of Gardner.

The landscape opened up as they distanced themselves from the city, presenting them with rolling hills and distant mountains. Houses were further apart, and the traffic was lighter. As they drove into town, they took in the downtown area with its rows of shops and restaurants, as well as old brick factory buildings that had been turned into condominiums. It was an equal mixture of opportunity and decline, with lavishly restored homes sitting side by side with houses slated for demolition. It seemed like the town was steadily deteriorating from its glory days, but was still trying to find a firm handhold.

At the turn of the previous century, Gardner was known as "Chair City," a nickname earned for its prolific furniture manufacturing. S.K. Pierce, the first owner of the Victorian, was one of the men responsible for the furniture boom.

Pierce was a self-made man. Growing up in near poverty, he worked in a local chair factory, carefully saving his money. In 1845, he bought out the owner and quickly began building his wealth. That same year he married Susan Jackson, the twenty-five-year-old daughter of a prominent Gardner townsman. They had a child together eleven years later, a son they named Frank. By 1875, S.K. was one of the wealthiest men in the entire country, and he set out to build a house more befitting his status.

The two-hundred-man crew worked around the clock to complete the massive mansion, finishing it in just a year and a half. The stunning results were a true work of art. As a furniture manufacturer, S.K. spared no expense with the woodwork inside and outside the house. Elaborate hand-carved moldings and doors graced every room, while crystal chandeliers hung from the ceilings. Tradesmen as far away as Boston came to install the fixtures and equipment. A Winthrop furnace was installed in the basement that heated every room in the house. Gas fixtures lit every room.

Even the servant's areas were given special treatment. His craftsmen created a lavish butler's pantry with floor-to-ceiling cabinets and built-in bins for flour and grains. S.K. should have been the happiest man in the world when he moved into his mansion but fate had other plans for him.

His wife Susan came down with a deadly disease known as erysipelas, an acute bacterial infection that affected her hands and face. Lesions appeared on her skin, ravaging her beauty and slowly eating her alive. She died a painful death in the house, just two weeks after moving in, leaving Sylvester alone with their twenty-year old son.

S.K. remarried two years later to twenty-eight-year old Ellen West, a woman who was thirty years his junior. She was an active member of the First Congregational Church in Gardner, as well as a member of the Afternoon Club, the ladies division of the Gardner Boat Club. She and S.K. had two children of their own, Stuart, born in 1879, and Edward, born in 1882.

After S.K.'s death in 1888, skirmishes flew between his heirs. Ellen took legal action against her stepson Frank for excessively spending against S.K.'s estate, stating that she was fully capable of handling the probate on her own. Her personalized safe still sits in the second floor landing, a testament to her importance in the household. Not many people had safes in the late 1800's, especially not women.

After Ellen died the house went to the three Pierce sons, but it didn't end well. Lawsuits flew back and forth between them for the rest of their lives, expensive evidence of the growing friction between them. Money could buy a lot of things, but it never brought the Pierce family the happiness they longed for.

Edward, the youngest son, ended up gaining possession of the mansion. He turned it into a boarding house, where rumors of prostitution and gambling grew rampant. The condition of the house declined, decade by decade. By the time Edward turned it over to the next owner, it was rundown and dilapidated, stripped of its former grace and glory.

The next owner put over a hundred thousand dollars into the mansion before he mysteriously abandoned it, leaving it standing vacant for twenty years.

It was no wonder the spirits were in such a state of unrest.

The house needed new owners; someone who could bring it back to the way it used to be without asking too many questions.

It had a lot of secrets, but not all of the ghostly occupants wanted them revealed.

Marble sink in the Butler's Pantry Photo by Jason Baker

Chapter 6

It was as if time stood still when they rounded the corner and saw the house for the first time.

"There it is," Edwin whispered under his breath. He stopped the car and stared.

The house was massive.

It stood three stories tall, dwarfing the other nearby structures. The yellow paint was peeling and fading, but the house commanded such a presence, you forgave any shortcomings. It looked like a grand dame, years past her prime, yet still a force to be reckoned with.

Lillian was practically bouncing in her seat.

"Oh my God, look at it!" she said. "It's beautiful!"

Edwin wasn't sure if beautiful was a good word to describe it. Money pit came much closer.

He felt his heart sink. It was nothing like he expected. It needed a ton of work.

Lillian didn't seem to notice the decay. "Oh my God. Look at the widow's walk! Isn't that amazing?" she nearly glowed from the inside out with excitement. Edwin smiled at her, trying to feel more excited about it. He loved seeing Lillian so happy, but he wasn't sure how they were going to manage it.

They parked and found their way to the back door to meet with the realtor and his wife.

The realtors introduced themselves as Warren and Janine.

Warren was tall and thin with glasses and short dark hair, while his wife Janine was a petite woman with short brown hair and intelligent eyes. Both were warm and friendly, quickly becoming close friends with Edwin and Lillian.

After the introductions were over, Warren pulled the keys from his pocket and moved towards the door. Lillian retrieved a camera from her purse and began taking photos of the outside of the house, but Janine stopped her.

"I'm sorry, but no photographs," Janine told them.

Edwin and Lillian exchanged puzzled glances. Edwin had never heard of a situation where a realtor wouldn't let them take photos of a house they were viewing. It seemed very odd.

The moment stole some of Lillian's earlier excitement. She wanted to show the pictures to her sisters. With a shrug, she put the camera back in her purse and followed the realtor into the house.

Janine moved ahead of them with a hurried step and flipped on a few light switches, beginning her banter about the house. The way she said it was practiced and polished, as though she recited it often without expecting any results from her efforts. It made Edwin wonder how many times she'd shown it.

As they already knew, the house was a Second Empire Victorian with both a basement and an attic. The main floor consisted of a kitchen separated from the formal dining room by the maid and butler's pantries. The Ladies Parlor and library room were on the other side of the house. The mansion had two entryways, one on the front for guests and one on the side for staff.

The second floor contained three large bedrooms, a bathroom, and two other rooms once were used as a nursery and nanny quarters. The third floor consisted primarily of servant bedrooms with the exception of the Billiards Room. Overall, the house was exactly 6661 square feet, a number that disturbed Edwin more than a little. He'd always heard that 666 was a sign of the devil. It made him wonder why they make it that precise size, unless it was unintentional.

While Janine showed them around the first floor, Warren enlightened Edwin with some of the stories about the house.

"Minnesota Fats used to play pool here with the owner," he told Edwin.

"Really?" Edwin asked.

"Oh yeah. S.K. Pierce had a lot of famous friends. Norman Rockwell, the painter, spent a lot of time here, as did President Calvin Coolidge, back when he was lieutenant governor of Massachusetts. You've heard of P.T Barnum, the circus guy, right?" he asked, and Edwin nodded. "He was a close friend too. He spent more time here than any of the others."

Edwin looked around, trying to imagine it. All those famous people once walked on these very floors. The thought was astounding. It made him forget the rundown appearance of the exterior for a few moments as he allowed himself to get caught up in the impressive history of the place.

If he was still worried about such a massive undertaking, those feelings faded quickly as he saw the smile on Lillian's face.

She spun around in a slow circle, her face tilted to the ceiling.

"This is my house," she told them. "I'm going to live here."

It was a moment that would remain with Edwin for a lifetime. He pushed away the last of his doubts. He'd do whatever he needed to make it happen for Lillian. It was good to see her smile so broadly. The past few months hadn't been easy for either of them.

She was right. They needed this.

"So, you want a tour?" Janine asked.

"Sure," they both said, as she walked towards a set of white doors just off the main entrance.

The minute Edwin saw them, his heart nearly stopped.

They were the same white doors from his dream.

As the realtor swung the doors open, Edwin could barely stifle a gasp. The room was exactly the same as in his dream. The only thing missing was the people.

He stared at the room, the visions from the night before flashing in his mind.

How could this happen?

How could he dream about a room that he never saw before, only to have it turn out to be a real place? His mind spun with the implications.

He hung behind the group for the remainder of the tour, trying to make sense of it.

Never in his life had anything like this happened. How could he have seen this very house in a dream? Normally, he would have said something to Lillian, but he didn't want to burst her bubble. He just trailed along as he desperately tried to wrap his brain around what was happening to him.

Janine and Warren led them up the grand staircase to the second floor. She opened the first door on the right, named the Red Room for its red wallpaper.

The room was simply breathtaking. Detailed crown moldings lined the ceilings, showcasing the beautiful red striped wallpaper on the walls. Beneath them, hardwood floors gleamed in the fading light. It wasn't difficult to imagine Victorian era people living there.

The next room they viewed was another bedroom directly across from the master bedroom, which would later be known as the Copper Room. It was adorned with the same beautiful woodwork, but it also had a built-in antique sink set in marble. Although the room was stunning, Edwin felt uncomfortable. His chest was tight as though he was having difficulties breathing. He felt a similar suffocating sensation in the master bedroom across the hallway from the Copper Room. He couldn't explain it, but he just didn't like the way the rooms felt.

They quickly toured the remaining rooms on the second floor, admiring the renovations the previous owner had painstakingly undertaken. She showed them the old nursery with the remnants of the dumbwaiter still in existence. Lillian opened the small door, marveling at the size of it.

"This used to be part of the dumbwaiter?" she asked.

"Yes, but it's been transformed into a closet. The previous owners thought it was too dangerous to have with small children in the house," Janine told them. She quickly escorted them to the door leading to the third floor.

She opened the door and they found themselves looking up a narrow staircase. Light from the windows filtered down the staircase, highlighting thousands of dust motes floating in the air, giving it a mystical appearance. As they walked up the staircase, they had to watch out for several framed paintings that leaned against the walls.

"What are these?" Edwin asked, pulling one of the paintings into the light, so he could see it better.

On the canvas was a lewd scene, depicting a naked woman whose bottom half was replaced with that of a cloven-hoofed beast. A demonic looking man threatened her with a sharp knife. The painting gave him a sick feeling in the pit of his stomach.

"Those belonged to someone who owned the house back in the 1960's," she said breezily, as if dismissing them. "I think his name was Jay Stemmerman."

Edwin crinkled his brow as he looked at them. They were dark and lurid like a nightmare, nothing he would ever hang on his walls.

The realtors quickly moved them the rest of the way up the stairs to show them several rooms used in 1875 for a variety of functions. The rooms were bare and sparse, not lovingly renovated like the rest of the house. She opened the doors, giving them a quick glance, before showing them the Billiards Room. The minute Edwin walked into the room, all feelings of anxiety left him.

The room had a welcoming feeling about it. Unlike the Copper Room where he felt strangely uncomfortable, the Billiards Room felt warm and inviting. It was a room he could see himself spending time in. He could almost imagine the huge billiards table in the middle of the room with men leaning over it, lining up their next shot as cigar smoke hung in the air.

"From what I was told, this is where S.K. Pierce entertained his famous friends," Warren told them. "Imagine playing pool with Minnesota Fats," he said.

Edwin could nearly feel the prominence resonating in the air. The house wasn't just beautiful, it was a silent witness to history.

If only the walls could talk.

As the last of the evening light faded, Janine invited them to walk up the spiral staircase to the widow's walk. They climbed the stairs, feeling a sense of dizziness as they wound around the staircase to the top. Once they arrived at the landing, their breath was simply swept away. The view was spectacular.

Windows lined the small landing at the top of the stairs, giving them a 360-degree view of South Gardner. A glorious sunset lit the horizon, sending rays of orange light cascading across the landscape. If they hadn't already made the pledge to purchase the house moments before, they made the decision right then and there.

They would buy the house no matter what it took.

The Billiards Room on the third floor

Chapter 7

Lillian couldn't stop thinking about the house.
Her house.
She revisited all the images in her mind, imagining herself living there. She could see the empty rooms filled with Victorian era furnishings and lush fabrics. Mentally, she began to redecorate it, changing around the kitchen so it was more functional, adding beautiful vintage curtains and fixtures.

She was disappointed to learn that the house was gutted before the prior owners purchased it. In the mid 1980's, workers came in with crowbars and dollies, removing all the Tiffany ceiling lamps and chandeliers. They ripped out the built-in cabinet in the library and sold all the antique furniture, including the massive billiards table on the third floor. She wished there was some way she could find them again and bring them back to where they belonged.

She began scouring the want ads, looking for the perfect pieces. She wanted ornate bedroom sets she could dress with velvet and satin, as well as end tables and vintage lamps harking back to the turn of the century. Her daydream was interrupted by her sister, Iris.

"Hey, Lil, you might want to see this," she called from the living room.

Lillian followed the sound of her voice to the computer, where she was staring at a video clip.

"Yeah, what?"

"The house is haunted," Iris told her. She refreshed the link on the computer and pressed play.

Lillian gasped as she watched the familiar golden yellow Victorian appear on the screen. A group of paranormal investigators walked through the rooms, talking about the history of the house with Mark Veau, the man who owned it before them.

She sat down in front of the computer, her mind racing a million miles a minute.

Haunted?

She was matter of fact about most things in life. As far as she was concerned, there were no grey areas. It was either black or it was white. She felt the same way about ghosts. She didn't believe in them. It only took her a few seconds to recover from the news.

People had a way of exaggerating things. She figured this was just one of those cases.

She shrugged. "Yeah, whatever," she told her sister. It wasn't something that even concerned her remotely.

She had no idea what was waiting for her.

The second house viewing came several weeks later.

It was August and the weather was much warmer. As the day faded to dusk, the humidity finally broke, leaving behind a light cool breeze. They got out of the car and stretched after the long drive from Boston.

South Gardner had a Friday afternoon feel to it. Cars buzzed by with their windows open, providing a backdrop of music. People made their way down the sidewalks, some walking dogs, others just trying to get from one place to another. As they passed, they all looked up at the looming mansion before warily glancing back at the prospective buyers standing in front of it. It was apparent that everyone in the neighborhood knew the history of the house.

Edwin and Lillian just smiled at each other.

One person's loss was another's gain. If the legends were keeping people away, then they might be able to afford it.

Edwin liked the feeling of the neighborhood. After living in fear for so many years in Dorchester, it would be nice to live in a town where he could let his guard down a little. He decided to walk around the house and kick the tires a bit. If there was something structurally wrong with the house, he wanted to find it before it was too late.

"It looks like someone did a lot of work to the house, but it still needs more," Edwin commented, looking up at the exterior. The previous owners painted the bottom floors, but the paint on the outside of the second and third floors was nothing more than dry, faded flakes. As they watched, a pigeon appeared from beneath one of the eaves, and then flew up to the roof.

Despite giving into Lillian's excitement, Edwin still had mixed emotions about buying the house. It would need years of renovations and nothing they did would stay finished for long. It was an old house, and old houses needed constant attention.

Could they handle it?

It was a monumental moment for him. After renting his entire life, he never thought he'd ever be a homeowner.

His thoughts swelled with pride.

If they did this, he would own a house... a mansion, in fact.

He couldn't wrap his mind around it.

If he had to make a final decision, it came as he glanced down at Lillian's beaming face. She was overjoyed. There was no way he could deny her that happiness. It would be a new chapter in their lives, a chance to start fresh.

Everything was falling into place for him. Just days earlier he learned he had the option to work from home. That meant that he was no longer tied to his job in Boston. He could work and live anywhere in the state as long as he had an Internet connection.

Maybe it was just meant to be.

Thoughts of a haunting couldn't have been further from their minds, but the house would soon supply them with a small sampling of things that were to yet to come.

Lillian pulled her camera out of her pocketbook. Since the realtor allowed them to bring a camera this time, she was intent on capturing every square inch of the mansion so she could show her family. After just a few shots, the camera suddenly shut down.

Lillian looked at it curiously. "The battery is dead," she said with disbelief. She remembered inserting fresh batteries just before leaving Boston.

How could this happen?

"What's the matter?" Edwin asked.

She showed him the camera. "The batteries died."

"Didn't you just put..."

"Yes," she cut him off and sighed. "Maybe something is wrong with the batteries."

Edwin took the realtor aside. "So why weren't we allowed to bring cameras in the first time?"

Janine rolled her eyes. "Because of the ghost hunters," she said, breathing the words out in a sigh. "You know this place is supposed to be haunted, right?" she asked, waiting for his nod. She went on to tell him a story about a woman who viewed the house earlier in the year.

"She disappeared, and I couldn't find her. I walked through every room until I found her in the kitchen with a tape recorder. She shushed me, telling me to be quiet because she was investigating. That was it for me," she said, fanning the air. "No more ghost hunters."

Edwin took a deep breath, hoping it wasn't true.

Unlike Lillian, he was on the fence about the paranormal. He watched some of the shows on television and figured there must be something to all the hype, but he also wondered if a lot of it was just scary stories meant to keep the ratings high. Surely, those things didn't really happen in real life.

Later Edwin discovered the true extent of the hauntings while researching the house at a local bookstore. He roamed through the paranormal section until he found a book on haunted houses in Massachusetts. As he flipped through it, he didn't expect to find anything. He nearly dropped the book when he saw it.

The house was right there on page twenty-six.

"Dear God…," he said. He found his way to a sofa in one of the reading areas and called Lillian from his cell phone. "The house is in this book," he said, his words running together to the point where she couldn't understand him.

"Slow down. Now, *what*? What house?" she asked.

"*Our house*. The one we want to buy. It's in this paranormal book, *Haunted Massachusetts* by a guy named Thomas D'Agastino." He started skimming through the paragraphs, reading things that made his mind numb. What he read nearly rocked him to the core.

"They're talking about our master bedroom. Supposedly, a man spontaneously combusted in there. Are you sure you want to do this?" he asked.

Lillian was quiet on the other end of the line. After a moment, he could hear her sigh. "It's probably just stuff somebody made up. Don't worry about it. We'll be fine," she said.

Edwin closed the book, but he couldn't close off the thoughts in his mind.

They signed the paperwork a month later.

Built-in flour bin and the dumb waiter in the Maid's Pantry

Detail of the Union Street doorknob
Photo by Jason Baker

Chapter 8

Although Edwin and Lillian signed the final papers on the house the day before Thanksgiving, they waited until April to move in because of the cold weather. Despite a massive furnace in the basement, the house wasn't insulated or properly heated. Walking inside the mansion during the month of December was like walking into a refrigerator. It was warmer outdoors than it was inside of the house.

Lillian couldn't stay away, though. She made excuses to make the trek from Boston, whether it was to bring carloads of household items or to shovel the walkways after a snowstorm. She managed to find a way to visit her Victorian mansion at least once a week.

She loved to roam around the rooms, admiring her beautiful house. She smiled broadly, the thought covering her with goose bumps.

Mine.

The word rang in her head like a golden note. She stood in front of the grand staircase leading to the second floor, while trying to imagine the history the house must have witnessed.

She could picture the extravagant parties. Women dressed in Victorian finery would have sipped tea in the Ladies Parlor, while the men smoked cigars over a game of billiards up on the third floor. Servants would bustle back and forth, caring for the guests. She endlessly explored each room, allowing the antique architecture to tell its story.

Guests would arrive through the eleven-foot-tall front doors. The side door, which opened on Union Street, was used for servants and staff. Lillian could tell by the way the side foyer was designed. They kept the interior doors closed to shield the main entryway from view, while allowing the hired help to access the kitchen, butler's pantry and servant's staircases, which lead to the second floor and the basement.

While most houses of this magnitude saved the lavish details for the main living areas, S.K. spared no expenses. Even the rooms typically used by the servants were adorned with the same beautiful hand-carved woodwork and doors. The third floor, which was primarily used for servant sleeping quarters, was less showy but still much more ornate than most homes of its era. It was obvious that the master of the house took good care of his staff, making his home a work of art from the basement to the attic.

Lillian was enchanted with the details. She found a hidden cabinet behind the fireplace in the master bedroom possibly used to hide liquor during the prohibition days. In the basement, she found one of the flower-shaped spears that once lined the roof tower. The more she looked, the more she found. It was like being presented with an intriguing mystery to solve.

She was especially drawn to the basement.

She wandered around the expanse, exploring the rooms. In its day, the basement would have been bright and sunny, with large windows in every room providing views of the grounds and gardens surrounding the house. Over time, the previous owners shuttered them closed to prevent vandals from breaking into the house.

She could almost hear the voices echoing through the space.

It its heyday, the space was filled with people working, talking and carrying out their household tasks. The massive double doors led directly to the outside. She imagined the gardener living in the room just to the right of the doors, hanging his coveralls on a hook before climbing into his bed for the night.

The Summer Kitchen was to the left of the double doors. A ten-foot long soapstone sink and countertop lined one wall, providing them room to work. Directly to the left of it was a brick kiln they used for cooking and burning waste. She could imagine the women dressed in their long aprons, lifting the heavy pots onto the kiln to heat the water they used for laundry, cleaning and cooking. Food would have been transported up to the kitchen in the dumb waiter. She could almost hear them humming as they worked, moving briskly to keep the household running efficiently. Children were most likely underfoot, chasing one another through the maze of legs, as the servants worked feverishly to keep the master of the house happy.

The rooms on the other end of the basement were a bit harder for her to decipher. One room was filled with old shutters. The old fieldstone foundation was visible here, obviously smaller than the actual footprint of the house. She later learned that another house once sat on the lot, having been moved down the street to make room for S.K. Pierce's mansion.

Across from the shutter room, she found a larger room that followed the contour of the bay window above it. It had a curious fireplace-sized hole that was bricked off, giving it a mysterious air. She wondered what it was.

She followed the line up to the ceiling. If it was a fireplace, it was missing a chimney.

"Hmmm...," she murmured to herself and moved onto the next room.

She walked into the room with the cistern, running her fingers across the rough brick trying to imagine how many other people had touched these very bricks over the course of more than one hundred and thirty years.

In the late 1800's, running water wasn't something most families had in their homes. They might have had pumps installed indoors, but they didn't have the benefit of turning on a faucet for running water. An elaborate channeling system in the attic caught rainwater and directed it to the massive brick structures. You could tell where the important people slept, because they had sinks in their bedrooms.

There were two cisterns. The one on the third floor provided a curious mystery to her. After she had the photographs developed, she discovered the name Edwin had been carved into the metal wheel at the top of the pulley. She showed it to Edwin after she noticed it, jokingly telling him they had to buy the house. It had his name on it.

The basement cistern was seven feet tall and twelve feet square, creating an open topped brick room within the room. The previous owners must have broken into it, because one of the walls had a rough doorway carved into it. She couldn't help but marvel at the ingenuity.

"The basement cistern"   Photo by Frank Grace (TRIG Photography)

Life was definitely different back then. It made her reconsider all the modern conveniences she took for granted. Back then, the wealthiest of the wealthy had a fraction of what came standard in most modern homes today.

Darkness was beginning to settle on the horizon, so she left for the day.

When she returned a few days later, something peculiar happened.

Even though they weren't planning to spend their Christmas holiday in the house, she still felt the need to decorate her Victorian mansion. She strung garland on the mantle in the Ladies Parlor, the same room that Edwin dreamt about the night before their first visit. She added silver reindeer and two large glass globes at either end. Satisfied with the way it looked, she left for the day.

When she returned the following week, one of the glass globes was in the middle of the floor. She stood there dumbfounded and stared at it.

"How in the world did that get into the middle of the floor?" she said.

She picked it up and put it back, making sure it was nestled in the greenery. She didn't think much about it until she visited the next week and found it in the middle of the floor again.

"What the hell?" she asked, looking around the room.

Was the house really haunted? Were the stories true?

She quickly dismissed the thought and laughed at herself for even thinking it.

There's no such thing as ghosts.

She packed up her things and headed home, still laughing at how easy she'd resorted to the ghost stories when there was probably a very rational explanation for it.

The Ladies Parlor fireplace - S.K. Pierce was a Freemason. Mason symbols can be found throughout the house, including on this fireplace.

Spiral staircase leading to widow's walk   Photo by the author

Chapter 9

Edwin was pleased to finally show the house off to their family. He couldn't wait to see the looks on their faces when they saw the grand Victorian for the first time. Lillian's younger sister Bridget and her eighteen-year old son Reo were the first visitors.

As he showed them the Ladies Parlor, Edwin noticed that one of the glass ornaments from the mantle was in the middle of the floor. He picked it up and placed it back on the mantle.

"How did that happen?" he asked, not ready to just walk away without questioning it.

Lillian sighed. "I don't know, but that's the third time I've found it there," she said.

Edwin stared at her, feeling a sense of apprehension rise up inside him.

How could an ornament make its way to the middle of the floor? Was it a ghost?

He brushed the thought away as quickly as it came. There had to be a rational reason for it.

He took it from the mantle and played with it for a few minutes.

"There must be a logical explanation. Maybe the floor is uneven," he said. If the ornament fell off the mantle, it could have rolled to the middle of the floor on its own. He placed the ornament on the floor and gave it a gentle push. It rolled several inches before it stopped, not coming anywhere near the middle of the floor where they found it.

"That's so strange," he said. It just didn't make sense. No matter how many times he tried, he couldn't get it to roll to the spot where they found it.

The thought made him uneasy, and he wasn't sure what to make of it.

If the ornament was able to get to the middle of the floor on its own, then why couldn't they duplicate it? No other factors made a difference. It wasn't like the windows were open or a heating duct blew air into the room. There was no way it could have happened, but yet it did.

What if the stories were true?

It had been much easier to dismiss the stories when they came from other people. Now that he'd seen something with his own eyes, it was harder to just laugh it off.

He tried to make eye contact with Lillian to see how she felt about it, but she had already left the room. Besides, he already knew how she felt about it. She was adamant in her beliefs about ghosts. She wouldn't believe in them until one walked up and introduced itself. He smiled at his own joke, and then looked up to find the others watching him expectantly.

He was always the one who figured things out and they were waiting for him to tell them what had happened, but there wasn't an easy way to explain this.

Instead of trying to explain something so impossible, he decided to change the subject.

"Is anybody hungry? I thought we could order a few pizzas," he said.

As everyone sat around the kitchen table eating, there was no mention made of the ornament. Edwin wondered if they didn't bring it up because they were afraid of hearing the answer.

Reo was especially quiet and it bothered Edwin.

"Are you okay," he asked his nephew. Reo nodded, never looking up from his pizza.

They were nearly finished with lunch when Lillian ventured down to the basement to retrieve something. She was gone for just a few minutes when they heard a tremendous crash coming from the stairs. It sounded like someone had fallen all the way down them.

Thinking the worst, Edwin leapt from his chair and ran to the staircase.

He expected to see Lillian lying at the bottom in a tangle of arms and legs, but the stairs were empty.

Bridget and Reo were right behind him. They stopped short as Lillian came up from the basement.

"What was that?" she asked.

"We thought it was you," Edwin said.

She shook her head. "No, I heard it from the basement too."

Edwin frowned, staring up at the staircase. His heart was beating hard from the fright.

Something had fallen down the stairs. There was no way they imagined it.

"There must be a logical explanation," he said for the second time that day. He couldn't imagine something large enough to make such a racket disappearing so suddenly, but there wasn't an obvious explanation.

They walked around, looking into all the rooms. Most of them were still bare, because the bulk of their furniture hadn't arrived yet. Nothing unusual stood out to them.

He shook his head and sighed. "I don't know what it was."

Everyone looked at one another curiously. It was clear they were all thinking the same thing.

The house was supposed to be haunted. Was this a sign?

If anyone was thinking it, nobody said it aloud. They walked back to the kitchen to finish eating.

"Well, that was interesting," Edwin said, trying to break the tension. He looked around at the group, seeing similar expressions on everyone's faces. They looked like they were ready to bolt at any second. He needed to calm everyone down, but he wasn't sure how to do it. He wasn't sure if he wasn't ready to bolt as well. Instead, he lifted the lid on the box. "Who needs more pizza?"

Bridget and Reo sat down at the table while Lillian stood behind them. Without warning, a three-foot-tall metal planter slid several inches across the kitchen floor. The sound was like thunder booming in the silence of the room.

Everyone jumped, their mouths agape.

"Did you just see that?" Lillian asked.

It was obvious they did, but no one could find the words to reply.

After a minute, Edwin got up from the table. He cautiously approached the planter and gave it a nudge. He fully expected it to be as light as a feather, but it wasn't. It was very heavy.

"How in the world did that happen?" he asked.

He pushed it back to its original placement, but an uneasy feeling came over him. Maybe the stories were true.

First the ornament, then the loud bang, and now this?

It didn't make sense. He thought about all those ghost shows he watched on TV. He discounted them as being amped up for viewers, but now he wasn't so sure. A sense of alarm began to rise in his mind.

Was this how it was going to be? How could they live with that?

He shook his head to shake the thought away. There had to be an explanation.

There just had to be.

Dusk was falling, blanketing the room in shadows. At that point, nobody wanted to hang around to see what would happen next. When Edwin suggested they start heading home, no one protested. They gathered their belongings and quietly walked towards the door.

As they passed the Ladies Parlor, Reo stopped abruptly.

The light was on in the Ladies Parlor. It shone brightly beneath the door.

"Lillian?" he said, pointing towards the door. He looked even paler since the planter moved.

Lillian turned and saw the light. Edwin was pretty sure Lillian had turned the light off when she closed the door earlier, but he couldn't be certain.

She opened the door and reached for the switch, but what she saw stopped her in her tracks.

The ornament was back in the middle of the floor.

The planter that moved across the floor

Chapter 10

The next week Lillian came through the door with her arms laden with boxes from the Dorchester house. The temperature inside the Victorian was cold enough for her to see her breath, but she brushed it off impatiently. She planned on unloading the car, putting some of the stuff away, and then heading back home in time for dinner, but those thoughts were whisked away the minute she stepped into the foyer.

Something about the basement called to her.

She wasn't sure what it was, but she felt drawn down there as if she was being pulled by an invisible string. As if moving in a dream, she set the box down near the grand staircase and made her way down the narrow wooden stairs, the smell of mold and mildew becoming sharper as she descended further into the depths.

The basement was endlessly dark, but she didn't mind it. She just stood there for a few seconds and let her eyes adjust. Finally, she pulled the cord on the light fixture, which was nothing more than a bare bulb dangling from the ceiling. A fan of soft yellow light radiated from the bulb, chasing the dark shadows back to the corners of the room.

Everything that happened to her during the last visit felt like a distant memory. She didn't give it any thought. It was a new house. There were bound to be things they didn't know about it. She lived in plenty of other houses where strange noises were eventually explained as mice in the walls or loose boards caught in the wind. They would figure this out soon enough.

Besides, she was on a mission.

She hated having to wait until April to get started with the house projects when there was so much they needed to do. If she could finish a little at a time over the winter, she figured she would be that much more ahead of the game later.

As she looked around, she took a mental inventory of the things she needed to do. Cleaning would be a top priority, followed by organizing. They could use the space for storage, something they never seem to have enough of at their old house.

She tried to put her finger on why the basement was so alluring to her. Maybe it was because it felt more genuine. The rest of the house was ornate and lavish, but the basement was where the real work took place. She could see it in the worn soapstone sink and feel it in the rough texture of the brick walls. The people who spent time in this basement were hardworking people. She imagined how they worked their fingers to the bone trying to make life easier for the masters of the house. She almost felt a kinship with them.

Nothing had ever come to her easily. She'd had to work hard for everything she had. Born in Puerto Rico, her family had relocated to the United States when she was a child. When she and Edwin first met, it was one of the first conversations they had. He had a similar story. He was also born in Puerto Rico in the very same hospital where she was born.

She pulled her thoughts away from her daydreams and looked around. There was so much history imbedded in those walls. The basement was a place where the house told its secrets.

As she explored the basement, she found remnants of the 1875 electric bell system that allowed people in the house to communicate with one another from different floors. Faded yellow tags marked the wires with locations in the house. Although it had long been disconnected, it spoke volumes of the life of the people in that time. Nowadays, if a house didn't have an intercom system, all people had to do was pull out their cell phones and send a text message to one another. So much had changed in a century. While she was happy with the modern conveniences of today, she felt a bit nostalgic about the era in which the earlier residents lived.

The unpacked box upstairs was immediately forgotten as she decided to get started with the cleaning instead. It would be one less thing to do later and besides, it would give her a chance to test the new shop vacuum she bought.

She wanted to remove all the nasty cobwebs. They coated the ceilings so thickly she could barely see the rafters beneath them. Every time she walked through, they caught in her hair. She wasn't necessarily afraid of spiders, but she didn't like the mess. It seemed like a good place to start.

She plugged the vacuum in and started vacuuming the back corner. As soon as she started, the machine turned off.

"What the heck?" she swore under her breath. She made her way back to the vacuum cleaner thinking that it might have come unplugged, but found the toggle switch was turned off. She turned it back on and the machine roared to life.

She returned to her vacuuming, only to have it happen again.

"Really?" she asked, looking around.

She turned it back on and had barely started working when it happened again.

"All right, I don't know if I believe in you guys, but if there's somebody here messing with me, please stop it. I need to get this finished," she said, adamantly.

She flipped the switch to the on position and continued vacuuming without any further interruptions.

She wasn't sure what to make of it.

One thing was for certain, she wasn't calling it paranormal without more proof. She filed it away in her mind along with the other unexplained events.

There must be an explanation.

Over the course of the winter, she made more trips to the house. Whenever she was down in the basement tackling her list of chores, she felt as though she was being watched.

It was a strange sensation, making the hair on the back of her neck prickle.

She turned around only to find herself alone.

"Is somebody there?" she asked.

The feeling was so gripping that it felt like a person should be standing there. A horrifying thought came to her. Maybe someone had broken into the house. She ran back up to check the doors.

She jiggled the handle on the side door and was relieved to discover it was still locked. She checked the front door as well, also finding it locked.

"That's so strange," she whispered to herself.

She just stood there in the fading light and looked around. The house was quiet except for the occasional sound of cars driving past. If someone broke in, they must have locked the doors behind them.

"Get a grip," she told herself, and she went back down to the basement. She wanted to finish the rack she was building, so she could start to fill it with gardening supplies on her next visit. She picked the directions up from the concrete floor, and tried to find the place where she left off, but the feeling of being watched just wouldn't go away.

She looked up again, finding the doorway empty.

"This is so frickin weird," she said.

Something fell over in another room. As she turned to stare in that direction, she saw a dark shadow dart across the doorway.

What the hell was that?

An uneasiness came over her, chilling her to the bone. She tiptoed to the base of the basement staircase and looked around. Shadows shouldn't move in a room where there weren't any windows. All the windows were boarded up. The only light source came from the bare bulbs that dangled from chains on the ceiling. She tried to make sense of it.

How could a shadow move in a room all by itself?

It made her uneasy but she refused to give into it. She waited her entire life to have her own Victorian and she would be damned if anyone or anything was going to take that away.

Maybe she just imagined it.

She was seeing these things because she expected to see them after hearing all the ghost stories surrounding the house. It was probably nothing more than a trick of the light. Besides, she had more important things on her mind. She had a beautiful home and she wanted to spend as much time there as possible.

She fell back to her go-to reassurance that always put things back into place for her.

There must be an explanation.

The next week she began organizing the Summer Kitchen. She brought the gardening supplies from the Dorchester house and was happy to get them onto the shelves she built. Thoughts of spring filled her mind with tulips and daffodils. She had no idea what the previous owners planted. Watching them come up would be like discovering a hidden treasure.

She had a lot of plans for the gardens. She wanted to plant more perennials and flowering bushes. A house this grand deserved some colorful garnishes. As she turned to grab the bag of flower seeds, she saw the dark shadow again.

This time it was enough to make her jump.

She had almost forgotten about it while lost in her daydreams about the garden.

Something was different about it this time.

It didn't dart away like before. It moved slowly across the room and floated up to the ceiling before it passed over her head. It was long and skinny, so dark she couldn't see through it.

"What the hell is that?" she whispered to herself.

She felt her heart begin to beat faster as the shadow lingered on the ceiling. Something about it was strange. It didn't float across the room like a normal shadow. It seemed to have deliberate motions, as though it was acknowledging her, allowing her to see it.

How could this be happening?

She waved her hand over her head, wondering if she was just seeing her own shadow, but it didn't change what she was seeing. The dark mass just hovered there, as if taunting her.

"What the hell?" she whispered to herself again, more perplexed than anything.

After a few seconds, it melted into the ceiling, disappearing as though it was never there. She wanted to pretend she hadn't seen it or blame it on something that made sense, but she couldn't. There wasn't a rational explanation for it. She just saw a ghost.

It was enough to set her stomach on edge. She packed up and left, not wanting to tempt fate.

On the drive home, the image ran through her head again and again. As the cars whizzed past her on the Mass Pike, she stayed in the far right lane, remaining under the speed limit as her mind tried to process what happened at the house.

Knowing that she saw a ghost meant she had to start believing in them. All her life, she rolled her eyes at people who told ghost stories. She lumped them together with all the other crazy people, like the ones who claimed they were abducted by aliens or saw Bigfoot. It just didn't make any sense to her.

"What the hell *was* that?" she whispered again.

Edwin looked up as she came in the door an hour later.

He was watching a paranormal show with her brother Will. He hated to admit it, but his interest in the paranormal had increased threefold since they bought the Victorian. There was something so intriguing about the concept. He wasn't sure if he believed or not, but it wouldn't hurt to learn a little more before they moved into their own supposedly-haunted house.

The show they were watching had documentation of a spirit child on film. Lillian came in just as they were showing the footage again.

"Hey Lil, check this out," Edwin said, pointing at the television screen.

The translucent image of a child drifted across a room on the TV.

Lillian took one quick glance and turned away.

"That's nothing compared to what I saw today," she said sharply and walked out of the room.

Edwin and Will exchanged curious glances.

"What was that all about?" Will asked.

Edwin stared down the hallway. He hated it when she did that, but he was pretty much used to it by now. That was just the way she was. If she didn't want to talk about something, nothing was going to convince her otherwise. He just let it go for the moment, but his mind still raced.

He was a researcher for an insurance company. His job was to get to the root of the problem and find a solution. He wasn't prone to jumping to conclusions. Before he could truly believe it, he needed to see more proof.

His mind was filled to the brim with uncertainty, though.

After the things they experienced, he was more confused than ever. Surely, there was a sensible explanation for all of it. He didn't know what it was, but it was better to look for valid reasons, than to succumb to the rumors and start believing in ghosts.

He wasn't even aware ghosts could do those things. He always imagined them as filmy apparitions that sometimes lingered at old houses. The idea that they could actually move furniture was unnerving. He wasn't sure what to think.

He wanted to talk it over with Lillian, but he didn't think she would be receptive to the conversation. She was always so dead set on her opinion of ghosts. The conversation would be over before it even began.

After Will left, he found Lillian in the kitchen cooking dinner. She had her hair pulled back into a ponytail as she dug her hands into a bowl of raw ground beef, mixing it by hand. Her signature silver earrings dangled from her ears, swinging with the motion.

He pulled a bottle of water from the refrigerator and sat down at the table.

She turned to smile at him as though nothing out of the ordinary had happened to her.

"I'm making meatloaf. You didn't eat while I was gone, did you?" she asked.

Edwin just shook his head, his mind still filled with thoughts of apparitions. Without knowing what she saw at the mansion, his mind began manufacturing a variety of options. None of them were any good. In fact, they were probably worse than what actually had happened. He took a swig of his water and decided to try again. Maybe she just didn't want to scare her brother.

"Will's gone now. Can you tell me what you saw?" he asked.

She turned, her face a perfect mask. "What do you mean?"

"What you saw at the house, at our house. You said you saw something worse than what we were watching on TV," he said, his voice rising in question.

"Oh that?" She pulled the ground beef from the bowl and plopped it down in a baking dish. "Nah. I don't want to talk about it." The tone in her voice was undeniable. She wasn't going to budge. "Can you hand me the aluminum foil?" she asked, changing the subject.

Edwin wouldn't find out about the dark shadow in the basement for several years.

When Lillian said she didn't want to talk about, she wasn't mincing words. Normally, her feisty personality was something he loved about her, but this time it just made him anxious.

What did she see?

*Dark shadow on the second floor in the Victorian
Photo courtesy of Conscious Spirit Paranormal*

Chapter 11

In April of 2009, Lillian and Edwin finally moved into their Victorian mansion. It was a joyous day. Friends and family gathered to help them make the transition. They rented a trailer and made quick work of it, making trip after trip until every last stick of furniture was moved. Music played from a radio in the kitchen, filling the air with a happiness Lillian could almost touch.

By the time they unpacked the last load, everyone was thoroughly exhausted. Even their two dogs weren't their usual selves.

Wendy and Nina were usually very happy-go-lucky Maltese dogs, content to be with their owners. This changed quickly as soon as they moved into the house.

Both dogs had an instant aversion to the grand staircase. They stood at the bottom and just stared up the stairs, the hair on the back of their necks rising.

"What's the matter, sweeties," Lillian crooned to them.

They turned and gave her a quick glance before turning back to the stairs with their hackles raised.

She took a few steps up the stairs and tried to call them. "Come on up!" she said in her sweetest voice, but the dogs wouldn't budge. With a sigh, she walked back down and scooped them both up to carry them up the stairs.

She found Edwin in his office. Cords and wires covered his desk like snakes as he worked on setting up his computer.

"Hey Hon, how's it going?" she asked, breezily.

Edwin looked up and mumbled something about printer cables. It was enough to make Lillian smile. When Edwin was deep into a project, he'd stick with it until he finished. Trying to interrupt him would be a fruitless effort. Instead, she just plopped the two dogs down on the floor.

"You two can hang out with Daddy," she told them and headed back to the landing to start on the boxes.

She started sorting through the boxes, looking for the box of linens they brought from Dorchester. She was elbow deep in the first box when she heard the telltale sound of toenails clicking against the hardwood floor. She looked up to find Nina and Wendy parked in front of her. They stuck closely to her for the rest of the afternoon, occasionally casting wary looks over their shoulders.

"There's no such thing as ghosts," she told them adamantly, but they still continued to cower.

As day turned to night, Lillian finished making up a bedroom for her and Edwin to sleep in the Red Room. She wanted to spend more time working on the master bedroom before they moved into it. She had wallpaper to strip, floors to scrub and a bedroom set to finish. Until she could get everything done to her satisfaction, they would simply use another bedroom. They certainly had enough of bedrooms to choose from.

The Red Room made the most sense since it was just off the landing and was the first to be furnished. She found a perfect bedroom set on Craigslist during the winter and was happy with the way it looked. She wasn't worried about the legends. If a woman died in there, then so be it.

Edwin was a bit more concerned.

"Hon, didn't a woman die in here?" he asked.

Lillian all but rolled her eyes at him. "Seriously Edwin. We don't even know if that's the truth or not. You know how people make stuff up. The house is over a hundred years old. For all we know people died in all the rooms," she said.

He looked a little wounded by her bluntness, so she gave him a smile. "It'll be fine. We'll just sleep in the Red Room for a few weeks, and then we'll move into our master bedroom, where that guy burned to death in," she said, trying not to laugh.

Edwin smiled this time and they shared a laugh. It was true, she thought as she started putting the linens on the bed. With a house this old, anything could have happened in it. It didn't mean that it was haunted, though. People died all the time. If everybody came back as ghosts when they died, the world would be full of them, all bumping into one another. The thought gave her a chuckle as she stuffed a pillow into a pillowcase.

It was an interesting piece of history, though. She wasn't sure how she would find out the whole story, but she intended to look into it further at some point.

As the story went, the house was used as a boarding house between 1926 and 1965. A woman who was known to be a prostitute allegedly used the Red Room to turn tricks. One of her customers wasn't happy with her services and strangled her on the bed. In order to escape the house, he stuffed her body in a closet to make his hasty escape. Since that time, people supposedly complained of having difficulties breathing in the room. Women especially felt a strong sense of discomfort, wanting to spend as little time there as possible.

They researched it and were not able to find any documentation to support the claims, but it was an interesting story. Despite the rumors, it was a gorgeous room, with detailed hand carved woodwork and lavish red striped wallpaper. The windows were six feet tall and stretched from the ceiling almost to the floor, allowing the room to become flooded with moonlight. She wasn't sure what to think about it. She knew the house had been a boarding house because of all the brass numbers on the doors, but she needed to see the death certificate before she truly believed a woman died there. People had a way of exaggerating things.

As they settled into bed for the night, both dogs climbed between them, happy for attention after a long day of moving. Lillian fell asleep with a smile on her face, content to finally be sleeping in her beloved Victorian. If there was a dead woman there, she'd have to wade through a whole lot of happiness to get to her.

Lillian had a routine each night at bedtime. She liked to kneel on the bed and then wrap two large blankets around herself. Then she would ease down on the bed, falling onto her stomach, making sure the blankets were tightly cocooned around her. The house was cold during at night, and she wanted to ensure she remained warm. Edwin smiled as he watched her. He had two blankets of his own as well, but he wasn't as fastidious about the process.

He had all but forgotten about the woman dying in the room by the time he slipped into bed. Setting up his home office had been much more trying than he imagined. He wished he spent a little more time marking the cords before he unplugged them at the house in Dorchester. He drifted off to sleep, ticking off a checklist of things he needed to accomplish the next day, unaware of the spirit activity surrounding him.

He woke up several hours later to the sound of the dogs growling.

He sat up, still half asleep, shaken by the sound. In all the years they'd had the dogs, he only heard them growl a handful of times. Maltese dogs just weren't prone to growling.

"Nina? Wendy? What's the matter?" he asked them.

Neither dog even glanced in his direction. Their attention was riveted on something in the hallway outside the bedroom door. Edwin stared into the darkness, trying to see what they were looking at.

His mind went into high alert.

Did someone break into the house?

At first, he didn't see anything, but as his eyes adjusted, he began to see a dark shape take form. It was tall and thin, and as dark as night. It moved slowly across the hallway towards a small table that sat opposite the Red Room doorway.

"What the hell?" he whispered to himself.

A satellite radio sat on the table beside a table lamp. A small blue light glowed from the radio's screen, sending a soft light fanning out on the table. As he watched in horror, the black shape moved past the light, completely blocking it out.

He felt all the air leave his lungs as he tried to remember how to breathe again.

Was he really seeing that?

He closed his eyes and then opened them again, but the shape was still there. There was no denying it. His legs began to tremble uncontrollably.

The shape turned towards him, as if drawn by his fear. He stared wide-eyed, unable to do more than breathe.

Would it come towards him?

Could it feel his fear?

He nudged Lillian, trying to wake her so she could see it too, but she didn't budge.

When he turned back around, the shape was gone.

The dogs continued to stare for a moment longer, and then put their heads down to fall back asleep, as though the crisis was over.

He eased out of bed, his bare feet hitting the cold wooden floor with a start. He wasn't sure if what he saw was human or paranormal. Both possibilities terrified him to the core. He turned the thoughts over in his mind. His first inclination was to think it was paranormal, but what if it wasn't? What if someone had broken into the house, thinking the house was still vacant? If that was the case, they were going to be sorry. It was one of the reasons he left Dorchester. If he couldn't feel safe in a small town like Gardner, he couldn't feel safe anywhere.

As he looked around for a weapon, he kicked himself for forgetting to unpack the baseball bat he kept by the door at the Dorchester house. He grabbed a silver candleholder from the table near the door, and then tiptoed out into the hallway.

He just stood there for a few minutes, letting his eyes adjust.

Light filtered in through the window over the stairs from a street light. It glinted across the spokes of the staircase, sending long shadows onto the stairs. A car drove past on West Broadway. He listened to the sound of the engine until it faded, but couldn't pick up on any other sounds.

Surely if vandals had broken in, he'd hear them.

He took a step towards the railing and peered down over the edge. The staircase was empty. He stood still, trying to pick out a sound that would give them away, but the house was silent. With a house this old, it was impossible to cross from one space to another without making some sort of noise.

He went into the nursery and flipped on the light. The room was filled with boxes, but was otherwise empty. He tiptoed down the hallway and checked his office, finding it exactly like he'd left it earlier.

As he turned, he bumped into someone.

A scream nearly made its way out his mouth before he realized it was Lillian.

"Oh my God," he said, feeling his pulse pounding in his temples.

Thank God he wasn't holding the bat.

"What are you doing?" she asked, peering around him to look in the office. He quickly told her what he'd seen. Together they checked the rest of the house, not finding anything amiss. The doors were still locked and the house was empty.

What the hell was that?

As they climbed back in bed, she went through her blanket process all over again, and then fell asleep within minutes. It took Edwin far longer.

He just lay there, trying to process what he saw.

This was more than a planter scooting across the floor or an ornament rolling across the room. It was an actual ghost moving through the hallway. How could that be explained?

His heart pounded as he thought about it.

Where did the entity go? Was it hiding behind a doorway waiting for him to fall back asleep, or did it go somewhere else? He thought about all the paranormal shows he watched in the past and tried to compare his experience to what he watched, but he still couldn't fathom it. Had it been a real ghost? What else was it capable of doing?

He must have fallen asleep at some point during the night, because he woke early the next morning, frozen to the core. As he opened his eyes and looked around, he realized his blankets had been pulled off him during the night and were lying in a pile several feet from the bed. He turned to look at Lillian who was still cocooned in her blankets. Events from the night before returned to him and he looked around wondering what was happening. Was it paranormal, or was it just his imagination?

Everything would change when it happened again the next night. Then he knew it was real.

It would continue every night for the first few weeks they were in the house, but that was only the beginning.

The house had formally welcomed them, but it was just getting started.

"The Copper Room"   Photo by Frank Grace (Trig Photography)

"The Red Room" Photo by Frank Grace (Trig Photography)

Chapter 12

The next morning, Lillian was up bright and early, ready to tackle the first of many projects. She enjoyed having a mental punch list to work on. It gave her a sense of accomplishment when she made it all the way through the list. Unfortunately, there was so much to do, she didn't even know where to start. Maybe she'd start by hanging some of the curtains.

She went into the bathroom to brush her teeth when she heard a strange but familiar sound. The piano at the bottom of the stairs played three notes. She lifted her head from the sink, thinking she must be mistaken.

Why would the piano be playing?

She spit out the toothpaste and walked into the bedroom. Edwin opened his eyes as she walked in.

"Hon, did you hear that?" she asked.

Edwin lifted up to his elbow. "Hear what?"

"The piano just played three notes, like dum-dum-dum."

She frowned, trying to make sense of it. She never owned a piano before, so she didn't know if this was common or not. Could there be a simple explanation? Maybe a mouse was inside and walked across a wire? She didn't know. She started down the stairs, intent on figuring it out. As she was halfway down the stairs it happened again.

"There it is again," she called.

Edwin climbed out of bed and joined her on the stairs.

"I thought I heard something, but I wasn't sure what it was. Did it play three different notes or the same note three times?" he asked.

"The same note three times," she told him. In the distance, she heard the sound of children laughing outside. Edwin glanced out the window.

"It's just kids playing outside," he told her.

"I know, but...," she said, her voice trailing off. In her mind, she pictured a small child standing near the piano, reaching over to toy with the keys. She looked out the window to find the children who were laughing. Was a voice in the wind any different than a phantom piano player? Just because she didn't see them, it didn't mean they weren't there.

Was it possible they had a ghost?

The thought gave her a cold chill.

She stared at Edwin, willing him to say it.

We have ghosts.

Edwin's face was a mixture of emotions, but he didn't say the words she hoped to hear. Instead, he ran his hands through his hair and down his face, something he did when he was tired. A part of her wanted to talk about it and sort it out, but another part of her wanted to just push it aside. She didn't want to start believing in ghosts. It was much easier to pretend it wasn't happening. Once she gave into it, it would make it real.

"That is strange," he said, offering no other explanations.

She shook her head, and then headed back to the landing to sort through a pile of boxes, putting the experience as far from her mind as she could. She didn't want to consider the possibilities. She couldn't imagine what people would say if they started talking about having ghosts in their house. Maybe it wasn't true. Maybe it was just something wrong with the piano.

They learned some disturbing news shortly after moving in. There were five confirmed deaths that happened inside the house.

It gave Edwin a chill just thinking about it.

He read them off starting with the earliest death, "Susan Pierce, S.K.'s first wife, died in the house in 1876, from erysipelas. S.K. Pierce died in the house in 1888, from typhoid pneumonia. Ellen Pierce, S.K.'s second wife, died in the house in 1902, from carcinoma. Rachel Pierce, the daughter of S.K. Pierce's youngest son Edward, died in the house from gastroenteritis in 1918, at the age of two."

Most of the people on the list were family members. There was no mention of the prostitute from the Red Room. He ended by adding, "Eino Saari died in the house in 1963, from smoke inhalation." His was the most curious death of all.

Eino Saari was a forty-nine-year old resident of Gardner. His father Matti and his mother Serafina were Finnish immigrants who moved to the Unites States just before Eino's birth. Eino left school in the fifth grade, and worked odd jobs before he enlisted in the military in World War II. He received an honorary discharge just a year later due to a head injury, which would leave him with a metal plate in his head. The plate caused severe headaches, which he often self-treated with alcohol. It was said that moonshine was his spirit of choice.

Eino lived in the house at the time it was a boarding house called the Victorian Inn. By all accounts, Eino kept to himself. He worked off and on as an auto mechanic at a nearby garage. He got along with the other residents of the boarding house, but he had a slightly dark side, as well. Often sullen and moody, he turned to his moonshine to ease his increasing depression.

On April 9, 1963, the Gardner Fire Department was called to the Victorian Inn after reports of smoke and flames were seen coming from the second floor. The firefighters extinguished the flames and to their amazement, the fire was contained exclusively to the bed, as well as to the person lying on top of it. The floors, ceilings and walls were mysteriously untouched by the fire.

While it was deemed a mattress fire, it was curious news for Gardner. Rumors swirled around town that a man died of spontaneous combustion, something relatively unheard of at that time. It was more than likely that his love of moonshine, combined with his careless smoking caused his death, but no one would ever know the absolute truth. It was reputed that Eino never left the house after dying, and that his spirit still wandered the hallways.

He died in the room they used as the master bedroom. It was the largest of the bedrooms, with two bay windows overlooking the streets below, a massive walk-in closet once used as a sewing room, and a beautiful dark grey marble fireplace with a hidden compartment behind it where Eino might have hidden his liquor.

Lillian and Edwin frequently noticed the smell of burning wood in the room. The scent would come on strong. It smelled exactly like a campfire, and then it would drift away seconds later, making them wonder if they really smelled it in the first place. It was one of the rooms that Edwin felt uncomfortable in when he first toured the house, but he didn't give it much thought at the time. Moving into the master bedroom from the Red Room was a welcome relief. It made him feel as though they were finally getting settled.

"The Master Bedroom" Photo by Frank Grace (TRIG Photography)

The first night in their new bedroom would prove to be similar to the terrifying nights they spent in the Red Room.

Edwin woke up to the sounds of the dogs growling again. He sat up and looked out into the hallway at the place where the dogs were staring.

Something black was moving around again.

He felt his breath catch in his throat. He didn't imagine it, because there it was again. He watched it move back and forth in front of the doorway, praying it wouldn't look his way.

It paused and a sense of fear froze him to the bed.

Dear God. Don't walk into the bedroom, he prayed.

The figure stood there for an eternity before it moved out of his sight.

After a few minutes, the dogs settled back down as if they knew the entity had left.

It was all a little unnerving for Edwin. Falling asleep became harder and harder. He would stare at the ceiling, wondering what was going to happen next. He spent many sleepless hours staring into the darkness, contemplating what he had gotten himself into this time. Lillian might not believe the house was haunted, but he was pretty certain it was. How else could he explain the things he experienced?

He wasn't seeing random shadows or light play. The shape he saw was the dark and definitive silhouette of a man. He started researching it on the Internet and came up with the concept of shadow people. What he found left him cold.

A shadow person was typically a dark shadow in the shape of a human being. Most people would see them out of the corners of their eyes, often dismissing them as a trick of the lighting or an overactive imagination.

Those who saw them up close knew better.

There were many different opinions about what they really were. Some people believed they were simply dark versions of apparitions. Others thought they were never human at all. A nonhuman entity wasn't something you wanted to mess with, as Edwin soon found. They were often evil and mischievous, sometimes bordering on dangerous. Some people even classified them as demonic.

Believing in demons wasn't something Edwin was comfortable with. He was barely getting adjusted to the idea of believing in ghosts. The fact that there were so many different classifications of manifestations was alarming. What was the difference between a ghost and a shadow person? Some people claimed that the difference could be tremendous. While an earthbound ghost was typically harmless, a shadow person of the nonhuman variety could host a world of trouble. Was that who was causing the sounds they heard in the house?

Was it the ghost of Eino Saari? Was he walking around in the middle of the night?

The thought was terrifying, and he wasn't sure what to do about it.

Should he just ignore it and hope it goes away? Should he try to reason with it?

Is there something that would appease it?

He wasn't sure what to do. It turned bedtime into a stomach-clinching venture.

How many ghosts did they have?

He would add another one to the mix the next morning when he woke up to a strange sound.

It pulled him out of his sleep slowly. As he woke, he could hear a woman singing.

He froze with his eyes closed, too afraid to open them for fear of what he might see.

The longer she sang, the more he relaxed. Nothing in the sound was frightening. In fact, the voice was beautiful and pure. It almost sounded as though he was being serenaded by angels.

He kept his eyes closed until the sound faded away, wondering if he imagined it.

When it happened the second morning, he gave up on the illusion that it was just his imagination. It was as real as the sounds of cars and trucks rumbling past on West Broadway Street. He strained to listen, but he couldn't pick out any words.

"Hon, do you hear that?" he asked Lillian one morning.

As soon as she rolled over, the chanting stopped.

He wasn't sure what to make of it.

Who was it? And what did she want?

It was just another layer of the house, presenting itself to him.

The activity made him anxious, but didn't completely unnerve him until it escalated.

Chapter 13

Edwin spent long moments wondering about what he'd been seeing on the second floor landing. He sat at his computer, thoughts wandering wildly through his mind.

Who was the ghost? Was it the man who supposedly self-combusted?

What did he want?

Would he just linger around the second floor landing, or was there more to come?

That was what really bothered Edwin the most. If he had to live with a ghost who floated around the hallway casting shadows on the wall, he could probably manage that. The terror came with the unknown. What else did the ghost have up its sleeve?

With the living, you usually had a good idea of what people were capable of. You could watch their facial expressions and gestures, or take a pulse from their previous actions. Being a wary person, it didn't take him long to decide whether to trust people or not. He went with his gut reactions, and he was usually very accurate with the assessment. With ghosts, it was much more difficult.

This one was elusive and retreating. It did things when no one was supposed to be looking. It pulled the covers off his bed when he was in the Red Room. It wandered around the second floor landing, causing the dogs to growl. A horrifying thought flooded his mind as he considered it.

What if there was more than one ghost?

What if something else was pulling the covers off him in the Red Room?

The thought was appropriately unnerving. Instead of trying to figure out what one ghost wanted, he most likely had a house full of restless spirits to decipher.

As he walked into the bedroom each night, the thoughts weighed heavily on his mind.

He knew so little about Eino Saari beyond the tragedy of his death.

What kind of man was he, and most importantly, what kind of ghost did he become?

Was he violent?

Was he prone to lashing out at people?

He found it increasingly difficult to close his eyes at night, leaving him at the mercy of the ghosts. What more could they do? He tried not to imagine them floating around the room, watching them, but the thought was almost impossible to avoid.

He closed his eyes, willing sleep to find him quickly, but it seldom did. He'd hear a sound in the corner of the room and spend the next ten minutes trying to analyze it. Was it a floorboard popping or someone tapping on a window? He would start to drift off again, and then he would hear what sounded like footsteps on the stairs.

After what seemed like hours, Edwin finally collapsed into sleep, only to be awoken very suddenly by the slamming of a door.

The sound was so loud and so forceful that the entire house shook with the impact.

The dogs began barking madly as he flew from bed and stared at the door.

His heart pounded in his chest as he tried to make sense of what was happening. A sense of chaos and shock filled the room.

"What was that?" Lillian whispered, sitting bolt upright in bed, her eyes wide.

Edwin was so stunned, he couldn't find the words for a few moments. He just stared at the closed door as his mind searched for a logical explanation.

"Hon?" she asked again.

"The door just slammed," he said distractedly and began walking slowly towards it. What could cause a door to slam with such great force? It couldn't be the wind because all the windows were closed.

Did someone break in?

Even after everything that had happened, his first reaction was that it was caused by a person. He didn't even consider that it might be a ghost. His Dorchester upbringing rose to the surface and he flew into action. If there was someone on the other side of it, he wasn't going to go easy on them. He yanked the door open, only to find the hallway empty.

He stared into the darkness, his heart beating heavily.

Nothing moved.

The house was quiet as he stood there listening. Surely if someone broke into the house, he'd hear some sounds. They couldn't hide forever.

He tiptoed into the landing and peered over the staircase, the same thing he did when he first saw the shadow person. He flipped on the light and looked into each room, satisfied they were alone. If there was someone there, they wouldn't have time to run away. No one was there.

That only left one thing.

It must have been a ghost.

His stomach tightened at the thought.

Was this the next level?

What would come next?

He came back into the room, not sure what to do. How do you combat an enemy who is invisible? If it were a living person, he could handle it. He knew what to do, but this was a complete unknown.

He became aware of Lillian sitting on the bed, watching him.

"Anybody there?" she asked. Both dogs were on her lap, their eyes riveted on the closed door as though they expected it to fling closed again.

"No," he started to say, when the activity picked back up again.

As if it was waiting for him to turn, the closet door beside the bed began closing and then slammed shut with another bang. The sound echoed through the room with the same velocity as before.

They both jumped, startled beyond words.

The dogs erupted with barks and growls.

Edwin didn't know what to do. He approached the closet door, anxiety rushing through his veins.

What would he find on the other side? And what would he do when he found it?

He flung the door open, only to find the walk-in closet empty.
What next?

That was the only thought he could hold onto as the night closed in on him.

He shut both doors and walked back to bed, his heart heavy with the prospects that hovered like a promise in their futures. There would never be any rest. They'd always be on their guard, waiting for the next horrible thing to happen.

He wasn't sure if he could deal with that.

It took him hours to get back to sleep as his mind played and replayed the recent events.

Was there a possible explanation, or was it something darker?

If it was an actual ghost, what more was it capable of?

If it had the ability to move a door with such force, what else could it do?

Apparently, Eino Saari wasn't happy with his new roommates. The house would begin showing them as the activity increased threefold.

This was only the beginning.

Chapter 14

Everything seemed better when dawn broke, sending golden rays of sunlight through the windows. Gone were the terrors of the night before. It almost felt like nothing more than a bad dream.

Edwin woke and just looked around the room, trying to make sense of what happened. Daylight had a way of smoothing over the edges. In the darkness of the night he would feel the hairs on the back of his neck rise, but by the light of morning some of it seemed explainable.

The way his covers kept falling to the floor in the Red Room was the easiest to clarify.

He was probably just restless as he slept in his new home. While he'd never done that before, it was still within the realm of possibility. Otherwise, why wouldn't Lillian's covers been removed as well? Surely, ghosts weren't particular about who they haunted.

The other things could be explained away, too.

The shadows he saw in the wee hours of the morning could have been his imagination. Nighttime had a way of making everything seem more sinister. He couldn't have seen what he thought he saw. Perhaps the headlights of the cars cruising along West Broadway Street were shining through a window, causing odd shadows to move around the rooms. The slamming door took a little more resourcefulness to explain, but it was still within the realm of reason.

He was just letting the stories get to him. That's all.

He rolled over and stared at the sun shining through the window, casting a warm rectangle of light on the oak floor. It was just a house. He couldn't account for everything that was happening to them, but he would. He just needed to spend more time figuring it all out, instead of blaming it on ghosts.

There had to be a rational explanation.

Edwin usually started his workday at around 11 a.m., and he worked late into the evening. He and Lillian weren't early birds, so the schedule worked well for them. As the days progressed, he found that he loved working from home. After years of working from an office setting, being home all day seemed like a true luxury. He could set his own schedule and completely eliminate the long compute back and forth to work each day. His commute was now less than thirty steps.

He ate a quick bowl of oatmeal and then carried his coffee mug up to the second floor, to the room that had once been the Pierce nursery.

He wasn't sure why he'd chosen the room, but it had a good feel to it. It was painted a deep royal blue, with windows facing Union Street and the side yard. The location was convenient and sunny. It was a bright space with plenty of room for his desk and files. He could easily look out to see if someone pulled up in front of the house, which was helpful with the frequent visits from plumbers and electricians.

Instead of pushing his desk up against a wall, he made it face the interior of the room. He liked being able to look up and see the entire room. This placement also kept the sun out of his eyes, and prevented him from daydreaming out the window, two things that were important for having a productive day.

The room had two doorways, one led to a smaller room once used as the nanny's quarters, and the other led to a long, narrow hallway leading to the second floor landing.

Work was busier than normal, which was good. It kept his mind occupied and prevented him from thinking about all the things that were happening to them in the house. He went from one call to another, completing reports and emails whenever there was a lull in the action. As the day began to wind down, he was busy wrapping up his projects, so he could spend time with Lillian that evening.

Without warning, something dark swooped in towards him.

As he looked up, he was shocked to find himself face to face with an apparition.

He gasped, nearly falling out of his chair.

There was no denying it this time. The ghost was as real as a live person.

He was frozen to the spot, terror pinning him in place as he stared at the apparition. It was a man with jet black eyes and bags beneath them. He looked as though he lived a very hard life. His face was thin and gaunt, and his plaid shirt was a flannel material. A pale white halo seemed to encapsulate him, making him look as though he was surrounded by light. What terrified Edwin the most was the look in the man's eyes. He looked angry, as though Edwin was violating his space, instead of the other way around.

Edwin flung himself away from the entity, hitting the floor with a thump.

He turned to look over his shoulder, but the apparition was gone.

He felt as though his heart leapt up into his throat.

Who was that?

Was it Eino Saari, who supposedly had spontaneously combusted in the master bedroom?

Was he the one who slammed the bedroom door?

Gone were all thoughts of trying to explain the incidents. In one fell swoop, he was thoroughly convinced. His entire body began trembling violently and he struggled to find his feet. As he pulled himself upright, his legs felt like rubber beneath him. He closed his eyes for a second and tried to get a hold of himself. The room felt like it was spinning all around him.

"Oh my God," he whispered.

What did he just see?

He made his way downstairs. The hairs on the back of his neck were still standing on end. The image of the face kept flashing into his mind. He found Lillian in the kitchen. He was so shaken, he could barely get the words out.

"You saw *what?*" she asked, sitting down at the kitchen table with him.

He told her what he saw. They both walked back upstairs to look, but the apparition was long gone. As he walked back down, he realized he wasn't even comfortable being in his own house.

If one ghost jumped out at him like that, what would stop another from doing the same thing?

Would he spend the rest of his days just waiting for the next spirit to appear?

The thought was unnerving.

It was getting close to dinnertime, so he walked across the street to pick up sandwiches, thinking that it might help him clear his head, and help him get some perspective on what was happening.

Daylight was quickly fading, leaving the sky swept with an array of colors. The cool air felt good on his face. Edwin took a deep breath, trying to steady himself. He would get through this. He had made it through worse situations before, growing up in Boston. There was nothing he couldn't handle.

As he crossed the street to get to the pizza shop, he noticed an ambulance pulling away. A small crowd had gathered. He could hear them whispering among themselves as they watched it drive away.

Edwin parted through the crowed, curious as to what had happened.

"Was that an ambulance just leaving here?" he asked the counter clerk.

"Some guy had a heart attack and died before the ambulance could get here," he said.

Edwin was stunned, all of his confidence swept away in a moment. He picked up his sandwiches and went back home.

Was the apparition someone from the house, or was it the man who just died?

What did it all mean?

Unfortunately, the mysteries of the mansion continued, one happening before Edwin and Lillian had a chance to recover from the last.

The house had proven its point to them. It was haunted.

There was no denying it.

Edwin's drawing of the entity

The Grand Staircase from above Photo by the author

Chapter 15

Thoughts of the apparition haunted Edwin day and night.

If it was capable of slamming doors and materializing in front of his face, what else was it capable of doing to them?

What next?

The words rang through his head like a mantra, following him through the dark halls of his house. Every doorway he passed became suspicious. He eyed it as he passed, expecting another specter to lunge out at him. He couldn't take it anymore. He needed to know what he was dealing with in the house. He finally broke down and called the former homeowners to see if they also experienced anything strange.

He knew very little about Mark Veau except for what the realtor told him. He knew he worked as a disc jockey at a local radio station, and that he was forced to sell the house after his divorce. Edwin watched the episode of *Ghost Hunters* Mark was a part of, so he knew what the man looked like, but he was still a little nervous reaching out to him.

For one thing, he hated admitting that the house was haunted.

He might have been able to pass some of the other activity off as normal, but there was no way to explain the apparition.

He was relieved to find Mark very cordial and willing to share his experiences. The stories Mark told him were all too familiar, deepening his doubts about living in the house.

Although Mark had never been fearful in the house, he experienced some of the same occurrences they had lived through. Doors in the house would often open and close all by themselves, and items often disappeared only to reappear somewhere else. This happened frequently with Mark's keys. He would always leave them in his designated place, only to find them somewhere else entirely.

Mark also told him about Mattie Cornwell, the young nanny who lived in the house and cared for the Pierce children. He said that a medium felt that Mattie was still in the house, caring for the children and watching over the house. The medium also reported that Mattie possibly had romantic inclinations towards her boss, S.K. Pierce and didn't want to leave him behind.

As Edwin listened to the stories, his blood ran cold. There was no denying that the house was haunted, but the fact that the previous homeowner had experienced similar things was a bit daunting. When Mark told him about the last spirit in the house, Edwin didn't know what to say. It was the saddest story he ever heard. A little boy spirit was trapped in the house, as well.

The first time Mark saw the little boy, he mistook him for his stepson. The boy was dressed in blue, and he ran past Mark towards the grand staircase. Mark turned, thinking his stepson got up from his bed, but he found the staircase empty. Mark then went upstairs to his stepson's bedroom, only to find him sound asleep. Mark told Edwin that he saw the boy in blue a number of times throughout the years.

The activity in the house quieted down after the appearance of the male apparition, which gave Edwin a much-needed break. While they still heard an occasional bang of a door, or footsteps on the stairs, at least nothing jumped out to scare them.

As spring moved into summer, they became busy with outside projects. They had a lengthy list of tasks they both wanted to accomplish while the weather was nice enough to allow it.

Edwin was mowing the yard one day when a man came up to him and started chatting. The day had grown hot and humid, with no relief in sight. Edwin happily took advantage of the opportunity for a break.

He shut down the mower and walked over to talk to the man, who introduced himself as Mike. He lived in the apartment building next door on the West Broadway Street side. They hadn't had a chance to really meet any of their neighbors yet, so Edwin was happy the man made the effort.

Mike seemed like a nice guy, but he definitely wasn't someone who would allow others to push him around. He had a tough side that he wore like a chip on his shoulder. He certainly wouldn't be someone who believed in ghosts.

What Mike said next stunned him. "You must have had your hands full last night."

Edwin gave him a puzzled look. "What do you mean?"

"With the little boy playing in your house last night," Mike said.

Edwin frowned. "Ummm....we don't have any children," he said, confused that the man would think they had children. He sorted through his memory, trying to remember if he'd ever been outside talking to a child, but couldn't. The only children they knew were now grown.

Mike ran his hand through his dark hair and peered up at the windows, his jaw tightened with apprehension. "A nephew, then?" he asked.

A motorcycle zoomed past the house, drowning out their voices, so they both stopped and waited for it to pass. Traffic along West Broadway was often heavy, especially in the mornings and evenings during rush hour commute. Talking outside was often difficult during those times with the house so close to the street.

"No, at least not a *young* nephew. My nephew is eighteen," Edwin said, wondering where this was going. His nephew Reo hadn't set foot in the house since the ornament incident. He doubted he would come back any time soon, either.

The man was growing visibly agitated. He turned and looked down the street towards his house, as if taking the time to gather his thoughts.

"Why?" Edwin asked, curious.

Mike turned to meet his eyes. Something about his expression made Edwin think he was a bit fearful. "Well, because I've been seeing a little boy running back and forth in the windows. He starts in this window," he said, pointing at the dining room. "Then he runs to this window seconds later," he said, pointing at the Ladies Parlor.

This was confusing to Edwin, because there was no way a child could dart back and forth between those two windows. A hallway and a staircase separated the two rooms. In order for someone to run from one room to the other, they would have to run through the doorway of the dining room, around the staircase, and down the hall into the Ladies Parlor. It made him think about what Mark Veau told him.

Was Mike seeing the little boy ghost?

"When did you see this?" Edwin asked.

"Oh, I see it all the time, sometimes during the day, sometimes at night, when I'm coming back from a run. I saw it all winter too," he said.

"I don't know what to tell you," Edwin started. "We don't have any kids, and there wasn't anyone in the house during the winter. We just moved in at the beginning of April."

Mike scowled. "You mean you weren't here all winter?" He waited for Edwin to shake his head before he continued. "Sometimes I see lights going on and off in different rooms." He pointed to the third floor window. "One will come on in that room, and then it'll go out. Then the light in this window will come on," he said, pointing to the window on the first floor. "It's almost like Christmas lights, the way they flicker on and off." He paused, as if sizing Edwin up. "And don't give me any of that ghost crap. I don't believe in that stuff. I know what I saw."

The conversation had dwindled down to nothing at that point. Lillian walked over to introduce herself. She had been busy working on a fire pit in the side yard. They stopped talking about the flickering lights and the little boy. Edwin and Lillian returned to their tasks in order to finish them up before her family arrived later for a cookout.

Edwin walked away, confused. No one was in the house all winter, except for Lillian on occasion, but there was no way she could have turned the lights on and off on various floors. It would take five or six people to accomplish what Mike was suggesting happened there. Were ghosts capable of doing those kinds of things?

He mulled it over for a few days before telling Lillian. They were on their way home from the grocery store when he mentioned it to her. She quickly shared her own story.

"You know, when we first moved in, I met another man from that same house. I think it's a boarding house or something, because I see a bunch of different people coming in and out of it," she said, as they pulled into the driveway.

She looked past the Victorian, through the trees at the boarding house beside it as if she was searching for an answer.

"Anyway, he told me it was nice that we were fixing the house up, and that he saw you upstairs painting all during the winter," she said.

Edwin shook his head. "That's crazy. There wasn't even any electricity in the house during the winter. It was like ten degrees inside. Why would I be inside painting?"

"I don't know," she said, her voice trailing out softly.

Edwin tried to make sense of it. He grabbed several plastic bags full of groceries from the trunk, looping them over one arm so he could close the lid. "You don't think it was the realtor, do you?" he asked, trying to find a logical explanation.

Lillian was quick to shoot him down.

"Why would the realtor come over here to paint after we bought the house?" she asked. "And besides, have you seen any new paint on any of the walls?"

Edwin had to admit that he hadn't. It was very strange. He wouldn't put the two incidences together until 2010 when another neighbor moved in on the other side with her own story about the little boy.

Things would continue to get stranger and stranger.

Andrew Lake, paranormal investigator and author

Photo taken in the master bedroom. Notice the light anomaly coming out of the screen in the back of the room. Photo courtesy of Andrew Lake.

Chapter 16

Summer was in full swing, bringing with it all the benefits and downfalls of the season. Since the house had no air conditioning, Edwin and Lillian spent their nights sweltering inside the warm rooms, with only window fans to ease the heat of the day. The screens were old and worn, preventing them from even opening many of the windows. They began spending more time on the porch with cool drinks or by the fire pit with friends and family who made the trek from Boston.

Random people often stopped by, entranced by the house, wanting to see more. Edwin would gladly offer a tour and listen to any stories they might offer about the house's history. He had one of the strangest visitors of all late one evening.

He opened the door to find a man standing on his porch. At first, Edwin thought the man was a salesman. Even after the man introduced himself as Andrew Lake, a paranormal investigator and author, Edwin was still waiting for a sales pitch. The man rocked him from his thoughts with one sentence.

"This house is haunted, you know," Andrew said.

Edwin's eyes widened at this. While he and Lillian were aware of the events transpiring inside the house, they hadn't shared their experiences with many others. Even their closest friends weren't privy to the stories for fear they'd think Edwin and Lillian were crazy. For the most part, they kept it all to themselves, hoping against hope that it would all settle down on its own eventually. Having someone stop and confirm it was earth shattering.

They stood on the porch talking for a moment. Andrew was writing a book about haunted locations in New England and was interested in adding a chapter about the Victorian Mansion. He He told Edwin some of the stories he knew about the house.

Edwin was shocked by the information. It was an earth shattering moment for him, one he would consider a turning point in his beliefs about the house. He shared his story with Andrew about the full body apparition that appeared in his office. By the time the evening wore down, Andrew agreed to return with a colleague.

When Andrew came back for his second visit, Edwin took him and his friend on a tour of the house. As they stood in the basement, looking at the old furnace, Andrew got a very strange sensation. Although he doesn't credit himself with being a person who is sensitive to paranormal presence, he definitely felt as though someone was standing behind him.

He turned around and looked behind him. Across from the massive octopus-shaped furnace was a collection of old, deteriorating chairs. They looked to be from the Victorian era.

"Sorry. I just had to look. It felt like someone was standing behind me," Andrew said.

Edwin's face took on a look of horror.

"I've always hated this area," Edwin told him and then told him about something that had happened to him recently. "Once when I was down here, I saw the outline of a man cross by right here and disappear into those chairs," he said pointing at the narrow space in front of the furnace." The experience frightened him so much, he avoided coming down to the basement as much as possible. When he did have to go down there, he kept his gaze locked at his feet and minimized the visit.

Andrew watched Edwin for a minute, a thought coming to him.

"Would you mind if I brought a psychic in here?" Andrew asked.

Edwin was so taken back by the question, all he could do was nod.

A psychic?

In his mind, psychics were a strange breed of people. All he knew about them was what he saw in movies and on television. He pictured them hovering over crystal balls, dressed in layers of scarves, cackling like Halloween witches. He was very wary about having one come into his house, but he agreed.

What could it hurt?

Maybe they'd learn something.

On a hot sultry August day, Andrew came back for a visit with the psychic medium. Andrew called when he was five minutes away to tell Edwin they were nearly there.

Edwin was in the master bedroom closet when he received the call, looking for a pair of shoes to wear.

"Sure, come on over," he started to say, when the screen from the window beside him suddenly flew from the window and hit the wall beside it with a bang. Edwin nearly dropped the phone.

"What was that?" Andrew asked, having heard the sound.

"Is it windy outside," Edwin asked. Looking out the window, the skies appeared to be calm. The day was stagnant and hot, with very little breeze coming through the windows. He knew the answer to the question before Andrew provided it.

"No, it isn't. In fact, this has to be the most still, hot, humid day I can remember. There isn't a bit of breeze blowing. Why?" Andrew asked.

Edwin sighed. "Because the screen just blew out of the window and flew halfway across the floor," he said. By the looks of it, it was going to be an eventful evening. The spirits were already letting them know their feelings on the matter.

When the two arrived, Edwin was very surprised at how normal the psychic really was.

Her name was Pam. She was petite with dark, curly hair and an olive skin tone. Her entire demeanor was nothing like what he expected. She was very personable, even sweet. She smiled and thanked him for allowing her to come into the house.

She took Edwin's hands in her own, but then dropped them suddenly, her face taking on an element of astonishment.

"Who's Isabella?" she asked.

Edwin nearly fell over. Isabella was his late godmother. She was the woman who was responsible for Edwin's existence in the world. She had introduced his mother and father to one another many years prior. Although she died when Edwin was six years old, he still felt a soft spot for the woman who brought his parents together.

"Did you say *Isabella*?" he asked.

The woman stared at him, transfixed. "She was a tiny woman. She liked to dress in leopard print," she said, then went on to describe her further. Edwin later called his mother and confirmed that she was correct on all accounts. It was as though his godmother was standing beside him and the psychic was describing what she was seeing.

"She wants me to tell you that she's with you, protecting you. She's your guardian angel," she said with a smile.

Edwin looked around him. After everything he experienced so far, he almost expected to watch her materialize out of thin air. Before he could even react to this, Pam started walking through the house.

It was almost as though she were being pulled in one direction, and then pulled in another. All the while, she was talking and telling them what she sensed. Edwin and Lillian exchanged puzzled glances.

What exactly were they experiencing?
Was this for real?

She was fairly quiet on the first floor, stopping here and there to stare into the air before dismissing it. "There's not much down here," she told them before heading up the grand staircase to the second floor. Much to Edwin's discomfort, she made an immediate beeline for the master bedroom.

She walked to the center of the room and looked around. At first, she didn't pick up on anything relevant beyond the fact that doors sometimes slammed and banging could be heard, but as they started to leave the room, she startled and stared at a spot near the ceiling.

"Moonshine," she said suddenly, pointing at Andrew.

Edwin and Andrew were surprised by the outburst.

"Moonshine?" Andrew asked her.

She narrowed her eyes. "Yes. Moonshine." She walked to the middle of the room. "I'm sorry to let the secret out, but there's been a man following us around. He made moonshine in this place. He died here. There was an accident. There was a fire here that I picked up on. He's a nice guy, a funny guy, but he's angry at me for telling you about it." she said.

Edwin and Lillian looked at each other, puzzled. It wasn't a far stretch for anyone to know of Eino Saari and his affection for moonshine, but they were curious by what she said next.

"You hid it in the basement, didn't you?" she asked the spot on the ceiling, smiling.

Edwin could almost feel the energy in the room swell. Every hair on his arm stood at attention as he watched her talk to an unseen entity. It unnerved him a little after all they'd experienced. He hoped she didn't do anything to anger Eino. The last thing he wanted was for him to pop up in his face again.

"Where did you get that scar?" Pam asked the air, and then nodded as if getting an answer. After a moment, she turned to them. "He was injured in a war. I think it was World War II. Do you know anything about him?" she asked.

Edwin nodded, telling her what he knew about Eino, shocked that she would be able to pick up on such details. Most people didn't know about Eino's head injury and the subsequent scar he must have had. The woman couldn't have found this information easily.

She pressed her lips together thinly. "Well, he doesn't care much for me," she admitted.

She then asked Edwin something fairly startling.

"Have you been hearing a woman singing in your ear?"

Edwin looked at her with astonishment. He'd barely even mentioned it to Lillian.

"Yes. It's sort of like chanting, but I can't make out what she's saying," he admitted.

He'd been hearing the voice off and on for the past few weeks as he was waking up in the morning. While the other events in the house terrified him, this one didn't seem to be as threatening. It was the most beautiful voice he'd ever heard. He just wished he knew what she was saying.

"She's trying to pass along a message to you. You should really try to listen harder to hear what she wants to tell you," she said, before moving onto the next room.

Edwin wasn't sure how to go about doing that, but he promised he'd try.

They made their way up to the third floor. Pam walked around the rooms, stopping to stare into each of them before settling on the Billiards Room. Everyone else just stood at the doorway, watching her. Edwin felt an equal mix of fascination and horror at the things she was telling them. It was as if she had a direct line to the afterlife. Everything she said was true, to his knowledge.

She narrowed her eyes. "There was a pool table right here," she said, pointing to the middle of the room. "The owner had a lot of very rich and famous friends who would come over to play pool with him. Am I right?" she asked.

Edwin nodded. It was one of the first stories he heard while viewing the house. It was a bit odd, though. Out of all the rooms in the house, he always felt the most comfortable here. It felt like a man's room, a place where men would sit around smoking cigars while sharing stories and laughs, even though the space was no longer outfitted for it.

She walked towards a closet that was tucked away in the corner, and stopped.

"There's a portal here," she told him.

Edwin had no idea what a portal was. All this paranormal stuff was new to him. He asked her to clarify, and she did.

"It's a doorway to the other side. They can come and go through here," she said.

It made Edwin stop in his tracks.

Several weeks ago, he had a strange experience in that very spot. While Lillian was working in her office, just across the hallway, he was in the Billiards Room trying to open one of the windows for some fresh air. As he stepped into a spot near the closet, he felt as though he sunk his foot into a pool of icy cold water. The sensation slowly climbed up his legs, making its way to his torso before chilling his entire body.

"Lillian, come here for a second," he said.

She just looked up for a second before returning to her project. "I'm busy. Can it wait a minute?"

He tried to explain what he was feeling, but it was clear she was in the middle of something and couldn't be interrupted, so he went to her.

As he came into the room, she looked up quickly, her expression marked with surprise.

"Where's that cold air coming from?" she asked, reaching down to feel her ankles. Even though the room was upwards of eighty degrees, it felt as if a block of ice had been dropped at her feet. It didn't take her long to figure out that it was coming from Edwin.

The coldness faded as fast as it came on, leaving the room sweltering hot once again.

What the psychic said chilled him even further.

Was that what he was feeling?

Things were just getting stranger and stranger.

The Red Room

Chapter 17

By September, Lillian was finally settled into the house. She knew every nook and cranny, knew the way the floorboards creaked when she stepped on them. She could walk from the bedroom to the bathroom without benefit of a light, knew where the every spice in her kitchen was kept, and which window provided the best morning sun.

She established several routines that helped guide her through her day. She awoke every morning before Edwin rose and made her way down to the kitchen to start a pot of coffee. The routines were comforting, something she could latch onto and allow them to carry her through the planned pace of the day. After the coffee pot gurgled, signaling it was finished brewing, she poured herself a cup and brought it out onto the Union Street porch, where she smoked her first cigarette of the day, enjoying the cool air on her face and the steady pace of cars passing by.

She nearly had the house squared away. All the boxes were unpacked, and the house was starting to look and feel like a home. She brought some of her decorations from Dorchester, but found they didn't fit the house as well, so she spent a lot of her days roaming around the town, finding the best shops and markets, searching for the perfect items to bring into the house. She wanted to be true to the Victorian origins of the house as much as possible. Decorating became one of her favorite pastimes.

She loved going to the local flea market in Gardner every Sunday. She walked the endless rows, her eyes scanning the tables filled with cast-offs. She found everything from furniture to table lamps at prices she could afford. Edwin laughed when she returned with their small Honda loaded to the brim.

Managing a house that large was a lot of work. It required much more coordinating and planning than what she was used to handling. Even though the previous owners had done great deal of renovating, there was still much to do.

It seemed like every time she thought she had everything organized and in its place, she discovered something else they needed, or something else that needed attention.

Or something would go wrong.

The house had fireplaces in most of the rooms, so she had them all cleaned. She even took it a step further and had the chimneys and fireplaces fixed so they were operational. Later, she was dismayed to discover that they weren't designed to burn wood. They were coal-burning fireplaces, something that would prove to be nearly useless to them once cold weather set in. They would have to figure it out before wintertime. There was no way she was staying in an unheated house.

She set up an office for herself on the third floor, in the spacious room across from the Billiards Room. The room had high ceilings, like the other rooms in the house, making the space feel even larger. She had a beautiful curved desk that she brought from Dorchester. While it completely overwhelmed the room at her old house, it seemed to fit in naturally here in the larger room. Like Edwin, she placed it so she could sit with her back to the window, so she could face the interior of the room.

The previous owners painted the walls a deep shade of blue. Chips of plaster flaked away in various places, making it look like stars on a velvety blue background. She wasn't sure what the room was used for in the beginning, but judging by the size and layout, she thought it may have belonged to the butler or someone with higher stature in the Pierce household. She liked the space. It had the same tall windows found in the rest of the house, providing her with sweeping views of Gardner. It was almost as nice as the view from the widow's walk, just above her.

The trees were beginning to transform into their full autumn glory, and the air was crisp, giving everything a fresh, new feel. Lillian always loved this time of the year. It made her think of home, family and the upcoming holidays they could spend happily in their new home.

As she was sorting through the monthly bills, she started hearing strange sounds in the hallway. She looked up, letting her reading glasses slip to the end of her nose. From her desk, she could see a small section of the Billiards Room and a slice of the hallway. Nothing seemed amiss, at least nothing she could see.

After the recent events, Lillian's original opinion on the paranormal had gone through a drastic transformation. All her lifelong beliefs crumbled like dust. It bothered her at first, but she was slowly adapting to the concept. After what they experienced, there was no denying they had ghosts in their house.

A part of her still pondered about the depth of the haunting. She wondered if a small grain of truth was simply overblown into a bigger story. She never met the former owner, but Lillian wasn't sure what to think about the stories Edwin shared with her. Still though, she saw some of the activity with her own two eyes. The dark apparition she saw in the basement was very real. What Edwin saw in his office was equally as real. She sighed and shook her head. She would consider the possibility, but was still looking for a reasonable explanation. One thing for certain, she wasn't going to let them scare her like they scared poor Edwin.

Lillian kept the thought fixed firmly in her mind. It was going to take a lot more than a dark shadow to chase her out of the home of her dreams. She waited her entire life to have her very own Victorian. If there were ghosts there, they would just have to make room for her, because she wasn't going anywhere.

She went back to her bills, sorting them into piles according to due date. As she was searching for her checkbook, she heard the sound again. It was as if someone was in the hallway, scuffling around.

"Edwin? Is that you?" she called, but there wasn't an answer.

The last time she saw Edwin, he was in the living room watching television. She glanced at the window, noticing that the sun was beginning to sink lower on the horizon. She glanced down at her watch, surprised to see it was already after six. She had steaks marinating in the refrigerator and her thoughts quickly turned towards dinner. As soon as she finished the bills, she wanted to go downstairs and start the grill. She pulled the checkbook out of a drawer and started making out the first check. The sound happened again.

"Hello?" she called out, watching the hallway for movement. This was ridiculous. What could that be?

She rose from her desk. As she reached the middle of the room, the door to the office very suddenly slammed in her face, as if preventing her from going into the hallway. She backed up slowly, and then pulled her cell phone from her pocket.

Edwin sat in his favorite chair in the living room downstairs, trying to stay focused on the television show blaring on the TV in front of him. The room they used as their living room used to be the dining room when the Pierce family lived there. Not having a need for a formal dining room, they converted it into a living room, bringing their comfortable black leather sofa and recliner from Dorchester to fill the space. It fit the room perfectly, even if it didn't match the Victorian decorating scheme Lillian had employed throughout the rest of the house. It was a comfortable space where they could relax and watch TV after a long day.

The summer was quiet for them, but he couldn't stop thinking about the stories Mark Veau, the former homeowner, shared with him. There were so many similarities, but there were many differences, too.

The first thing that bugged him was that the Veau's frequently saw the little boy.

Besides the occasional knock or footsteps on the stairs, they weren't sure they'd even encountered him yet. The only ghost Edwin had personally met was the creepy guy in the office, who he thought was probably Eino Saari claiming his space.

Seeing the apparition was life altering for him.

It not only changed his beliefs, but it stole some of the confidence he had in their safety. Even though things had been quiet recently, he still found himself watching the doorways, studying the shadows in the corners of each room, and flinching at every sudden movement. A dog darting into the room made his heart race, whereas before he would have simply smiled.

The dogs still had an aversion to the stairs. Despite everything they tried, including throwing their favorite treats onto the steps, the dogs refused to walk up them. It would have made more sense if the dogs had never been around stairs before, but that wasn't the case. When they lived in Dorchester, the dogs went up and down the stairs without issue. Something about these stairs set them off.

As the show went to a commercial break, the dogs trotted into the room and jumped up onto the chair beside him. He stroked their silky fur, thinking how strange it was that they'd given the dogs such appropriate names.

When they got their first two Maltese dogs years ago, they didn't give any thought to their names. They named Casper after the friendly ghost, because his coat was snowy white. Wendy just seemed like a good companion name. Now it seemed odd, as if it was foreshadowing their current lives. Since Casper died shortly before they purchased the house, they were back down to two dogs, Wendy and Casper's daughter, Nina.

A loud car zoomed by on Union Street, the sound momentarily drowning out the television. Both dogs looked up with alert faces. They were far edgier than they were back in Dorchester. They no longer played like they used to. He could remember a time when they would chase toys, or play tug-a-war with a rope toy, but they didn't do any of that now. They spent most of their time staring at the doorways and shadows, much like their owners.

It made Edwin remember a story Mark Veau told him. Mark knew a man named Bill Wallace, who was an empathic medium. Bill told him that S.K. Pierce didn't like dogs, and that they weren't allowed to run freely in the house. It was enough to give Edwin pause for thought.

Was that who was making the dogs so anxious, or were they just reacting to being in a new home?

The television show ended, making Edwin realize he had completely missed the ending. , He thought about getting up to refresh his drink, but before he could rise from his chair, both dogs began to growl at the doorway leading to the grand staircase. His heart immediately raced.

What now?

Was something going to pop out of the shadows like a jack-in-the-box to scare him again?

It was as if the ghosts knew he was afraid, so they used it against him every chance they got. He imagined them snickering every time he jumped, wanting to see just how far they could push him before he hit his limit.

As he stared at the doorway, he heard the sound of footsteps coming down the stairs. He relaxed a little, thinking it was Lillian. She said she would be down by six to start dinner, and he was starting to feel the first rumblings in his stomach. He started to rise from his chair to help her in the kitchen, but paused. The footsteps stopped, as if in the middle of the staircase.

"Lil?" he called out, but nobody answered.

The dogs growled a little louder, their eyes riveted to the doorway.

He could feel the hair on the back of his neck rise.

Not again.

Seconds later, the footsteps started up again. The dogs nearly went ballistic, hopping off the chair so they could bark at the doorway.

"Hon, is that you?" he said again.

There was no answer.

"Wendy, Nina! Come here," he said.

The dogs raced back to the chair and lunged into his lap, trembling, as if thankful to be pulled away from guard duty at the door. He wasn't sure how much more of this he could take. How could he ever be comfortable in his own home when someone was intent on scaring him every waking moment?

It was as if they were toying with him, giving him a few months of solitude before starting in again. Every time he began to feel comfortable, they pulled the rug out from under him once more.

Another show started on TV, so he tried to get back it, thinking he would give Lillian a few more minutes before he went to find her. Seconds later, he heard the footsteps again.

The dogs jumped from his lap and began barking at the door again. Edwin rose from his chair to look, but the hallway and stairs were empty.

What the hell?

He stared out into the hallway, his gaze traveling up the empty staircase. It felt as though someone was standing there watching him. He could almost feel the eyes boring into his head. With a sigh, he pulled the door closed and returned to his chair, trying to get a grip on his pounding heart. If they were going to live here, he was going to have to find some way to deal with it. As it was, he dropped nearly ten pounds after seeing the apparition. He wasn't sure if he could handle any more of this.

He no sooner got to his chair before the shuffling sounds started again. He froze in his chair, his mind racing a million miles a second.

When was this going to stop?

He nearly jumped out of his own skin when his cell phone suddenly rang. It was Lillian, calling from the third floor.

"Edwin, get up here NOW!" she said.

He braced himself in the chair, fearful about what she was going to tell him. "Why? What happened?"

"Just come up here, please?" she asked, her voice strained with fear.

He made it to the third floor in record time, his mind overwhelmed with the possibilities. He found her sitting in her office with the door shut. Unlike her normal cool, breezy demeanor, she was definitely rattled. She looked at him with wide eyes as he came through the doorway, almost as though she had been expecting something else to barge into the room.

"What happened?" He joined her behind the desk, alarmed at the look of fear on her face. It took a lot to unnerve Lillian.

She told him what happened.

Despite what had just happened to him, he went into researcher mode and tried to debunk the slamming door. It was a comfortable gesture, but one he wouldn't find any solace in. He opened the door and gave it a little push. It edged forward a few inches but stopped. He tried it again, giving it a harder push, but it only moved a little bit further. Finally, he gave it a good hard push, causing it to slam shut.

"That's not even as loud as it was," Lillian told him, staring at the closed door.

She abandoned the bills and they went downstairs to the living room.

"I'm just going to sit for a minute, and then I'll start dinner," she said, but as soon as she sat down, another sound jolted them.

This one was much closer.

It sounded like someone threw plastic cups onto the floor inside the butler's pantry, just to the right of the fireplace. The door was closed, but the sound was so loud, it could have almost been in the room with them.

Cups hitting the floor?

They could both clearly imagine the red plastic beverage cups being tossed onto the hardwood floor. The sound was unmistakable, but when they went there to look, they found nothing. Everything was still neatly in its place. If they even owned any plastic cups, they were tucked away inside a cabinet.

They just both looked at one another.

Where was the breaking point?

When would they simply just have enough?

Lillian's office

The dining room   Photo by Frank Grace (TRIG Photography)

Inside the widow's walk   Photo by the author

Chapter 18

The house quieted down for the next few weeks, as if it was conserving its energy for the next attack. Edwin could almost imagine them scheming and planning the next horrifying event He could almost hear their whispers as they watched him with evil smirks. He found that he truly hated being in the house alone. When Lillian left to run errands, he holed himself up in his second floor office and worked until she came back. On the rare occasion when Lillian stayed overnight to visit her family, he dreaded the prospect of spending a night alone in the house. He left every light in the house on until she came back.

Sleeping had become a huge undertaking, as well. Every night, they were woken by the sounds of the dogs growling .

When they jolted awake, they found Wendy and Nina glaring into the dark hallway, growling at something neither of them could see. Edwin felt the hair on the back of his neck rise as he watched them. They wouldn't growl if they didn't see something, but what where they seeing?

Other nights, Edwin and Lillian would wake up to find the dogs fixated on other areas, as though the ghostly visitors were roaming around the room. One night Nina and Wendy watched something near the closet for nearly an hour. The following night, their attention was drawn to a spot near the fireplace. No matter how hard Edwin looked, he couldn't interpret what the dogs were seeing. Every time he opened his eyes, he fully expected to see an apparition jump up into his face. It got to a point where he just stopped looking. He closed his eyes and tried to ignore it until sleep finally found him.

One night in mid-October, the activity escalated once again.

As they walked into their bedroom, they noticed the smell of burning wood again. The odor permeated through the air, stronger than an intangible phantom scent.

Was it Eino Saari?

After all, he had burned to death just feet from where their bed now stood.

"Do you smell that?" Edwin asked Lillian.

She came closer, tucking her hands together as she focused on the smell. "Yeah. It smells exactly like a campfire burning," she said, as if amused by it. Edwin was intrigued, but was far from amused. He wished the ghosts would just stop with all the scare tactics and leave them alone.

They got into bed and pulled up the covers. Edwin gave her a little kiss goodnight, like he always did, and they settled in for the night. The night was cool and still. As he closed his eyes, he listened to the comforting sound of traffic on the streets outside. The steady hum was interrupted by a thump on the floor above him.

He opened his eyes and stared at the ceiling.

What was that?

He stared into the darkness, trying to make sense of the sound. It almost sounded like something was knocked over on the third floor. Blood began thumping rapidly though his veins.

After several minutes passed, he closed his eyes again.

Maybe he imagined it. Or maybe it was just a shutter thumping closed in the wind.

He had barely closed his eyes when he heard another sound above him. It was followed by another sound, linking them together into something he understood. It sounded like a child running back and forth across the floor.

He nudged Lillian. "Hon, did you hear that?"

She moaned and then shifted over until she was lying on her back. He could see the profile of her face against the light from the street lamp outside. She stared at the ceiling, obviously listening.

"Yeah. It sounds like little kids running up there," she said.

There was nothing in her voice to suggest she was afraid. Edwin couldn't understand how she did it. She had nerves of steel. She recovered quickly from her fright in her office, almost too quickly. While most people would have been traumatized for months, she brushed it off with a shrug. She wasn't going to let anything get to her. It was as if she just erased it from her memory and moved on. He wished he could be that way. The activity in the house consumed his every thought.

After a few minutes, he heard the sounds of Lillian's breathing deepen as she fell back asleep. He sighed, amazed she could do that. *How could she just fall asleep when someone was walking right above them?*

There was no way he was getting back to sleep. While Lillian's nerves were made of steel, he felt like his were ready to burst out of his skin. The unknowing paralyzed him.

What if it was just a squirrel that had somehow gotten into the attic? He listened to the sounds, trying to make them fit the logical assumption, but he couldn't. The steps were too heavy, too loud to be a small animal. It sounded exactly like footsteps.

What if it wasn't a squirrel?

He stared at the ceiling, wondering. He knew he should probably go up there to check it out, but he couldn't bring himself to do it. After all the strange occurrences, they never found anything when they went to look. He wasn't sure he even *wanted* to find anything. Thoughts of the apparition returned to him and he shivered, despite his will to suppress the fear. He imagined himself tiptoeing up the dark stairs to the third floor, the room lit by nothing more than moonlight, and he shivered again for good measure. What would happen if he peered around the corner and actually saw something else? What then? Could he sleep another night in the house knowing that a ghost might pop out of the darkness at any moment? No. Staying in bed was the best option. He would go look in the morning, by the full light of day.

As if taunting him, the sound began getting louder, the footsteps more pronounced.

What first sounded like one child running soon became three.

The fear became so real, it wrapped him in a cold sweat. He felt his heart pounding like an iron drum, but he was too afraid to move.

What next?

As if in answer, the footsteps drifted into the room.

He clearly heard them walking from the fireplace to the edge of the bed. Through the light from the windows, he could see the room was empty, but the sounds continued. His head began spinning.

Should he reach for his cell phone and use the light to get a better view?

He was too afraid to even reach his hands out from under the covers.

What if someone grabbed his arm?

The footsteps grew closer. He could hear them walking around the bed. Back and forth they went. The footsteps came right up to the bed and stopped, as if someone was standing there, watching him.

Was he losing his mind?

He just lay there clenching the edge of the covers, praying for it to be over, listening to the sounds of Lillian's breathing and the hush of traffic outside.

After about twenty-five minutes, the sound of footsteps began to fade until they finally disappeared.

The ghosts had accomplished their goals.

They scared Edwin within an inch of his life.

And they planned to do it again, very soon.

Chapter 19

By November the weather became cold and brutal. The house had very little insulation, and the central heating system in the basement was useless. They spent a good chunk of money having it cleaned and prepped, only to fire it up and watch it burn through an entire tank of oil in just two weeks. It seemed as though all measures of heating the huge house was only in vain. Every ounce of heat they pumped into the house was whisked away by the old, drafty windows.

They purchased two pellet stoves, putting them in the rooms where they spent the most time during the day and evening. One went into Edwin's office on the second floor, and the other went in the kitchen. That left the rest of the house unheated. As October faded into November, they found themselves lingering in the heated rooms, only leaving for brief moments. Nights became trying, since the bedroom wasn't heated at all.

To stay warm, they had multiple blankets on the bed. Lillian had her two favorites, and Edwin had two of his own, with the dogs snuggled between them, creating another pocket of warmth. Edwin would smile as he looked at her. After she tucked herself in, all he could see was the tip of her nose poking through the thick layer of blankets.

All of this changed one cold November morning.

Edwin woke up feeling Lillian shivering beside him. He was surprised to find her blankets on the floor. If it was odd, he wasn't awake enough to consider it. He simply gave her one of his and fell back to sleep.

An hour later, he woke up again, this time to the sound of humming.

It reminded him of the strange chanting sound he heard off and on for several months, but this was different. He rolled over and opened his eyes.

Lillian bustled around the bedroom gathering the clothing she wanted to wear that morning. This alone was strange, because Lillian was resolute in her morning habits. She typically didn't do anything until she had a cup of coffee and a cigarette. Afterwards, she would come back upstairs and start getting ready for the morning. After spending so many years together, he knew better than to try to talk to her beforehand.

They had a small electric heater in the bathroom that would take at least a half hour to warm the room above freezing. Bathing was always a quick, hurried affair, because the room seldom reached more than fifty degrees. It appeared that Lillian took a bath without bothering to heat the room first.

The fact that she was up and moving about the bedroom was strange, but even more surprising was the humming. In their twenty-four years together, Edwin never heard her hum, especially not in the morning. It sounded like a lullaby.

He squinted at her, wondering where she was going. When she just worked around the house, she usually wore her standard uniform of jeans and a sweatshirt. Today, she was dressed up in nice clothing, complete with her silver dangling earrings and bangle bracelets.

"You going out?" he asked, but she barely brushed him with a glance. Still humming, she headed out of the bedroom and walked down the stairs, the sound of her feet on the steps his only indication of where she was going.

He just stared at the space where she'd been. It was odd that she hadn't answered him.

The alarm on his clock began sounding, so he rose from bed and began getting ready for work. His day was filled with phone calls and reports that he needed to finish. Most days he was so busy, he found himself looking up at the clock, surprised to discover hours passed since the last time he got up from his chair.

During one of these breaks, he looked out his office window at the driveway and was surprised to see Lillian's car still there. With the way she was dressed, he figured she was out running errands. He took his headset off and listened for a moment, trying to hear the telltale sounds of her bustling about the house, but the house was quiet. All he could hear was the popping of the pellet stove and the window pushing against the old walls of the house, making it creak and groan.

At that moment, his office phone rang again, pulling him back into his work. He slipped the headset back on and disappeared into the world of insurance. By early afternoon, he could feel his stomach rumble. He rose from his desk and stretched his back, trying to work out the stiffness in his muscles from sitting for too long. A quick glance out the window showed him that Lillian's car was still parked in the driveway.

"That's strange," he whispered to himself.

He walked up to the third floor first to see if she was in her office, quietly working on paperwork, but the entire floor was empty. He didn't find her on the second or first floors either. A sense of panic mounted inside him. Lillian was usually so unvarying in her habits that he usually knew where she was at any given point during the day.

"Where the hell is she?" he asked himself. He walked to the windows to see if she was in the yard, but she wasn't. Finally, he thought of the basement. He couldn't imagine why she had dressed up to go to the basement, but it was the only space in the house he hadn't yet checked.

As he came down the narrow staircase, he could hear an odd sound.

It sounded like someone was digging.

He found her in the Summer Kitchen, hunched over the brick kiln. Soot was flying as she dug into its depths.

"Hon? What are you doing?" he asked, concerned.

She leaned up just enough for him to see her face all covered in soot and ashes. Her silver earrings swung from her ears, as if keeping time with her motions. She had a blank look on her face as she stared at him. It was almost as if she didn't recognize him for a second.

"I don't know what I'm doing," she said.

He just stood there, transfixed. This was so unlike Lillian, it alarmed him. She was always particular about keeping her good clothes clean, and here she was covered with grey soot.

The second thing that bothered him was the blank look on her face. Lillian was a decisive person. She did everything with a purpose. Bending over a kiln digging with a garden trowel wasn't something she normally did, and by the looks of it, she'd been at it for hours.

"Are you okay?" he asked, moving towards her.

Something in her expression snapped. "Just leave me alone and let me finish!" she roared at him.

Started by her reaction, he backed away.

Something was going on with her, but if she was going to yell at him, he'd just leave her to it.

"I'll never figure out women," he mumbled to himself as he stomped back up the stairs.

He went back to his office and picked up where he left off. After twenty minutes, he heard the sound of footsteps on the stairs. He looked up, fully expecting to see another apparition pop up into his face, but it was Lillian. She came into his office with a huge smile on her face. She was covered in grey soot from head to toe.

"Hey Edwin! I found something!" she said. Her entire demeanor had changed. She was almost giddy with excitement, her eyes twinkling as she held her hand out.

"You found something?" he asked, squinting at the grey object in her hand.

"Yeah. It's a pelvic bone." She handed it to him.

He turned it over and examined it. It appeared to be a bone, but he had no idea how she knew it was a pelvic bone. To his knowledge, neither of them had ever seen one before. He handed it back to her and quickly looked it up on the computer. The image that came up was very similar to the bone in Lillian's hand.

"How did you know it was a pelvic bone? Have you ever seen one before?" he asked.

She shrugged. "I don't know. I just knew, that's all."

He watched her for a moment, confused at everything that had transpired that morning. This just wasn't like Lillian. She wasn't one of those women prone to moodiness. She was very upfront and honest about the way she felt. If she was angry, she let you know. If she was sad, you'd know that as well, but usually she was her normal happy-go-lucky self. This Lillian was someone he didn't know.

"What else did you find?" he asked, almost afraid to hear what she was going to tell him.

"I found the clip from a garter belt!" she exclaimed happily. "Oh, and some newspaper clippings from 1910. They were buried above the level where I found the pelvic bone, so it must be even older. And, I found a few more bones, but they're just tiny pieces."

Edwin watched her. Something wasn't right. He could feel it in the pit of his stomach. She had soot smeared across her forehead and her good clothes were pretty much ruined, but she was smiling. He just tucked it away in the back of his mind, not sure what else to do with it.

The next day he brought the bone to a doctor. He had a routine appointment with his general practitioner and wanted to see what his doctor thought about it. The doctor agreed with Lillian's evaluation that it might be a pelvic bone. It was small though. If it were a pelvic bone, it had belonged to a child. He took a photo of it and promised to share it with a friend who specialized in orthopedics.

"The kiln" Photo by Frank Grace (TRIG Photography)

Lillian spent the next few days in a strange frame of mind.

Edwin watched her pacing back and forth, her brow creased as if she was deep in thought. She wasn't herself, not by any measure of the word. It was almost like she was sleepwalking at times.

"I have to know what it means," she told him.

He didn't understand what she was talking about. "What does *what* mean?"

"The bone!" she snapped. Her entire demeanor was off kilter. She was obsessed with the bone, carrying it around with her like a totem. "It has to mean something that I found it. Some child died in this house."

He wasn't sure what to make of it. The entire situation had been so out of character for her, starting with the morning when she got dressed to go out, but went into the basement to dig for five hours instead, and ending with this strange fixation on what she found. She went from zero to sixty in a single breath. One minute she was denying the existence of ghosts in their house, and the next minute she was mourning their loss.

She spent long hours moping around the house, staring into the shadows as if she was trying to glean information from the very walls. He tried to talk to her, but she just brushed him off.

"I'll be okay. I just need to figure this out," she told him, so he left her alone.

Several weeks later, she was nearly out of her mind with questions. The orthopedic surgeon reported that the bone did look like a human pelvic bone. He said he needed to see it to make a full analysis. The news wasn't enough for Lillian. She finally worked up the nerve to bring it to the police station.

As soon as she announced who she was and what she had, a group of officers nearly enveloped her, asking questions about the house. It was apparent the Victorian was a local legend. They wanted to know where she found the bone as well, promising to send someone down to take a look at it. She left the station feeling optimistic. If someone died in the house and their bones were burned in the kiln, she wanted to get to the bottom of it.

Edwin was feeling some of her concerns. Times were different back in the early 1900's. Records weren't as carefully kept as they are today, and what they did keep was often damaged by flood or fire, or misplaced. If a child disappeared, it could have gone unnoticed. He began wondering about that child. What would cause someone to burn a child's bones in a kiln instead of giving them a proper burial? Was this child one of the ghosts haunting the mansion?

When the police lieutenant showed up, the trail of answers would stop almost immediately.

He met them at the door with an expressionless face. Unlike the other officers at the station who were excited about the prospects of finding bones in the basement, he was all business. He walked to the basement and took a few photos of the kiln area, then left shortly afterwards with the pelvic bone, promising to send it out for evaluation.

"What happens if it's a human bone?" Lillian called after him.

He barely turned as he answered. "Then we open an investigation," he told her as he got into his car.

Lillian and Edwin looked at one another with exasperation.

It would be yet another mystery they would never solve.

Several weeks later, they called the police station, only to be brushed off. "The bones weren't human. We sent them to New York for evaluation," they were told.

They later learned just how weird this situation really was. Normally, they would send something like this to Boston for evaluation instead of New York. At this point, they would never learn anything more.

Lillian thought, if nothing else, it was a message. The bone may not be human, but that didn't mean there weren't others down there somewhere. It was a cry for help.

Lillian kept up her vigil in the basement, spending long moments in the Summer Kitchen.

She mourned over the child's loss as if it were family. Despite what the police told her, she knew that a child died in the house. Instead of giving him a proper burial, they burned the child in the kiln; a kiln they used for destroying refuse. It just felt so wrong.

What could have happened to him?

She paced back and forth in the basement, her gaze landing on the tall brick cistern. Someone cut a doorway into the side of it, but back in the early 1900's, it would have been a brick room filled with rainwater. What would have happened if a child climbed to the top to look inside, and then tragically fell in?

Would they have pulled him out, crying over his limp body?

Surely, they would have reported the accident. From what she knew, no one ever reported the drowning of a child in the cistern. Two children drowned in a pond that was not far from the house, way back in the house's early history, but she didn't think that was related. Her mind gnawed over it again and again.

There must have been a reason why she found the bones. She felt it as strongly as she knew her own name. Someone had called to her, pulling her out of bed, moving her through the house like a marionette until she found him. It felt like a dream. She could remember the time she spent digging, but it was as though her mind was somewhere else, separate from her body. As her hands worked, digging into the kiln, her mind had drifted to another place. While it should have bothered her, it didn't. It felt like something that was just meant to happen.

She carried the photo of the bone down to the basement with her and set it on the steps.

"What does it mean?" she asked, searching the shadows for an answer.

"Please tell me. Are you glad that I found those bones?"

Does it set you free?

She caught movement out of the corner of her eye and turned to look at the steps.

The photo of the bone wafted off the stairs. It glided back and forth in the air, as if carried on a breeze, before it sailed into the Summer Kitchen and landed on the floor beside the kiln.

She just stood there and looked at it.

In her mind, it was answer enough.

"You're welcome," she told the shadows, before walking back upstairs to start dinner.

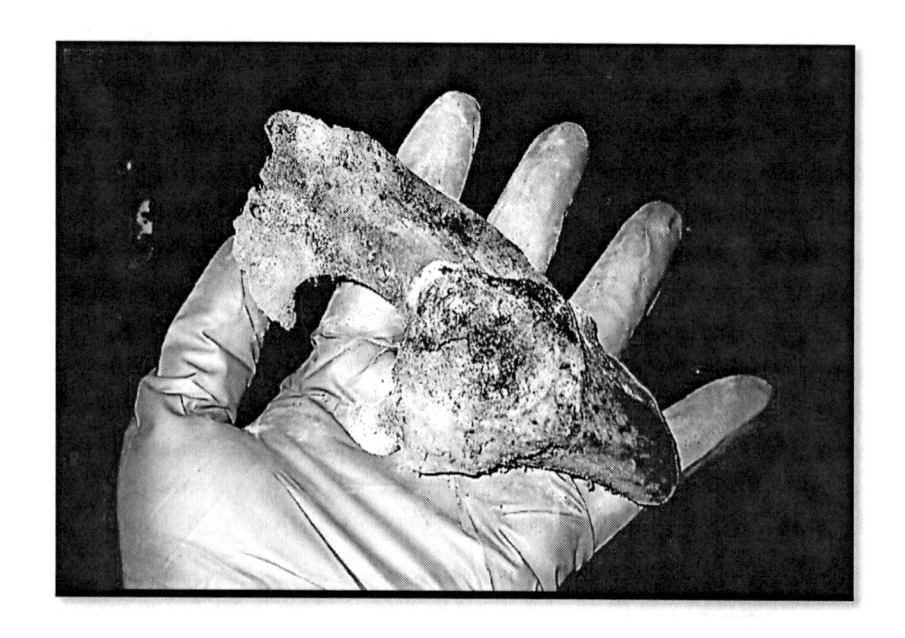

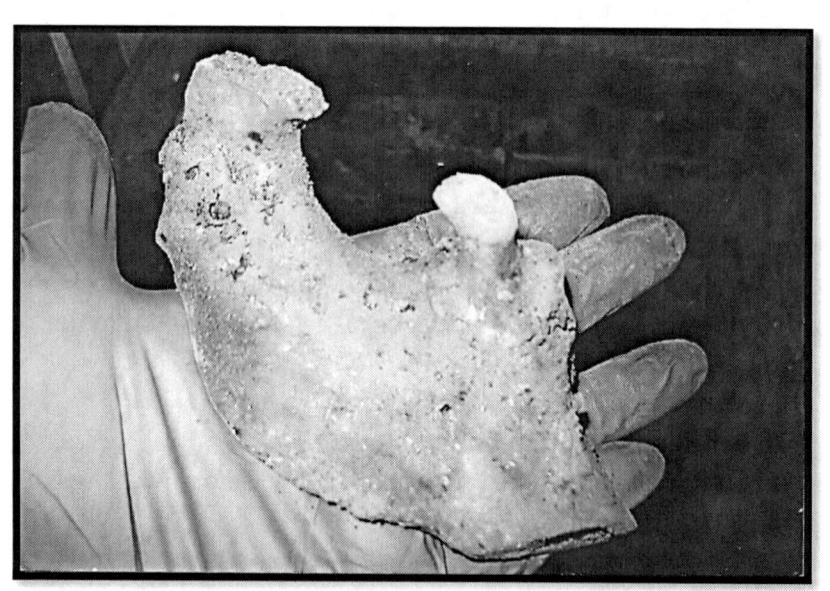

Photos of the bone found in the basement

Chapter 20

Several weeks later Edwin woke to the sensation of Lillian's elbow in his ribs. He jolted awake and became aware of the sound of the doorbell ringing downstairs. The room was so cold, he could see his breath huff out in front of him.

He looked around the room, blinking to clear his vision. The light that trickled into the bedroom was thin and light. All he wanted was to crawl back under the covers for another few hours, but Lillian elbowed him again.

"Hon, somebody's at the door," she said.

He glanced at the alarm clock on the nightstand. It was only 7 a.m.

"Who the hell is at the door at 7 a.m. on a Sunday?" he started to say, when he was interrupted by three loud bangs on the bedroom door. The sound was maddeningly loud. It was as if a wrecking ball was slamming against the door.

Edwin nearly jumped out of his skin.

What the hell?

The dogs went crazy, barking at the closed door. His mind was a blank as he sprang from bed.

He raced for the door, his anger rising to the surface. The sound was far too loud to be from a ghost. He threw open the door, but nobody was there.

Lillian sat up, the covers falling to the side.

"Nobody's there?" she asked, her voice filled with disbelief.

"No," Edwin said, edging into the hallway, looking around at the empty landing. It was freezing in the house, but he barely felt it. His mind raced with the implications. There was no way to explain this. Even if someone had pounded on their door, there's no way they could have run away in the five seconds it took him to get to the door. And besides, how would they get in? The only other person who had a key was Lillian's brother, Will, but he wouldn't have done that. He would have stood outside on the sidewalk and called them on the cell phone, like any reasonable person would do.

He stared across the landing, trying to piece it together, his mind still foggy from sleep.

Was it another ghost?

Was this the next scare? Would he turn around only to find an apparition grinning in his face?

How could they make such a loud noise? Was that even possible?

It hadn't just been a small tap on the door. It had been so loud, it caused the windows to rattle.

"Go check the front door. I heard the doorbell ring three times," Lillian said.

Edwin raced down the grand staircase and pulled the front door open. Nobody was there either.

He ran to the side door, but the porch was empty, as well. He walked out onto the sidewalk in his bare feet and looked up and down the street. The morning was still and calm. Sunlight peered through the clouds like the fingers of God. He shivered, wrapping his arms around himself. The South Gardner Hotel across the street was open for breakfast. Several early risers were making their way up the wooden steps, chatting happily among themselves. The faint aroma of bacon drifted in his direction. He turned and looked back up at the house behind him, his heart pounding.

Nobody could have rung the doorbell and then pound on the door, only to vanish into thin air. He walked back into the house and found Lillian on the landing.

"Who was it?" she asked.

He just shook his head.

How do you explain something like that?

Should he tell her it was just one of the ghosts acting up again? He couldn't even form the words in his mouth without grimacing.

It made him think about his father. He always said that when something happens, there's always a reason for it, something that had been validated to him after Lillian found the bones in the basement. Maybe the house was trying to tell them something.

Or maybe it just wanted them to go away.

Either way, he had to know.

He stared up the grand staircase. Light filtered through the lace curtains on the landing window, leaving half the landing in shadows. He stared into them, wondering if someone was standing there staring back at him. Had someone woken them for a reason? Were they trying to warn them? Was the house on fire? The thought made him spring into action. He ran from room to room looking for something amiss.

"What are you doing?" Lillian asked, watching him race past her back up the stairs.

"Looking to see if something's wrong. Somebody woke us up for a reason," he said, then spent the next ten minutes inspecting all the rooms. When he came back down, he was slightly winded and thoroughly shaken.

"Find anything?" she asked, her blanket wrapped around her shoulders. Her breath fogged the air in front of her. It would take hours before the sunshine brought the indoors temperature up above freezing.

He shook his head, staring into space, his mind spinning.

Threes. It happened in threes.

He knew from his research into the paranormal that things often happened in threes to mock Christ and the Holy Trinity. Usually though, it happened with demonic hauntings. The more he thought about it, the more instances he was able to come up with. Every night when the dogs woke up, it was around 3a.m. The piano played with three notes. The doorbell rang three times, before there were three loud bangs on their bedroom door. What did it all mean?

He didn't share this thought with Lillian.

He looked up to catch her watching him. A part of him wanted to talk to her about all of it like they usually did, but something held him back. He wasn't sure if he was afraid the ghosts in the house would hear him and somehow make life even more insufferable, or if he was afraid of frightening Lillian. Either way, he couldn't find the words to even begin the conversation.

Lillian finally broke the moment. "I'm gonna go make some coffee," she said as she brushed past him, leaving him to his thoughts.

He just stood there for a minute, letting it all sink in. He never dreamed something like this would happen to them. It made him angry. It was their house. Why couldn't they just live there? Why go through all of this?

As he went about his day, he couldn't stop thinking about the morning's events. Even though he kept himself busy with projects, a part of him still waited for something to happen that would explain the rude awakening. Was it a warning? Or was someone just letting their presence be known?

On a deeper level, he wondered if they were just trying to separate them by scaring him away, so they could have better access to Lillian.

One thing was certain: he couldn't explain it.

Chapter 21

Lillian's experiences with the resident ghosts always differed from Edwin's. Once she embraced the possibility of the haunting, they began to touch her on a deeper level. Instead of scaring her, like they often did with Edwin, they approached her emotionally, taking advantage of her maternal nature. She began to envision them as children.

It made complete sense to her. Many of the encounters had a playful element to them, almost like the pranks a playful child would pull. Many of them happened daily, if not several times a day, and were seldom threatening in nature. It was almost as if a child was trying to garner her attention. She sometimes felt a tug on her shirt at child level, but when she looked down, nobody was there. Other times, she heard footsteps running up and down the stairs, but the stairs were empty when she went to check. Instead of scaring her, it amused her, turning something potentially terrifying into an intriguing mystery.

The first of the playful experiences happened in the basement.

By April, the warm rays of sunshine poured through the windows, filling the rooms with light. The activity had quieted down for a while. After the slamming doors, nothing happened for several months, besides the occasional sound of footsteps on the stairs.

It was as though the ghosts were pacing themselves, allowing Lillian and Edwin to grow comfortable again before springing the next surprise on them. Lillian wasn't sure what to make of it, but she refused to let it rattle her. If she wasn't afraid of it, then it couldn't touch her.

Somewhere in her mind, she wondered if fear motivated them. When they slammed a door and got a big reaction, it seemed to encourage them to do it again. She couldn't control how Edwin was going to react to the ghosts, but she wasn't giving them anything to work with.

Revitalized by the new season, she began spending more and more time in the basement, organizing her tools and gardening supplies. If shadows lurked on the walls, she didn't notice. She had a project and nothing was keeping her from it.

It was important to her that everything had a place. One of her biggest pet peeves was to search endlessly for a lost item. If everything had a home, then she'd know where to find it when she needed it. She purchased an assortment of bins and jars for her screws and nails, and spent most of the morning separating them into compartments. Around noon, she decided to take a break. She sat a half-filled jar of screws on the soapstone counter and went outside to smoke a cigarette. When she came back down, the jar was gone.

"Where did it go?" she asked, looking around, irritated. She knew she left the jar on the counter. The lid was still sitting there. Edwin must have come down to the basement while she was outside.

She marched up the stairs to find him in his office, more than a little irritated that he would act so inconsiderate. When you use something, you put it back so the next person can find it.

"What did you do with the jar full of screws in the basement?" she asked. Logically, since they were the only two people in the house, he must have moved it.

Edwin gave her a puzzled look. "What jar?"

"The jar in the basement. Somebody moved it while I was gone. What did you do with it?"

He continued to look at her with confusion. "I didn't do anything with the jar. I don't even know what you're talking about," he said, but she wasn't convinced. Finally, he got up from his chair and followed her to the basement to help her look.

They searched the entire basement, but couldn't find it. After a while, she put her hands on her hips and looked around. If she didn't move it and Edwin didn't move it, who did?

It took nearly a year before she discovered the answer.

The next room over from the Summer Kitchen was the room with the cistern. Even though it was the room where they kept their washer and dryer, she hadn't been able to fully explore it. Part of this was due to the issue with the lighting. Instead of having a bulb fixture on the ceiling, it had one on the wall beside the door, which left the rest of the room blanketed in shadows. The other issue was water. She had peered into the cistern on several occasions, but couldn't walk inside because it held several inches of stagnant water. One day, she happened to look in to see that the water had finally dried up. She walked inside with a flashlight, eager to finally look around. She stepped inside and her gaze landed on a curious sight. The jar full of screws was sitting on the ledge of the cistern, covered in a year's worth of cobwebs.

She stared at it for a long moment, puzzled.

Who put it there?

It felt like a joke. Like someone deliberately hid it from her.

Did the little boy do it?

Interior view of the basement cistern
Photo by Frank Grace (TRIG Photography)

There were no records of a little boy dying while living in the house. So where did he come from? Did someone cover up his death? Was that his pelvic bone she found in the Summer Kitchen?

"Can you show yourself to me?" she asked.

It didn't seem like an impossible request. After all, he showed himself to other people in the past. Why wouldn't he show himself to her?

"Please?" she begged, but he never appeared to her.

It was almost as though he was taunting her. He wouldn't show himself, but he often left signs of his presence in places where she would find them. A stand saw that disappeared from the side yard reappeared a year later beneath one of the heavy bureaus in the bedroom. A set of keys mysteriously appeared on a living room table after vanishing from the kitchen table. It was as if he was following her around the house all day, playing one prank after another.

One day Edwin had to drive into Boston to the office, leaving her by herself in the house for a few hours. She didn't mind the time alone. The house didn't frighten her in the least. If nothing else, it would give her a chance to get some work done without interruption. His car was barely out of the driveway before she was up on a ladder, trying to find a way to snake the wires down for the Internet.

They had Internet upstairs in Edwin's office, but she wanted it on the first floor, too. She could have hired someone to do it, but they'd already spent more than they could afford on other projects. Besides, she was up for the challenge. How hard could it be?

As she was running a cable down the inside of a wall in the butler's pantry, she happened upon a curious find. It was a handful of old wallpaper scraps stuffed inside the hollow of the wall.

She pulled them out and carried them to the kitchen table for closer inspection.

It was apparent the wallpaper was from the turn of the century. The scraps were frail, but still very lovely, with pale blue flowers on a white background. She turned a large piece over in her hands, smiling at the find. It was as though the house was sharing some of its secrets with her.

She was eager for Edwin to get home so she could show him.

Wendy and Nina followed her from the kitchen into the butler's pantry and sat with their heads on their paws, watching her climb back up the ladder to finish the task. She got the wire all the way down to where she wanted it and carefully snaked it through the opening.

"We can do this, can't we girls?" she said to the dogs. They looked up, hopeful for attention.

There was so much work that needed to be done with the house, she'd need to learn how to do some of it herself in order to finish it. Hiring workmen to come in for something simple was out of the question. She was pleased that she'd managed this small task herself.

She looked back down at the dogs. "Wanna go outside?" she asked.

Both dogs sprang to their feet, which was answer enough.

She grabbed her cigarettes off the table, casting a quick glance at the wallpaper on the table.

As she stood out on the front porch smoking, she thought about it, wondering why someone would hide wallpaper in the wall like that. It was almost as if they wanted her to find it. Were they encouraging her to make the kitchen look like it looked in the late 1800's? Could she even find a similar wallpaper pattern?

She finished her cigarette and snubbed it out in one of the planters on the porch. It was noon in Gardner, which meant the traffic on West Broadway was heavier than normal. As people drove past, most of them looked up at the house, as if hoping to see a face at the window. She shook her head and smiled. If those people only knew what they had already lived through.

They still kept the haunting to themselves. Most of the people they knew would think they were crazy if they started blabbering about ghosts. A car honked and she waved before herding the dogs back inside.

She closed the door as the dogs ran ahead of her into the kitchen. She followed them into the room, her mind already focusing on the next task to tackle. She sat her lighter down on the table beside her cigarette package and stopped short. The wallpaper wasn't on the table any longer. It was in the middle of the floor.

"Wendy? Did you do that?" she asked, as Wendy came over to sniff the pile of paper.

The dog looked up at her and wagged her tail.

"Bad dog! You leave that alone," she said, scooping the paper back up and putting it back on the table.

Wendy just looked at her. Usually when she'd done something wrong and was scolded, she'd tuck her tail between her legs and look up at her with a guilty expression. This time she just stared, as if wondering what her owner was talking about.

Lillian sighed. "Just leave it alone, okay?" she said, before moving into the living room. She straightened the pillows and gathered several glasses from the coffee table. They were up late the night before watching TV. She was usually particular about straightening everything up before heading up for bed, but last night, she was just too tired.

A bowl filled with the scraps of wallpaper

As she walked into the living room with the glasses, she stopped short.

The wallpaper was back in the middle of the floor.

Her mind spun as she stared at the pile.

The dogs couldn't have moved it. They were both still in the living room. They hadn't left her sight for a second.

Her gaze slowly wandered around the room. Was it a ghost?

"Who did that? Was it the little boy?" she asked into the air, not really expecting an answer. She spent the past months trying to get the little boy to show himself, and it was obvious he was going to remain silent.

Hearing her voice, the dogs trotted back into the kitchen, their toenails clicking on the hardwood floor. All of a sudden, she heard the sound of footsteps on the servant staircase, just outside the kitchen.

Both dogs went barreling out of the room, barking.

She followed them through the doorway and looked up the staircase. Nothing was there.

"What are you two barking at?" she said, shaking her head.

If there was something there, the barking wasn't going to change anything. She couldn't imagine anyone being frightened by two little white fluff balls.

"Come on back to the kitchen," she told them. They both took a long look at the staircase, and then followed her into the kitchen. She started to get them a treat from the cabinet when they raced back to the staircase, barking again.

She followed them out again. They were both fixated on something near the ceiling at the top of the stairs. By the way they were staring, it was clear they were seeing something she wasn't. Was it the little boy?

"You can come out and talk to me, you know," she started to say when she was interrupted by an ear-shattering roar. It rumbled through the house, nearly rattling the windows with its intensity. It was more than a growl. It sounded like a savage lion, ready to attack.

The sound stunned her. Even though she swore she wasn't going to give them a reaction, she couldn't help the shriek that rose out of her. She scooped up the dogs and rushed back into the kitchen.

Her heart was pounding as she stared at the closed door, fully expecting it to swing open at any moment.

What the hell was that?

It couldn't have been the little boy. This was something much darker.

It was something evil.

She could feel it fill the air with electricity. Even the light shining through the windows seemed dimmer. She just sat there until Edwin came home some hours later.

It was evident he was exhausted by the look on his face and the slouch of his shoulders. He'd barely taken off his jacket before she started in with the stories. While the wallpaper was intriguing, she was still spooked by the loud roar.

What did it mean?

Who did it?

Were they trying to scare her out of the house?

Edwin obviously wasn't in a mood to deal with it. The house seemed to be losing its charm with him.

"What do you expect? We live in a haunted house," he said.

She just stared after him as he made his way upstairs to prepare for bed. Normally they were sympathetic of each other's experiences, but it was beginning to weigh them down. After a long period of slight occurrences, they thought the worst was behind them. The fact that it was starting up, especially with something so frightening, wasn't exactly welcome news.

She retreated to the living room and sat up watching television until almost one in the morning, trying to get her mind off the roar. After one yawn too many, she finally pulled herself up off the sofa, collecting her empty glass and bag of snacks off the coffee table. Nina and Wendy retreated upstairs with Edwin when he went to bed, so she was all alone on the first floor.

As she came into the kitchen, her mind on nothing more than bed, she saw a familiar sight.

The wallpaper was back in the middle of the floor.
She stared at it, wondering what it meant.
She was going to find out all too soon.
The house wasn't finished with her.

Photographic rendition of the boy in the basement.
Photo by Jason Baker

Collage of the rooms Photo by Frank Grace (TRIG Photography)

Chapter 22

April and May flew by quickly with very little activity. June was in full swing, providing them with all the blessings of summer with hardly any of the burdens. The trees were filled out with lush green leaves, and the grass was a healthy carpet. The lilac bushes near the front of the Victorian were in full bloom, filling the air with their fragrant scent.

A new family had just moved in next-door, into one of the houses separated into apartments.

Edwin noticed the new neighbors right away because of the boy standing at the edge of the lawn. He looked out his office window while he was working to see the boy staring up at the side of the house. The boy appeared to be nine or ten with brown hair and an earnest face. Edwin gave the boy a wave. After a few seconds, the boy waved back before disappearing back into his apartment.

Several days later, Edwin saw him standing there again. Something about it intrigued him. The boy wasn't simply admiring the architecture. It was almost as if he was looking at something, or even watching something…or someone. Edwin would learn what he was staring at shortly after meeting the boy's mother.

Katie was a young woman with sandy brown hair, bright blue eyes, and a warm smile. She was the kind of person you liked in an instant. She walked over while Edwin and Lillian were getting out of their car, coming home from running errands. After introductions were made, she asked a strange question.

"How old are your children?" she asked.

Edwin was a bit taken back. This was the second time someone thought they had kids.

"We don't have any children," he quickly told her. It didn't seem to satisfy the woman. She began looking around as if searching for something. "What are you looking for?" he asked.

She gave him a sheepish look. "I was looking for toys…outside toys."

He just stared at her for a moment before he understood what she was saying. She hadn't believed him that he didn't have any children. Why would he lie about something like that?

"Do you want to come in and see the house?" he offered, thinking that if she saw the house and the lack of children inside, she'd understand that he was telling the truth.

Her eyes lit up. "I'd love that. Do you mind if I get my son, Joshua?" she asked.

"No, of course not," Edwin said.

Edwin and Lillian exchanged puzzled glances. They were used to people stopping them to talk about the house. They were even fine with giving impromptu tours. They loved their house and enjoyed sharing it with people who admired it, but something about this just didn't seem right.

When Katie returned a few minutes later, she had a boy in tow that Edwin recognized as the boy who had been standing in the yard staring up at the windows. Typical of kids his age, he was wearing a Red Sox shirt with his denim shorts. Katie introduced Joshua, and then admitted the truth behind her questions.

"Joshua has been seeing a little boy in the window," she said.

Edwin immediately broke out in goose bumps. It brought him back to the day he met Mike, the neighbor on the other side of his house. He also saw a little boy run back and forth between the windows. Could this be the same little boy?

He wanted to ask him more questions about what he saw, but Lillian beat him to it.

She knelt down to the boy's level and smiled warmly at him. "Do you have a name for this little boy?" she asked. "Or did you see what he was wearing?"

Joshua studied her face for a moment before looking back up at the window.

"I see him upstairs. He has a white shirt on and black shorts," he said.

Edwin jumped in, astounded by the details. It was very similar to the story the previous owner had told him, except for the color of his outfit. Mark Veau always saw the boy dressed in blue. "What color is his hair?" he asked.

"Yellow."

Edwin felt his knees nearly give out on him. All accounts of the little boy said that he had blonde hair. It was almost too much for him to absorb.

"When you see him, is he always wearing the same outfit?" Edwin asked.

"Yeah. He wants me to come over and play in the big hallway, but his mommy won't let him," Joshua said, sounding sad at the prospects.

Edwin recoiled at his words. No wonder Katie was asking if they had kids. She probably thought they had a little boy locked away upstairs.

"Let's go in and I'll show you the house," Edwin said, ushering them towards the Union Street door.

The minute he opened the door, Joshua raced down the hall and up the grand staircase, not pausing until he was in Edwin's office. The others followed behind, stopping as they watched Joshua stare out the window at his house.

"Is this the window you see him at?" he asked.

Joshua nodded. "I see him at the window below this one too," he said. His words gave Edwin more chills. The window below his was the kitchen.

Joshua ran out into the hallway and looked at his mother. "This is the hallway he wants me to play in. See, I told you it was big enough to play ball in."

Edwin and Lillian exchanged a surprised glance. How was the child communicating with the little boy? Telepathically? It was almost too much to comprehend.

They finished their tour, reassuring Katie that they didn't have a child locked up inside. After they closed the door behind them, Edwin and Lillian just stared at one another in disbelief.

Was this really happening?

The story of the little boy was the most enduring story attached to the house. It was also the most heart wrenching. Why would a little boy still be lingering there? And why would he interact with a child who had nothing to do with the house, putting thoughts into his head and changing his behavior?

Edwin looked out his window in the following days, and even weeks, to find Joshua sitting on his bicycle, staring up at the house. It seemed like an obsession. Katie said that Joshua was a very outgoing little boy who loved to play sports, but as far as Edwin could see, the only thing he did was stare up at the house.

One day, he was surprised to see a moving truck next door. He caught Katie as she was packing the last few items into the truck.

"I can't take it any longer," she said. "It's tearing him apart. He's not the same happy little boy he used to be. I have to protect him."

And with that, Joshua's family moved away, protecting him from something they couldn't see but knew was very real. As it turns out, Joshua was the lucky one.

The house attempted to overtake him, but the love of his mother was far stronger.

Not everyone escaped so easily.

Chapter 23

Everything that happened to them seemed purposeful.

It was almost as though the house chose them from the very beginning, luring them in like it did many others, and then showing them what it wanted them to do.

The first thing it did was convert them from skeptics to believers.

Then it began molding their behavior. It used fear to motivate Edwin, while it worked on Lillian's maternal instincts.

The next thing it needed was witnesses.

At times, Edwin felt like he was fighting a losing battle. Every time he thought he had a handle on the house, something would happen to change it. The house would go very quiet for long periods of time, and then something would happen out of the blue to wake them out of their blissful peace. A door would slam in a vacant part of the house, or footsteps could be heard coming down the staircase. Then, weeks would go by without any activity at all. Was it something they were causing? Did the ghosts dislike something they were doing?

Was there anything they could do to appease them?

Edwin didn't like being a hostage in his own home, but if making a small change was enough to keep them happy; he was willing to do it. He started keeping a log of the activity, trying to pinpoint some sort of cause, but nothing really stood out. It didn't matter if it was a full moon or a crescent moon. The time of the month had no effect, either. As a researcher, he needed answers, but they weren't readily available. He soon turned to social media for help, hoping that others could help him make sense of everything that was happening to him.

The thought of doing this terrified him. It would give all the naysayers a voice to criticize them, allowing them to consider him and Lillian in the same light he once viewed those who believed in ghosts.

After he set up the Facebook page for the Haunted Victorian Mansion, there was no going back. It was like a giant snowball rolling down a massive slope, gathering speed and velocity, until it took down anything in its path.

The results were far more explosive than Edwin expected. Paranormal groups from far and wide started flooding him with requests to investigate the mansion.

"What do you think?" he asked Lillian.

She gave him a sidelong glance, a sure sign that she wasn't comfortable with the idea. Lillian was always the pragmatic one of the pair. She wasn't as prone to impulse decisions as he was. She'd think it over, turning it over in her mind until every possible ramification could be analyzed. He knew it would be up to him to convince her.

"We just let people walk around our house, with all of our things in it? What if they broke something or took something?" she asked.

While he didn't like that aspect of it, the overall concept was still very alluring. After all, they learned a lot from the psychic who came to tour the house earlier. Maybe another group could provide more information. They weighed Lillian's concerns with the possible benefits and decided to give it a try. If they didn't like it or it presented more issues, then they could just stop.

Several local groups came in right away, including a group Mark Veau recommended. They set up infrared cameras all over the house with wires trailing down the stairs and into the Ladies Parlor, where they usually set up a base camp. There, someone would sit and watch the cameras. Edwin would lean over their shoulders, amazed at the visibility. As dust particles flew past the cameras, he grew leery.

"What is that?" he asked.

"Probably just dust. A group just walked through there, which kicked up dust. The IR light is just catching it and making it illuminate," the investigator told him.

When another group came in, they grew excited about the particles, calling them orbs. They told him that it wasn't dust, that it was spirits floating around the room. Edwin didn't know who to believe. The more he experienced, the more confused he became. It was quickly apparent that there weren't any set rules for the paranormal field. The opinions were as varied as the investigators. It was rare that two groups had the same ghost hunting philosophies.

One group brought in a psychic medium, who was quick to take Edwin aside.

"Your wife has been talking to the spirits, hasn't she?" she asked.

Edwin wasn't sure what to make of it. Yes, Lillian did often walk around the house trying to communicate with the little boy spirit, but it wasn't something he was necessarily going to share with a stranger, psychic or not.

He just nodded, and the psychic medium continued.

"She needs to be careful. Ghosts aren't always truthful. Sometimes they will pretend to be something very benign like a child to get your trust. That's how they get in, how they gain access to people. She should be very careful, because not all of them are what they seem."

This gave Edwin pause for thought.

What if it wasn't a little boy? What if it was something much darker?

He tried to talk to Lillian about it, but she wasn't interested in hearing it. Her mind was made up.

As summer turned to fall, people trickled into the mansion, providing clues to the haunting.

Unfortunately, none of them would prepare the couple for what was coming next.

Doors in the basement leading out to the lawn
Photo by the author

Chapter 24

Lillian stood at the window watching the snow fall from the sky. It fell softly, as if it was coming from a giant flour sifter. It had a timeless feel to it, as if everything in the world had suddenly paused while the snow floated down. Traffic became lighter as the snow got deeper. Only the occasional grate and roar of a snow truck disrupted the perfect silence. The second winter was turning out to be worse than the first.

She wasn't used to the slowed-down pace that winter insisted upon. Back in her old life, she was a true Type A personality. When she wasn't busy with a project or task, she was thinking about starting one, planning it out with the precision of an architect. Being idle felt like living with her hands tied, and she hated it.

As winter descended, the rooms grew very cold. If a water glass was left on a table overnight, it would be frozen solid by morning. Navigating through the mansion became akin to going outdoors during the winter. She had to bundle up in layers of clothing before she could venture out of the kitchen to the rest of the house.

She spent much of the winter days cooking in the kitchen where it was warm. She made soups and breads, chicken dishes, and some of their native Puerto Rican dishes. Her cooking filled the room with the tantalizing aromas of garlic, paprika, onions, and cilantro, but eventually she grew restless. She desperately needed to see something else besides the same four walls.

Several times a day she would pull on her winter coat and mittens to leave the warmth of the kitchen and wander around the house, making sure everything was okay. She checked windows and ceilings to make sure there weren't any new leaks, retrieving items she needed along the way. She wouldn't last for long, though. Her body was more comfortable with summer than it was with winter. She returned a few minutes later frozen to the core, to stand over the pellet stove to warm herself. How would they survive living in a house that was largely unheated? There was so much to do and so many repairs that needed to get finished. How would they find the time and the funds to do everything they needed to do to the house? The thought was almost overwhelming.

She hated the worries that consumed her days. She missed the way her days used to fall into place, one after another. Happiness used to be something she didn't have to look for - it was just there, ripe for the picking. Now she found herself wondering where it went and how she got to such a place.

They were supposed to be happy in the house, but it was causing nothing but issues. Combined with the mortgage she still paid on the house in Dorchester, they were always scraping the bottom of the barrel. As soon as money came in, it went back out. Maybe it was time for her to look for another job. It had been years since she worked after quitting her last job to take care of her mother. As she looked around the house, she wondered if she could do something here. The thought of opening an antiques store was very appealing. She loved tracking down timeless pieces of furniture. Maybe it was something she could do for a living.

She surrendered the thought as she heard footsteps on the stairs.

In any other house, she would naturally assume it was Edwin, coming down for a break after working all morning, but in this house it could be anything. She let the curtain fall across the window and just stood still, listening. The house grew quiet again.

So much had happened to them in the last year. It was enough to make her head spin. Soon after the paranormal team conducted their interview, the local Fox News station asked to come inside for a tour.

They led them through the house as Edwin regaled them with his stories. Lillian had to smile as she watched him. He was very good with the tours, and he really seemed to enjoy doing them. It was almost as if he became another person as he assumed the role of master of the house, leading the group through the haunted rooms. Several nights later, Edwin and Lillian watched the story on the news. They had mixed emotions.

> *To watch the news clip, click the link below or type the link address into your computer's browser*
>
> *http://www.myfoxboston.com/story/17743352/real-haunted-house-tour-of-the-victorian-mansion-in-gardner*

While it was fun sharing their stories with other people, it was also a little nerve wracking, too. Once they let the cat out of the bag, they would open themselves up for ridicule and public persecution. People who didn't believe in ghosts may say they were just doing it for the attention. Others might laugh at them or call them fools, something she could fully appreciate. If she hadn't lived through the events herself, she would have laughed too after watching the news clip. What they didn't count on was the outpouring of public support.

Most people believed them and wanted to experience it for themselves. Edwin and Lillian soon found themselves flooded with requests for investigations. Some of the information they would come to learn as a result was disturbing, at best.

It was beginning to feel as though she lost her choices on what to do with the house. Things would continue to progress until they tumbled out of control. Lillian was no more than a participant on a wild ride.

One thing was obvious: there was far more going on in their house than what she could see.

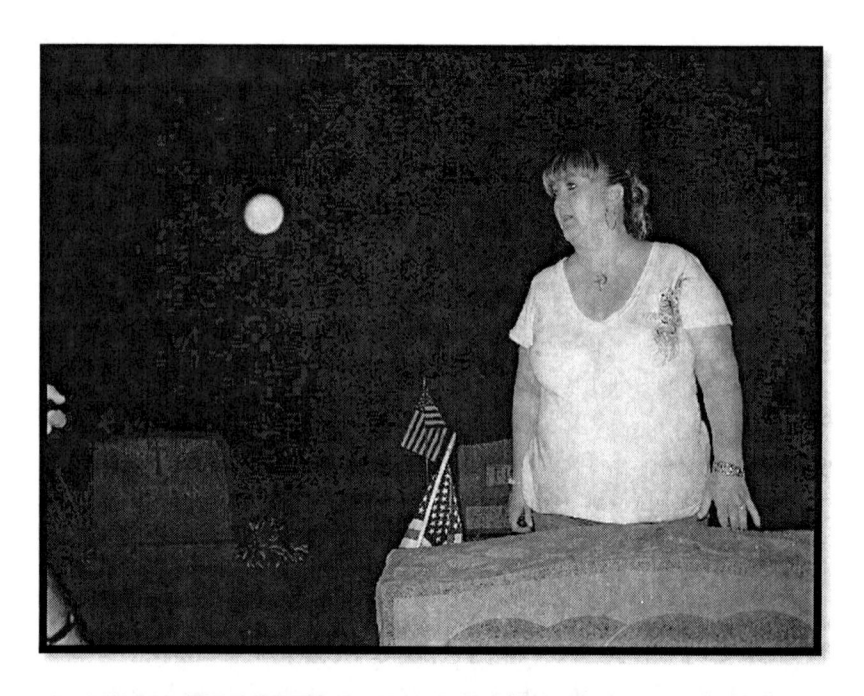

Kim Huertas in a photo captured during the Fox New segment.

Chapter 25

Kim Huertas was the second psychic mediums invited to the house.

When Fox News contacted her and asked her to participate in the segment, she jumped at the chance to explore the old Victorian. She knew very little about the house prior to her visit, but that changed quickly.

She brought her team members from Harvest Moon Paranormal, a group she co-founded in 2009 with her husband. As she walked into the Red Room, she began getting impressions of the ghosts who haunted the room.

She saw a woman from contemporary times who she identified as a prostitute. She wasn't certain of the exact time frame, but she felt it was closer to the present than it was to the Victorian era. The impression of the woman was very fleeting because the man who murdered her came forward much stronger.

Kim saw him as having reddish-brown hair with a thick mustache that curved down the sides of his mouth. He was tall and thin and considered himself a lady's man. Something about him set her nerves on edge. He was spiteful and arrogant, someone who would kill people without a second thought. As she sat on the bed, it immediately began shaking. Members of the news team had to pull her off, but she wasn't safe even then. The chair she sat on also began to shake.

"I need to leave this room," she told the crew, as the room seemingly spun around her.

She made it to the foyer and the spinning slowly subsided. A photograph taken of her at that moment captured a glowing white mist surrounding her. She wasn't the kind of investigator who put a lot of faith into misty photographs, but she felt that this one was definitely paranormal considering what she had just experienced. This was more than just dust or moisture reflecting in the flash of the camera.

Kim's experience with the paranormal started in her childhood. Ghosts came to her at random times, seeking her out because they recognized her as someone they could communicate with. There was seldom an escape from their presence. She often worked privately with local police departments, helping them with missing person cases and unsolved murders. In her years of investigating, she saw many things, but she wasn't sure what to think of the Victorian.

She never visited a location that was haunted by so many different entities. There were so many levels to the house and so many periods the ghosts came from. It made her dizzy just thinking about it. There was a strong sense of sorrow and tragedy lingering there, but it lived alongside some much darker energy. The negative energy seemed to control some of the other ghosts, keeping them there against their will, holding them hostage.

By the time she left, she made contact with eight separate entities. She identified them as S.K. Pierce, Mattie Cornwell, the little boy, the man and woman in the Red Room, a servant who had a baby out of wedlock, as well as the two negative entities in the basement. The sheer number of lingering ghosts was shocking enough, but she was even more astonished at how advanced many of them had become.

Typically, most ghosts weren't able to manipulate their environment. They just hovered nearby, taking it all in, and seldom interacted with the realm of the living. It took a tremendous amount of energy and ability to do the things she witnessed at the Victorian. The fact that there were so many ghosts with powerful abilities concerned her. She wasn't surprised to hear about the encounters Edwin and Lillian experienced. In fact, she was surprised there weren't even more. The darker energies worried her the most though.

Dark energy went by its own rules. It fed on the energy of the living and then used it against them for the sheer sake of causing harm. She worried about Edwin and Lillian's welfare, but there was little she could do about it except to warn them about what they were facing. Not only was it dark, but it was also very powerful. It would take an entire team of mediums to make a dent in the darkness.

Before they left, one of her team members experienced the negative energy firsthand.

As her group exited the Red Room, they stood on the landing for a moment discussing what they'd experienced. One of the women on her team suddenly felt invisible hands grab her by her face and neck and fling her backwards down the stairs. If two other team members weren't standing there to catch her, she would have fallen backwards down the stairs. She was shaken by the experience, but shook it off and continued with the investigation.

They explored the rest of the mansion, having encounters in almost every room. Kim wasn't sure what to make of the house. It was the most paranormally active location she'd ever witnessed.

Once they left for the day, their experiences didn't end. Without explanation, every member of her team began having strange incidents happen to them at their homes. It started with the telephones.

Kim would try to phone a team member only to have the call go right to voicemail. She left a message, but it wouldn't record. She didn't realize it was happening to all of them until one of her team members finally got through to her, angry that she hadn't returned her calls. While Kim had never had anything like this happen before, she suspected that it could be paranormal in nature. Ghosts often interfered with electronics, especially those as advanced as the ones at the Victorian. Her group saw firsthand how the ghosts could drain batteries in an instant and then use that energy to perform a physical act, like manifesting, or moving objects. When the team got together, she learned just how widespread the activity really was.

Every member of her team experienced issues with their telephones. Messages were left but never received, phone lines were suddenly filled with static, and strange things began happening at each of their homes. Items disappeared, only to reappear somewhere else, and dark shadows would flit across walls without any plausible explanation. They went through and did a thorough cleansing of each team member's house until the activity lessened.

Kim returned to the Victorian several times, feeling drawn to the location. There wasn't a single room in the house that wasn't haunted. She took a team down into the basement and felt her stomach clench as soon as she reached the bottom of the stairs. There was something very dark down there. The room with the tunnel was especially disturbing.

"Something really bad happened down here," she said. She saw an image flash in her mind of poker games, gambling and anger before the image turned towards children cowering, fleeing for their lives. She wasn't sure what to make of it. It was possible that more than one horrific event happened there, and the two impressions were coming to her, one on top of the other. In her mind's eye, she saw the man from the Red Room leering at her in the darkness. When she turned to her left, she saw an actual face emerge from the darkness.

"Holy shit!" she gasped, but when she blinked, the image was gone. She could feel the energy swirling around them, surrounding them with a deep darkness that chilled her to the bone. When one of her team members snapped a photo, they discovered a white mist hovering above her. Was this the entity?

The house had a secret. She didn't know what it was, but it was extremely powerful. It lingered in the house, protected by a darkness it couldn't escape. Until they learned what it was, they would be haunted forever.

She would find herself thinking about the house and about Edwin and Lillian, worrying for their safety. They were such novices in the paranormal world, and they were far too trusting of others, which was a dangerous combination. If they listened to the wrong advice, it could be disastrous for them.

Several weeks after they left, she began getting a strong feeling that something was wrong with Edwin. When she called him, she found out that he had been in a recent funk. The house was getting to him.

She returned with her team and immediately felt what was wrong.

"Have you had more teams in here investigating?" she asked him. In her psychic mind's eye she could clearly see a group of people sitting in a circle, trying to summon a spirit. "It's not good when people do that," she told him. "They bring things in – things you don't want here at this house." She urged him to watch the teams more carefully, even volunteering to come and oversee all future events. Before they left, she took a series of photographs of Edwin. In each of them, his image grew darker and darker, until the last shot was nearly black. He was disappearing in the frames. She pulled him aside.

"Edwin, you have some very powerful entities in here. You need to do a thorough house cleansing and get them all out," she advised. While she didn't think the house minded Edwin and Lillian, she knew that it was pulling their energy and was affecting their moods, turning them both into hollow versions of the people they used to be. She urged him to get away for a few days and rebuild his energy, even if they just went down the street to the Super 8 motel. Before she left, she gave him one more piece of advice.

"Nobody should live with a ghost in the house. I don't care if it's someone's dear old grandma. They need to move on. You can't have them here," she told him, but was afraid it was falling on deaf ears. Something had a hold of both of them, and until they were able to break away from it, things would just continue to get worse.

It would get worse before it would get better. She only hoped they would both survive it.

Arlene and Tom D'Agastino

NEPURs team photo

Chapter 26

Soon after the Fox News show aired another paranormal research group came in to investigate.

New England Paranormal United Research Society (NEPURS) is a widely respected paranormal team located in Putnam, Connecticut. Founded by Thomas D'Agastino and his wife, Arlene, the group focuses on helping people with their paranormal issues.

Having invested over thirty-one years in the field, Thomas amassed over a thousand investigations. He also wrote ten books on the subject, including *Haunted Massachusetts*, the book that gave Edwin his first insight into his haunted home's history.

Thomas was already familiar with the Victorian Mansion, having investigated there in March of 2006, when the former owner was in residence. He put together a dream team of investigators, many with years of experience between them. They began experiencing activity almost immediately.

During that 2006 investigation in the master bedroom, Mark Veau was telling them the story of Eino Saari. At the time, they were under the impression that Eino was of Portuguese decent instead of Finnish. He was telling the group how Eino would toast his friends before taking a drink, saying "porteo," which meant "for you," or "to you," in Portuguese. Thomas was running his digital recorder during this discussion and was surprised to later learn that Eino agreed with the toast. They recorded a clear "porteo" on their digital recorder, capturing Eino's voice.

Thomas felt that with Eino's experience in the war, he may have picked up the term, despite the fact that he wasn't Portuguese.

Thomas also caught a glimpse of Mattie Cornwell, the former nanny.

They were standing in one of the bedrooms when Thomas saw a young woman walk past the doorway on the second floor landing. Thinking it might be Mark's teenage daughter, he didn't think anything of it until he asked Mark if his daughter was upstairs.

Mark went to the stairs and called down, only to discover that his daughter was downstairs the entire time. They searched the second floor, but didn't find any explanation for the mysterious visitor. He only saw her for several seconds, but noticed that she had dark brown hair pulled back in a bun, and she was wearing a black dress.

When Edwin called Thomas in September of 2010, PURS was quick to respond. They returned to the house days later. Once more, they experienced strange occurrences. One involved a camera.

They set up several video cameras on the second floor. One was located in the second floor hallway, pointing towards the nursery, and the other was inside the nursery, pointing out towards the hallway. At one point in the night, something bumped the camera inside the nursery. Because the second camera was pointing towards the room where the investigators were standing, they could clearly see that everyone was accounted for at the time. To their delight, it was all recorded on the cameras.

They also captured several relevant EVPs.

EVP stands for Electronic Voice Phenomena. Ghosts often communicate on a different frequency than human speech. While we can't hear them with our ears, digital recorders will often catch them for us to clearly hear when we play them back.

Among the audio recordings is an eerie message that sounds like "Look under our beds." They also captured a whisper stating the name "David," in the Ladies Parlor while no one was around. The name didn't resonate with Edwin right away, but later investigators would also capture the name, a name in reference to the man who may have killed the prostitute in the Red Room.

They returned in March of 2011 to investigate further and captured even more evidence, including repeated growls on the third floor. Later, Tom's wife Arlene asked, "Is this what happened in the past?" The voice box responded with "Business." She was also reading Tarot Cards at the time, something she has a 99 percent accuracy rate with, and the card she pulled at that moment was the "business" card. Was she channeling the ghost of S.K. Pierce?

History would show that S.K. was a prominent businessman in his time. Besides his investment in the furniture manufacturing business, he was also a board member in several banks in Gardner. Business had made him the wealthy man that he was, so it wouldn't be difficult to imagine him retaining that characteristic after death, as well.

Thomas was also able to clear up a few misconceptions through his detailed research. The house was never a brothel, which is something that Edwin was told when they first moved into the house. S.K.'s son, Edward, converted the mansion into The Victorian Inn in 1926, and it functioned as a guesthouse for many years, before becoming more of a boarding house later in its history. While it's likely that objectionable behaviors might have occurred there during the boarding house days, it was never strictly set up as a functioning brothel.

Thomas's feelings were that the house was haunted, but that Edwin and Lillian were never going to fully clean it. Like Kim Huertas, he felt that the haunting went too deep and the ghosts were too far developed. They could calm the energy down, but it would have to be something they needed to learn to live with, or they would have to sell the house and move on.

Edwin found his advice to be sound but sobering.

They didn't want to move, so what did that leave them?

If they did move, could they just walk away and leave the issue with the next owners of the house? It seemed like a never-ending saga. He wasn't sure he could do that to someone else.

To view the evidence, click the link below or type the link address into your computer's browser:
http://www.nepurs.com/purs/investigations/the_victorian.htm

Carl Johnson with Edwin Gonzalez (above) and with Dina Palazini at the Victorian Mansion during a presentation (below)

Chapter 27

Many people recognize Carl Johnson from his years on the hit television series, *Ghost Hunters*, but his experience in the paranormal world extends far beyond the television screen. A seasoned paranormal investigator and lecturer, he specializes in demonology, which is the study of demonic lore and tradition.

By his definition, demons are non-human entities that exist outside the human realm. They often act like ghosts, but generate much more power, and are often hostile towards human beings. Evidence of a demonic presence includes foul, unexplainable odors, abrupt personality changes, and scratches that appear suddenly on the body.

Carl's research and involvement in the paranormal world began in his childhood while growing up in a haunted house. The first phenomena his family experienced came when he was just four years old. His mother was holding a full glass of water when the glass suddenly became empty. They looked around, trying to find an explanation for the occurrence, but they couldn't find anything to explain it. Soon more phenomena began to happen. Items disappeared, only to reappear in other locations. The family began hearing odd noises in the house, as well.

When Carl was a teen, he and his sister began experimenting with an Ouija board, trying to make contact with the ghost. Much to his surprise, as they moved the planchette around the board, it spelled out the name, "Sylvia," followed by the word, "cellar." Thinking the entity wanted them to go down to the basement, they walked to the top of the cellar stairs. As they stood there wondering if they should go down or not, they heard three raps on the wall beside them. The experience startled them, so they put the board away but it wasn't the last they heard from the entity. Soon after, the haunting became far more prevalent. Furniture moved to different locations in the basement, and they began witnessing a woman dressed in old-fashioned clothing drifting through the rooms of the house.

Carl later had an experience that would cement his belief in the paranormal world. After recording music in the basement, he realized that he captured an odd voice on the tape. When he played it back, he couldn't quite make out what the female voice was saying. He gave the tape to one of his friends, who sped it up nine times the original speed. When they listened to it, they were amazed at what they heard. A very clear female voice said, "Carl...help me." The experience awakened Carl's curiosity regarding ghostly phenomena, leading him on a diverse and fascinating journey into the world of the supernatural.

While attending classes at the Rhode Island College, Carl and his twin brother Keith joined a local paranormal team. This eventually led Keith to place an ad in the local newspaper, offering help to anyone experiencing a haunting. Amazingly enough, their first case involved an inhuman entity.

The case led them to an eighteenth-century farmhouse in Harrisville, Rhode Island, the home of Carolyn and Roger Perron. After witnessing some of the phenomena the Perron family was experiencing, they knew they needed some help with the investigation. They reached out to famed demonologists Ed and Lorraine Warren, who they met at a college lecture. The Warrens eventually took over the investigation. Their haunting experience led to the 2013 hit movie, *The Conjuring*.

Carl and Keith went on to become members of The Atlantic Paranormal Society (TAPS) paranormal investigative team. They remained with TAPS for eight years. During that time, they appeared on the SyFy Channel series, *Ghost Hunters*, for three seasons of the show.

In 2009, both Carl and Keith departed from TAPS and created their own separate groups. While Keith founded the New England Anomalies Research (NEAR) team with his wife Sandra, Carl joined the Beyond the Veil Paranormal Research group, founded by Dina Palazini, an empathic medium, author and paranormal researcher. While both brothers specialize in demonology, their focus in the paranormal field was often quite diverse. Joining separate teams allowed each of them to follow their own path in the paranormal field. While they still support each other in their individual endeavors, being in different paranormal groups gave them a chance to break their own ground as individual investigators. During his time with Beyond the Veil Paranormal Research, Carl appeared on five episodes of The Animal Planet's series, *The Haunted*, as well as The Travel Channel's documentary, *Most Terrifying Places in America*. They also founded the *Big Rhodey Research Project* in Rhode Island, which explores and researches the mysterious sightings of a bipedal creature that people commonly refer to as a Sasquatch or Big Foot.

Carl first visited the Victorian mansion in March 2010, along with Thomas D'Agostino's group, the Paranormal United Research Society (PURS).

Most paranormal investigations are nothing like how the television programs portray them. They spend a great deal of time setting up equipment, followed by long hours sitting in the darkness, trying to capture evidence of a haunting. That night at the Victorian, Carl noticed that the house was abnormally cold, which made the investigation more difficult. They left the warmth of the kitchen to explore the house, only to return an hour later, frozen to the bone.

During the investigation, Carl wandered away from the group to spend some time in the master bedroom where Eino Saari perished in 1963. As he stood there, he heard a man say, "Hey, you!" He stood stock-still, pondering what he just heard. At first, he thought it was a team member, but then he realized he didn't hear any footsteps preceding the voice. He walked out into the second floor landing only to find himself alone. After tracking down the rest of the team on the first floor, he confirmed that no one was nearby when he heard the words spoken. He wondered if he had managed to connect with none other than Eino Saari.

Fascinated by the mansion, he returned to the Victorian in June 2011 to participate in a Victorian style séance. A local psychic medium that frequented the mansion set up the séance. While the house was far warmer than it was on his last visit to the Victorian, the investigation was far from typical. Fourteen people attended the event, with eight people sitting at his table, including Dina Palazini.

The medium who led the séance began asking questions, and the group received immediate responses. Carl expected to hear raps on the table, but the knocks came from the walls, instead. After nearly a half hour, he started to rise from his seat, but was shocked to feel cold hands on his shoulder pressing him back down to his chair. The medium leading the séance explained that the male entity in the house was targeting him, seeing him as competition. While he didn't experience any other paranormal phenomena for the rest of the evening, it left him with a lasting impression of the mansion.

"An old house can be an organism in itself. You can almost feel it breathing. There's a darkness to the house," Carl said, and then he added, "If this house isn't haunted, it ought to be."

As the group broke up to take a break, Carl found Lillian in the kitchen. The minute he saw her, he knew something was amiss. She turned and showed him a medallion cupped in the palm of her hand.

"Somebody gave me this Saint Benedict's medallion, because it's supposed to keep me protected," she said, noticeably agitated. "I had it pinned to my jacket with a safety pin. I just heard a sound on the floor and looked down to find the medal on the floor." She showed him her jacket, where the safety pin was still pinned. "Somehow it came off the pin without the pin being opened."

Carl thought it was strange, but had no suggestion on how it happened.

Were the ghosts sending her a message?

They would never know for certain, but as the events continued to unfold, it became clear they weren't finished with Edwin and Lillian.

Edwin and Lillian were captivated by the information they gathered from the paranormal investigations, but it made them realize how little they actually knew about the house.

Most of what they knew was information that was passed down through the ages, much of it exaggerated or untrue. Lillian thought about hiring a historian, but they were barely meeting their monthly bills. One day as she was shopping for a bedroom set, she ran into a woman who would provide her with many of the answers she needed.

Eleanor Gavazzi is a seasoned historian and author with a spirited nature and friendly demeanor. When she ran into Lillian at the furniture shop, an instant friendship formed. The two chatted amicably, quickly discovering they had something in common. Both shared a love of old houses, especially those with a sordid past. Lillian told the older woman about the mansion she lived in and invited her over for a visit.

Eleanor knew the house was haunted after her first visit. Besides being a historian, she is also a psychic medium. The dead communicated with her on a regular basis. They drifted in, attracted to her energy, and shared their tales.

When South Gardner was sponsoring a block party, Eleanor volunteered to come and help Edwin with tours of the Victorian. She dressed in a long skirt, shawl and hat fitting of a Victorian era lady. As soon as she came in, she felt an instant connection with the former lady of the house, Ellen West Pierce.

Being a psychic medium helped Eleanor get to the information she often needed. At times, she felt as though she was led to the documents she wouldn't have found otherwise. Other times, the ability gave her a direct line to the parties involved. In this case, the ghost of Ellen Pierce was keen to make her acquaintance, seeing her as a possible peer from her era due to her costume.

Eleanor felt bad for Ellen after sensing the inner turmoil Ellen had experienced during her life. Despite her desires to become one of Gardner's wealthy elite, she would never truly enjoy her elevated status.

After S.K.'s first wife Susan died from erysipelas in 1876, he was quick to find another wife to replace her. He mourned for the socially-accepted period of two years, and then married Ellen West in 1878. By all accounts, young Ellen was beautiful and socially connected. She was also 30 years younger than her 58-year-old husband.

When she moved into the grand mansion, life would never become what she hoped it would be. S.K.'s son, Frank, disliked her immediately, feeling as though she were coming in to replace his mother. He was also upset that his father married a woman who was only six years his senior. Not wanting the young man to feel pushed aside, his father sent him on a three-month European tour, which was recorded in the newspapers and celebrated in the community. However, it would never be easy between the two. A fancy European trip wouldn't put their disenchantment with one another to rest.

After S.K.'s death in 1888, Ellen inherited the bulk of her husband's estate, sharing the ownership of his business with Frank. Many battles would ensue between the two over handling of expenses, resulting in several documented court cases. Ellen's safe, which sits on the second floor, was evidence of her importance in both the household and the business. She was responsible for accounting for much of the monetary demands of the home and business.

After his father's death, Frank also pushed to obtain custody of his younger brothers; possibly hoping to have control over the property and inheritance they received from their father. Ellen fought this tooth and nail. No one was taking her children from her, especially not someone like Frank. She won the case and maintained custody of her children, despite his best efforts.

Eleanor felt a sense of sadness about the woman. Nothing was what she expected. She came into the family hoping to make her mark in the community, expecting the world in return. She fulfilled her responsibility with her husband by providing him with two more sons, but she was never fully accepted into Gardner's high society. Despite her involvement with local charities and church events, they would always see her as S.K.'s trophy wife.

Eleanor was invited to spend the night at the Victorian the night of the block party, but she wasn't comfortable with the thought. The house scared her. She didn't like going anywhere by herself. When the evening grew long, she was tired and was eager to get to sleep. She needed to be well rested for her chiropractor appointment the following morning. Lillian offered to put her up in one of the bedrooms upstairs, but Eleanor wasn't keen about the idea. She ended up settling down on the reclining leather couch and ottoman in the living room.

Thoughts of sleeping in the house terrified her. She wasn't sure why she agreed to it. If nothing else, she wanted to be prepared in case something terrible happened. She slept fully dressed, keeping her packed bag by her side and her cell phone tucked in her shirt. If something did happen, she would be ready to bolt out the door.

She was only asleep for a few moments when she felt a tingle work its way up her body. She opened her eyes to see a weird distortion in the air in the doorway leading to the grand staircase. The shape was low and small, almost the size of a tiny child. She watched it move into the room and approach her chair. To her amazement, it slowly climbed up on the chair and settled against her. It was a child.

It certainly wasn't what she expected, sleeping in a haunted house. She thought that if an entity came to visit her, it would be one of the darker ones in the house. The prospect of meeting a child spirit was alluring. She sat there for a long time with the small child taking comfort on her lap. After it left, she found herself drifting back to sleep. She woke early the next morning to the sound of rapping, followed by the jingle of keys.

She opened her eyes. *Did she just hear that?*

She froze in her chair, her mind spinning. The feeling she got wasn't the same warmth and comfort she got from the child the night before. This one scared her. The fact that the sound was so distinct and undeniable set her nerves on edge. She held her breath until she heard it again. At this point, she'd had enough. She jumped up and left.

As if drawn back, she returned to the mansion later that day.

The boy on the stairs was calling to her.

She had been aware of him the day before during the tour. He was playful, but cautious, preferring to watch from a distance. While she was giving the tour, a young boy who was on the tour ran up to her and hugged her legs. She asked his mother if this was something he was prone to doing, but the mother just shook her head in disbelief. He was normally shy around strangers. Eleanor looked up, her eyes drawn to the staircase. She saw the boy sitting there, watching them.

Had he influenced the other child?

Thoughts of him remained with her all day as she ran errands. When she returned, she brought something with her that she thought the boy might enjoy. It was a ball.

"What's that," Lillian asked her, when she greeted her at the door.

"It's a ball. I brought it for the little boy," Eleanor said, then proceeded to head to the grand staircase. She tossed the ball halfway up and watched it bounce slowly down the stairs. She could feel the boy's joy at having a ball to play with, so she tossed it over and over again, finally retreating to the library room to bounce it some more.

Lillian came in while she was doing this, a curious expression on her face. "What are you doing, Eleanor?" she asked.

Eleanor wasn't sure herself. She just knew that the boy enjoyed watching the ball bounce. It was as though she couldn't stop. Lillian finally took the ball away from her.

"I think that's enough," she told her older friend.

Over time, Eleanor would return again and again, providing them with a plethora of information about the house and its occupants. She dug deep into the historical records, finding information that had never been uncovered. In the end, she had to put some distance between herself and the house. Every time she visited, she was influenced by the ghosts who lingered there. They would lead her to do things she wouldn't normally do. She felt it was in her own best interest to stay away from the mansion as much as possible.

(L) Edwin with Eleanor Gavazzi   (R)Ellen Pierce's safe

Footsteps Paranormal with members of NE GHOST

Night vision photo of the basement during the investigation

Chapter 28

Armed with the documentation from Eleanor, Edwin and Lillian felt they were much closer to finding out the truth about the hauntings. They now had names and a history to follow. The next logical step for them was to turn to the paranormal teams to see what they could add to the mix.

The next group they invited to the house was a local team, Footsteps Paranormal, organized by a woman named Sandy MacLeod from Hubbardston, the next town over. She brought nearly twenty people to investigate the house.

The group arrived with cameras and paranormal investigative gear. They also had two psychic mediums with them, something that fascinated Edwin. While the investigators were able to get documented evidence in the form of photographs and audio recordings, the psychics seemed to get to the heart of the hauntings, something he was desperate to understand.

Towards the end of the evening, one of the psychics took him aside and gave him her impressions.

She connected with many of the spirits in the house. She was aware of S.K. Pierce, Mattie Cornwell, the little boy, and Eino Saari. What truly bothered her though, was what was going on in the basement.

"There are secrets being kept down there. I kept getting the word 'secret' over and over again," she told him. "Something happened down in that basement, and it involved children," she said.

Her words left him cold inside.

Secrets.

It was the same thing Kim Huertas had told him.

What kind of secrets could it be?

She saw children going through the tunnel to work in the factory, many against their will.

Edwin had a hard time imagining someone of S.K. Pierce's stature allowing that to happen, but it wouldn't be the last time a psychic picked up on a similar image.

She told him some of the same things the other psychics had alluded to. The house was full of layers. Ghosts from the Victorian era were merged with ghosts from the 1960's and beyond. She felt they often conflicted with each another, causing chaos in a world that should be silent. She also picked up on the same thing as Kim Huertas, which was that many of the ghosts in the house were advanced in their abilities, making them far more dangerous than anyone should have to handle.

Her words were frightening, especially because of the validation from other investigators and psychics who shared the same feelings.

"What can we do?" he asked. They raised their eyebrows and shrugged. Convincing normal ghosts to move along wasn't difficult for a talented psychic medium, but the ones in the house were far from normal. There wasn't much anyone could do.

She warned him to be careful in the basement because of the dark energy. He knew what she meant, because he felt it more than once.

It would start out to be a prickle on the back of his neck; the sensation of being watched so strong, he couldn't ignore it. He swiveled around expecting to find someone standing in the shadows, but the room would always be empty. As much as Lillian loved the basement, Edwin hated it.

He had to go down there several times a week to grab a bag of pellets for the pellet stoves. As he made his way down the stairs, he kept his eyes adverted to the ground in front of him. Once he made it to the bottom, he would practically run to the room just beyond the old boiler to grab the pellets and go. The last thing he wanted was to see the shadow person again.

Presumably, it was where Edward slept.

Edwin found this to be disturbing on more than one level.

He always thought that wealth brought good fortune, but according to what he learned from Eleanor, S.K. Pierce's wealth brought nothing but pain and misery to the family. Edward's life story was one of the saddest tales she ever heard.

Edward was S.K. Pierce's youngest son. After his mother died and his brothers moved away, he inherited the Victorian mansion.

He married a local woman named Bessie had two beautiful daughters, Annette and Rachel. Unfortunately, the happily-ever-after scenario wouldn't last long. In 1916, his youngest daughter Rachel died from gastroenteritis, a very strong bacterial infection that brought symptoms of diarrhea, vomiting, and fever. Some would refer to it as Spanish Influenza, but doctors didn't discover the first cases until 1918, a full two years after Rachel died. More than likely, the influenza that took her life was another strain altogether.

Psychics often picked up on a small girl who often ran across the floor on the third story hallway. She would provide sweet greetings on digital audio, but seldom said or did anything more. Sometimes she could be convinced to move a ball back and forth, but she never entertained the ghost hunters for very long, as if the effort was too much for her to manage. Considering Eleanor's story about a small child climbing on her lap, Edwin wondered if this ghost girl was Edward's daughter, Rachel.

To make ends meet, Edward and Bessie turned the mansion into a boarding house, originally called the Victorian Tourist Home, which was later changed to the Victorian Inn. It would run successfully for many years with Edward and Bessie at the helm.

After Bessie died in 1951, the Victorian took a downward turn. The family fortune was all but gone, and the house was quickly crumbling to pieces. Edward continued to manage the boarding house until 1965, until it was transferred out of the Pierce family for the first time since it was built.

As the house began its swift decline, Edward became friends with a man named Jay Stemmerman. Jay's sister worked as a maid in the house. When she saw that times were getting tough for her employer, she contacted her brother to invite him for a visit.

The two became friends, spending a good amount of time in the library room playing cards. Although no records can be found to document it, many people feel that Edward lost the house in a card game to Mr. Stemmerman. Edward then became a tenant in the house that had once been his own, choosing to live in the basement where he could spend his days in solitude. Eleanor felt that this wasn't the whole story. She felt that Edward turned the house over willingly to Mr. Stemmerman, most likely out of necessity.

In reality, the old mansion was rotting away. Perhaps Jay pointed out to Edward that he didn't have many choices. He could either let the house sit and rot until it was unlivable, or he could turn it over to someone with more resources, someone who could fix the house and still provide Edward with a place to live. He may have sold it for a dollar, or have just signed it over. Eleanor didn't feel that Edward was in the right frame of mind to make such a decision, but his options might have been as limited as Stemmerman suggested. He needed the help and it would be foolish for him to turn it down. A fair amount of psychics picked up on a negative energy in the basement, leaving many to wonder if it wasn't Edward, who was angry at the hand life dealt him.

Another ghostly resident that psychics would pick up on time and time again was the prostitute who was allegedly murdered in the Red Room.

After hearing the story for the first time, Edwin turned to Eleanor to research the history. While she couldn't find any records of a prostitute, or even a female who was not a member of the Pierce family dying in the house, she had little doubt that it happened.

Although the house was never officially a brothel, many things happened that weren't documented, especially in the days when it sat empty. After Jay Stemmerman moved back to Florida, the house was abandoned for over twenty years. Getting inside it was just a matter of climbing in through a basement window. Eleanor felt that people probably came and went frequently, trolling the local playground, which could be viewed from the widows walk. She felt that children were abused there, brought in on the premise of seeing the house, but ending up with a far different reality. She felt it the strongest on the steps leading up to the widows walk, a place many other woman would feel uncomfortable, too.

She thought the prostitute in question was a woman who frequented the bar at the South Gardner Hotel across the street. Perhaps she met customers at the bar and then brought them to the house because of its close proximity and ease of access. Eleanor saw the woman as being in her late thirties, with a streetwise demeanor and a sense of impatience. She was the kind of woman who was eager to get things done. She hated sitting around waiting. Eleanor thought that the woman's name was Rita, or something similar, and she saw her with long auburn hair and a thin build. The man who murdered her was a large man with a slow wit. Eleanor didn't think he killed her on purpose and panicked when she died, dragging her body out of the house to dispose of it elsewhere. This differed from the impression that Kim Huertas got, but that was often the case with psychics. Ghosts came to each of them differently, sharing both truths and lies, depending on their mood. Just because they told one psychic one thing and another psychic something else didn't mean there wasn't a kernel of truth hidden beneath all of it. It was just a matter of interpreting it.

It helped Edwin piece together some semblance of the haunting. He'd always wondered how a woman could have died in the house without it being documented. It would have become town wide news, making it into the archives as prominently as the story of Eino Saari. Her body must have been moved after her death so it was never connected to the mansion.

One thing the psychics would often contradict each other about was the time when she was killed. While most felt she was contemporary, some felt she was there earlier than what Eleanor felt. Many thought she worked at the house during the days after Bessie's death. If there was a code of standards, it all but disappeared once Edward began managing the house on his own. He let in people like Eino Saari, a man who was well known around town for his heavy drinking. Perhaps the mysterious prostitute came in during that period of time, using the mansion for prostitution, but residing somewhere else. This would explain why her death didn't show up on any of the public records.

Whoever she was, her soul was felt by countless mediums that came to visit the house. Many female investigators couldn't spend time in the Red Room without getting an uncomfortable sensation in their chests. They reported feeling tightness as if the air was suddenly sucked out of the room, and they gasped for air before quickly retreating to the hallway. Others with more empathic psychic abilities would feel a strong sense of sadness, the sensation so strong they were often brought to tears.

Like Kim Huertas, many picked up on the man who killed her, a man who was frequently called "David." They felt he lingered in the house, and he was responsible for controlling several of the other spirits. One psychic felt he once held a position of power in the house, either as an owner or a manager of the property.

Edwin wasn't sure how it all interconnected, but deep in his heart, he knew it was true.

While it didn't slow down the activity, it helped him piece together the reasons behind it.

Many people had died in his house. He wasn't sure if they were looking for closure or for someone to simply know their story. Either way, he hoped that finding out the truth would bring them all some well needed peace.

As word got out, more and more paranormal groups wanted to experience the Haunted Victorian Mansion, as it came to be known. One such group was East Coast Paranormal Research Team out of Cumberland, Rhode Island.

Although they had a psychic medium on their team for specific situations, they preferred to investigate like scientists, obtaining proof of the paranormal through collecting tangible data. Typical of other paranormal groups, they had an experience right away.

As they were walking up the grand staircase to the second floor, Jeff Bartley, the founder of the group, was pushed. He felt the distinct impression of fingers on his back, giving him a slight shove. He turned around, thinking it was one of his team members, only to discover that no one was behind him. That same night they also heard the sound of a woman screaming. The voice was heard by all members of the team.

Was this the woman from the Red Room?

There seemed to be a connection between the two events, but Jeff wasn't sure what to make of it. If she was the one who pushed them, it showed an aggressive side to her. Was the scream a residue from the moment when she died? It would stand to reason that she would be angry, but why would she feel the need to push random people? They pressed on, moving to the master bedroom.

They connected quickly with Eino Saari. Edwin had filled them in on Eino's passion for liquor and the details of his grisly death. They turned on their digital recorders and began asking questions, hoping to capture a ghostly response. They started the session by asking Eino if he ever went across the street to the South Gardner Hotel for a drink. One their audio recording, they heard the very clear response of "yep."

It was apparent how much Eino loved his liquor. Other investigators would record similar responses to the question, something that was also documented by personal accounts from people who knew Eino when he was alive.

Happy with a response, they moved down to the first floor and began investigating in the library room. In the S.K. Pierce days, the room was used as a sitting room. It now housed all of the photos and memorabilia from the sordid history of the house.

They set up a flashlight and used it to communicate with the resident ghosts. Ghost hunting teams often used the practice as a quick method of obtaining responses. They would ask a question, and then instruct the ghosts to turn on the light as a positive response. They immediately began getting quick replies.

Like most investigators, Jeff has seen the flashlight technique provide inadequate responses. Sometimes it seems to go on and off in a random pattern, something they quickly dismiss as coincidence. This time the responses were immediate and concise. There was no doubt that someone was operating the flashlight.

They doubled back to ask the same questions in another manner and would always get the same response. By the responses, he felt as though he were talking to Mattie Cornwell, the nanny. It was the first time he ever got such fast responses, even if she didn't disclose anything they didn't already know.

She confirmed her name, age, and position in the household, which was interesting in itself. When they began asking more personal questions, she simply stopped responding.

The group moved on to the basement. Intrigued by the investigation, Edwin joined them on several of their sessions. Even though he wasn't fond of the basement, he followed them down and sat in the dark while they conducted the investigation.

"Why don't you ask a question," Jeff told Edwin.

Edwin wasn't altogether comfortable talking to the dead, but he was curious. He asked if anyone wanted to talk to him and got the response of "Eino."

It was a curious response, since no one else had ever encountered Eino Saari in the basement before then. Immediately, he remembered what Mark Veau, the former owner, had told him. Apparently, Eino hid his moonshine beneath the servant's stairs. Maybe he was just going down to check on his liquor. If felt as though some of the history of the house was starting to unfold for them during the investigations. Each one brought them a small glimmer of the truth. He only hoped that they could one day piece it altogether to construct the full story.

Investigations are often draining for the investigators, prompting the need for period breaks. During one of their breaks, Jeff and another team member went outside to get some fresh air. As soon as they sat down on the front porch steps, a woman walked past with a child. The little boy looked up at them, and then told his mother, "See, I told you there was a little boy here."

Jeff immediately looked around expecting to see a child behind them, but the porch was empty. He shook his head as the woman quickly ushered the child away. It made him wonder what the boy saw. Was the ghostly apparition of a boy standing right behind them?

Like so many others, he felt drawn to the Victorian, and returned several times to investigate. He felt it was the most active location he ever investigated, and he was thankful for the experience.

East Coast Paranormal Research Team with Edwin Gonzalez

Cameras set up and ready to go in the library room

New England Paranormal Society

Chapter 29

Lucky Belcamino, founder of New England Paranormal Society also investigated the Victorian with her group. A self-described biker chick, she is also a sensitive medium, someone who can sense ghosts and spirits, as well as communicate with them. Her first paranormal experience came after her mother died. She saw her appear at her bedside shortly after she passed away, telling her "You've got it and you'll know when to use it." Lucky found this to be true as she began investigating the paranormal. Messages or impressions often came to her as she sat in the dark, talking with the dead. While most people were quick to discount the messages, Lucky learned to trust them. They often led her closer to the truth behind the haunting.

There was always a story to tell. Most ghosts didn't linger on because they lived a full and happy life. Most of them stayed because something very traumatic happened to them, removing them from their living existence before they were ready to go. Some remained because they wanted their story to be told, while others remained to look over something or someone they loved and couldn't bear to be separated from.

Both times when she investigated the Victorian, she had experiences. She encountered the little boy in the library room and a male spirit in the Billiards Room. Several members of her group also detected the smell of cigarette smoke. A quick look out the window proved that no one was outdoors smoking, and the scent disappeared as quickly as it came.

After a presentation and tour of the house, they split into groups and began investigating the house. While they were in the Red Room, one of the attendees felt a heaviness in her chest and had a difficult time breathing. They later learned that other women have experienced the same feelings in the room.

She also captured strange light anomalies in the closet. They left a string of bells on the doorknob and heard them ring on more than one occasion. Psychically, she picked up on a hostile woman inside the room, which was different from what Edwin had heard in the past. He always heard that the woman was protective, but the man, David, was the aggressor. He wasn't sure what to think anymore.

Was she the one pushing people on the stairs?

After what he learned from Jeff Bartley's team, he had to wonder.

Lucky's group moved to the third floor, but the widows walk proved to be trying for her. The minute she started up the winding stairs, she couldn't go any further. Something felt wrong about it and she had the distinct impression that she shouldn't go up there. She decided to go anyway. Halfway up the stairs, she heard a man's voice telling her to "get out." When she got to the top, she felt dizzy and nauseated. The sound of footsteps could be heard coming up the stairs behind her, but when they looked, nobody was there.

An investigator from their team named Debbie went into the house by herself while everyone else was outside. She wandered up to the third floor and began filming the cistern room. As she filmed, the Victorian sofa moved several feet. She raced outside, telling the team she wasn't going back up there. Later in the investigation, they also caught a curtain moving in the dining room, which was followed by the basement door in the kitchen opening on its own.

Video below (for E-Readers or computers).

Click to watch to the video or copy and paste onto your computer's browser:

https://www.youtube.com/watch?v=jbawC7sjCcs&list=WLnYdyu5SSc89OZiBwqGici0O5cjTZ1j6m

Lily Colon at the Victorian prior to the event

Lily Colon attended the event as well. It was her very first ghost hunt, so she was excited to be participating. When the group was divided into smaller groups, she found herself with several others on the second floor in the Red Room. Like many women, the group couldn't stay in the room for long. They felt a sense of dizziness and had difficulty breathing. As they walked back out into the hallway, they looked back in the room to see that the closet door was hanging open. Lily was one of the last ones out of the room and remembered it being closed. While they didn't see the door actually open, it was enough to make them wonder if they'd just experienced something paranormal.

Her group then relocated to the basement. Lily was unnerved the moment she began descending the dark stairs. She wasn't sure if it was just a natural reaction to the creepy basement setting, or if she was picking up on an entity.

As they reached the bottom, one of the women jumped, telling the others she heard something in another room. Lily didn't hear the noise, but made her way into the room. Feeling nervous, she stayed at the back of the group and stood there filming the session with her camera. She wouldn't realize until later that she actually captured footage of a shadow person darting through the group.

Video below (for E-Readers or computers).

Click to watch to the video or copy and paste onto your computer's browser:

https://www.youtube.com/watch?v=YT2hDHYFcII&feature=youtu.be

The second time Lucky investigated at the Victorian, she experienced a hostile force on the grand staircase. As she was walking up the stairs to get her equipment she felt a push, which almost sent her back down the stairs. She turned to look, fully expecting to see someone behind her, but the staircase was empty.

Edwin was concerned about all the reports of pushing on the stairs. Even though neither he nor Lillian had experienced it, just the possibility left him fearful. Were they just waiting for the right moment? He thought about it every time he went down them. It was like living with a ticking time bomb.

In the master bedroom, Lucky's group also encountered Eino Saari.

Lucky's team experienced a small dose of his frustration and anger.

She brought a small bottle of whiskey and some cigarettes she wanted to use as trigger objects to encourage Eino to communicate with them.

"Hi. We're here. Hopefully, you'll communicate with us," she said, and then realized they left the whiskey and cigarettes in the car. She ran outside and when she came back in, one of the investigators smiled.

"Don't worry. We don't need whiskey. We'll just take him across the street to the South Gardner Hotel," she said. They captured an EVP at that moment, telling them, "I've already had my whiskey, bitch!"

The voice was anything but friendly. It made Edwin wonder if Eino was the shadow person he often saw in the hallway, making the dogs growl. However, it wouldn't come together until another psychic came to the house to fill in some of the missing pieces of the puzzle.

During the night they smelled cigarette and cigar smoke in various parts of the house. The smell was illusive. As soon as they smelled it, the scent would promptly disappear. It was as though someone was following them throughout the house during the investigation.

Below are audio sessions from their investigations:

Click to listen to the audio recording or copy and paste onto your computer's browser:

https://soundcloud.com/ccbelcamino/sets/vm-feb-2014

Click to listen to the audio recording or copy and paste onto your computer's browser:

https://soundcloud.com/ccbelcamino/sets/vm-3-22-14-recordings/s-yhwoU

Founders Lucky Belcamino and Candace Craft Belcamino with Edwin prior to the investigation

The third floor cistern room, where Lucky's team captured video footage of the sofa moving on its own accord

Andrew Lake surprised Edwin with another request to visit the Victorian. When he first visited the mansion in 2010, he was the first person to confirm the hauntings to Edwin. After returning two more times, once with a psychic medium, he helped Edwin understand more about the hauntings.

On his fourth visit, he brought another psychic medium, a woman named Stephanie. She wasn't a psychic by profession, but had inherited the ability from her mother. Andrew made sure she didn't know anything about the house before her visit.

As she walked around, she began picking up on small things, but it wasn't until the end of the tour before she truly surprised them.

"The man who built this house is really upset with the things that are going on in the house right now," she told Andrew.

"How so?" Andrew asked.

"Apparently, as he says it, there are a bunch of fools and idiots that keep coming into this house and expecting them to perform for them, like circus animals. He's talking about the ghost hunters. They come in here and they're rude. They act like it's a carnival or circus in here. He's mad that Edwin is allowing them to come in. He says, 'Enough of this nonsense. Tell Edwin to get this house fixed like it was. Enough of these fools and idiots coming in here!'"

When they walked downstairs, she walked into the library room, went directly to the photo of S.K. Pierce and pointed him out. "This is the man who was talking to me," she said.

She also suggested that they find a reputable ghost group to lead the paranormal investigators instead of allowing them free reign throughout the house. That way they could monitor the investigations and insure investigators weren't overstepping their boundaries by being rude or bringing things like Ouija boards into the house. In hindsight, it was good advice that Edwin should have taken to heart.

An EVP captured later confirms this. A male voice strongly states, "Don't talk to her."

A female responds to him with, "I won't."

Was it S.K. Pierce?

Click to listen to the audio recording or copy and paste onto your computer's browser:

https://soundcloud.com/jonimayhan/mbr-gb-dont-talk-to-heri-wont

S.K. Pierce

Chapter 30

Heather Anderson came to the house multiple times as part of a paranormal group. Being a psychic medium, the experience would always be different for her than it was for other members of her team. She could see and feel what was usually hidden from everyone else, and they used her wisely.

Heather Anderson

Her team leader asked her to do a preliminary walk around the house to see what she felt. He then set up their cameras and equipment in the spots where she felt the ghosts lingering the strongest. It helped them gather more evidence, and it gave them better access to the resident ghosts. There weren't too many places they could hide from a gifted medium like Heather.

Like the others before her, she felt a child, a young female, servants, and a man who had been burnt. However, the one that would provide the biggest impact for her was the woman from the Red Room.

Like Lucky Belcamino, she felt that the woman in the Red Room was angry and aggressive. She thought the woman may have been a prostitute, but she also felt she acted as a madam for other ladies of the evening during the period that the house was a boarding house.

The longer she was at the mansion, the more the woman in the Red Room concerned her. She saw her as a woman in her late thirties, with dark hair, who was filled with absolute, raw rage. If anyone was ever pushed or harmed on the second floor, she felt this woman was the one responsible. This entity hated the living more than anything else. She wanted them out of the house, so the dead could continue to manage their domain. She wouldn't relent until every last living person was gone.

This was concerning to both Edwin and Lillian. So many psychics said the same thing. What could they do about it, besides move? Heather wasn't certain, either.

"She's very advanced," she told them. A ghost like the Red Room woman was capable of almost anything. If she was able to push people down the stairs, the activity may lead to scratching, or even worse. That, combined with her sense of rage made her an extremely dangerous entity.

Heather's group finally made its way to the third floor. While there, she kept getting glimpses of a man falling from a window. At the urging of the group's leader, she attempted to channel the person to learn more about what happened to them.

Channeling can be a dangerous venture for a medium. It involves opening up your body and allowing another entity to step inside and take over. While she had never attempted it before, she was confident she could handle it. It felt like the right thing to do at the time.

"If it gets too heavy, just push him back out," a teammate suggested.

She closed her eyes and allowed herself to be quieted from the inside out. After a moment, she felt the woman from the Red Room move into her body, instead of the man she expected. It wasn't the person she'd hoped to channel, because the rage filled her from head to toe, making her feel the burning, churning sensation of pure hatred.

Bob, another team member, stepped forward and started asking questions. Instead of asking Heather what she was feeling, he began to speak directly to the woman herself. She felt an immediate sense of agitation.

"What did you do to the man?" he asked, getting right into her space. He grabbed her arms just below the shoulders and began to shake her.

She just came unglued. The woman that lurked inside her body roared to the surface.

She wanted him OUT!

He was the one who strangled her in the Red Room so many years ago.

She gave Bob a tremendous push, and he went flying. He reeled back nearly twenty feet towards the window. If Heather's husband wasn't standing there to catch him, Bob would have gone through the window himself.

The push was so traumatic that he reinjured his shoulder, which was healing from a recent surgery

Everyone stood there with wide eyes as Heather began to come out of it.

All the "what ifs," swirled around each one of them. If Heather's husband wasn't standing by the window, Bob may have repeated history by falling to his death. If Heather couldn't come out of it, what else could she do with the angry woman inside her? What if it was just practice for the angry woman? Who would she attempt to take over next?

Heather was so shaken she had to be helped out of the house. She sat on the back steps, feeling dizzy and sick. She felt like she was violated all the way down to the very core of her existence. She was nothing more than a passenger in her own body while the woman held the reins.

It would take her two weeks to recover.

During that time, she felt the woman return, wanting to take over her body again. Heather pushed her away each time, and then followed up by burning sage in her house to try to move the negative energy elsewhere. It took her weeks to finally push the woman away and even longer to get over the experience.

It would be the first and last time she ever attempted to channel an entity.

The window on the third floor landing

    Lillian wandered up to the third floor. Even after Heather's experience, she didn't feel a sense of danger up there. The area felt calm to her, almost as calm as the basement, another place where investigators felt uncomfortable.
    She didn't get it. Why would the ghosts of the house fill some people with fear, while it did nothing to other people? Did it pick and choose the ones it liked? She wasn't sure, but she couldn't find any reason for it.
    She dismissed the thought as her mind filled with numbers.

The electric bill was due, the mortgage was due, but the plumber had pretty much wiped them out after the pipes were clogged again. They hired someone to patch the roof to stop some of the leaks, but it wasn't going to hold for long. They needed a new roof soon. The thought filled her with despair.

She wasn't sure what they were going to do.

As she made her way up the narrow staircase, the wind howled as it swirled around the building, blowing gusts of snow through the cracks in the windows. She reached the landing and heard a strange sound. She was used to hearing odd noises in the house. It had become almost commonplace, but this one was different. She stood still until she could identify it. It was the sound of pigeons cooing. She followed the sound to the ceiling in the long room just off the cistern room. She scowled, feeling the anger rise inside of her. The pigeons must have made nests inside the eaves of the house.

It frustrated her because she truly loved animals. When she visited her sister's house, she always brought a loaf of bread to feed the ducks at the pond. It was to a point where they saw her coming, and nearly knocked her over to get to the bread. She hated the thought of doing anything to hurt the pigeons, but they were literally destroying the house.

"What can I do about them?" she asked aloud, feeling foolish as the sound of her own voice echoed back at her. There was no answer. She sighed and looked out the window at West Broadway, which was quickly disappearing beneath a blanket of snow.

Getting rid of the pigeons wasn't easy. She poured dish detergent around the window eaves because someone told her it was an effective deterrent. It worked for a few days, but once the rains came, the pigeons came right back again.

She even placed a life-sized plastic owl on the roof, but they adapted to that as well, often perching on top of its head. Finally, in desperation, she purchased poison. She looked at the bag sitting by the window. It would be so easy. She could mix it with bird seed and sprinkle it on the eaves outside the window.

"I hate doing this, but I have to kill these birds," she said to no one in particular.

At that precise moment, she heard a loud thump from the other side of the room, the room where the cistern was located. As she turned the corner, she saw a mirror fall to the ground. Thinking it had just slipped from the nail, she went to rehang it, only to discover that it hadn't slipped off the nail. The nail was still firmly in place, as was the round holder on the back of the mirror. In order to fall from the nail, it needed to be lifted and then dropped.

She took it as a sign and threw away the poison.

She had to find another way to kill the birds.

Winter continued with a record amount of snowfall. A December 20th snowstorm blanketed the area with over a foot of snow. Another storm repeated the gesture the day after Christmas with yet another foot. While the snow was beautiful to look at, it made Lillian feel isolated and lonely. She hoped to spend the holiday at her new house surrounded by friends and family, but it just wasn't meant to happen. Nobody wanted to spend the most joyous day of the year in an unheated haunted house. Instead, she and Edwin drove to Boston to spend it with her family.

On the rare occasion her family made the trek west, they would often experience strange occurrences at the house. It got to the point where many of them refused to return. She found herself reluctant to call them, fearful of hearing the pleas for her to come home.

"Just sell that house and come back home," her mother told her.

"I can't, Ma. Not yet," Lillian said, wondering herself what she meant. They did have a lot of money tied up in the house, but that wasn't the only reason why she couldn't let go. Something in the house called to her. She felt as if she had to more to do.

It wasn't something she could put her finger on, but she knew she needed to stick it out. She couldn't just walk away from the house. Despite the lack of heating and the paranormal activity, it was her dream house.

While most of her family was fearful of the paranormal activity, her sister Bridget was the exception. She seemed to enjoy the opportunity to antagonize them.

"Be good," Lillian warned her the last time she came for a visit.

Bridget was known for outwardly provoking the ghosts, trying to get a response.

"I just want to see them. If they're really here, they need to come out and show themselves," she said. Lillian arched her eyebrows, hoping her sister wouldn't get more than she bargained for. She hid a smile as she wondered what her sister would do if a full-bodied apparition appeared in front of her face, like it did to poor Edwin. It might be a different story then.

Lillian was working on laundry all morning. As she headed down to the basement to switch the loads, Bridget followed close behind her. When she moved the wet clothes from the washer to the dryer, they heard a noise coming from another room.

"Wanna check it out?" Lillian offered playfully.

"Of course," Bridget said with an evil smile.

They walked down the short hallway past the servant's staircase, and turned left into the big open room that was known as the tunnel room. Although she remembered what the psychics and investigators felt in the basement, she didn't feel it.

If nothing else, the basement was the most comfortable place in the house for her.

She wondered if it had something to do with the way the basement looked. She had to admit, it did look creepy down there. Unlike the rest of the house, the basement looked like a typical New England cellar. Rafters lined the ceilings, and the brick walls were lost in shadows.

Lillian paused at the doorway and looked back at her sister.

"Have you seen the tunnel entrance?" she asked.

Photo of the tunnel in the basement that led from the house to the furniture factory across the street before it was bricked over.

The bricked-over entrance as it currently looks

"I don't think so," Bridget said. Unlike the rest of her family, Bridget wasn't frightened by the stories about the house. She was much like Lillian had been in the beginning, wondering if people were just exaggerating the truth.

Lillian led her into the tunnel room and showed her the place on the wall where the entrance was blocked off. It was a small space, looking more like a covered up fireplace opening than a tunnel.

"You're sure that was really a tunnel? Bridget asked, always the skeptic.

"That's what they tell me." When they moved in, they heard it from the realtor. Several of the psychics who came into the house picked up on it right away, as well.

"Why would he have a tunnel here?" Bridget asked.

It was a good question, and one Lillian didn't have an answer to. She knew the tunnel existed. When the former owner dug up the sidewalks, they encountered it and dropped a time capsule into its depths. Why the Pierce family would need a tunnel was beyond her.

"I don't know. I guess there were once a lot of tunnels in Gardner, mostly because of the snow in the winter. S.K. Pierce's furniture factory was on the other side of the street, so he built this tunnel to get back and forth," she said, but she always had to wonder about the logic behind that reasoning. Why would a multi-millionaire crawl through a dusty old tunnel to go to work, when he could simply walk out his front door and be fifty feet from his factory?

She thought about what the psychic medium told them about using the tunnel to shuffle children workers back and forth. That didn't make any sense, either. Why children? Maybe it wasn't illegal, but that was just part of the culture back then. She saw the photos of women and children caning chairs. It was far less work to put the woven seats on chairs than it was to manufacture them.

It had to be something else.

Maybe a child was hurt near the tunnel?

Was this one of the house's dark secrets, the same secrets the two psychics mentioned?

Was that what happened to the little boy? Was been fatally injured somehow? Did they burn his bones in the Summer Kitchen to hide the evidence? The thought gave her a chill.

She hoped not.

Bridget put her hands on her hips and looked around. She had a defiant look on her face that worried Lillian. One of these days, she was going to get a response that could force her to use a bit more respect towards the ghosts of the S.K. Pierce house.

"If there are really ghosts here, come out and show yourself. I don't believe all this crap," she said.

She was answered by a tremendous bang near the servant's staircase.

Lillian jumped, despite herself. "What the hell was that?"

They raced from the room and just stood speechless at what they saw. One of Lillian's sneakers was lying on the ground. This was strange on two accounts. The first was that she kept her shoes in a box under the main basement staircase, which was at least twenty feet away. The second was that the shoe hit a piece of plywood leaning against the wall. In order for her shoe to do that, it would have to shoot twenty feet across the basement, before making a ninety-degree turn to slam into the wood.

This was impossible.

She walked over to the main basement staircase. The other shoe was still sitting in the box beneath the stairs. She just looked at her sister in disbelief. It felt like a sign, and an unfriendly one at that.

"Let's go upstairs," she suggested to her sister.

Bridget, who was uncharacteristically silent, quickly followed her.

The basement would continue to be a source of intrigue.

And it wouldn't be the last time something unexplained happened there.

Terri Harlow investigating the basement at the Houghton Mansion
Photo courtesy of Terri Harlow

Terri Harlow, the founder of Conscious Spirit Paranormal, visited the house on several occasions, intrigued by the activity. Terri's involvement in the paranormal world began during her childhood, growing up in an old Victorian haunted house.

As a child, when she went to bed at night, she always kept the closet door partially opened, so it created a barrier between her and the hallway outside her bedroom door. Her mother confirmed her belief when she saw a female apparition, dressed in white, coming through a bedroom door.

Prompted by the early experiences, Terri began investigating the paranormal in her teens, starting out at cemeteries and soon branching out to houses and haunted venues. In 2009, she founded Conscious Spirits Paranormal with a group of people, who by chance were all mediums. She's found that when their group visits a haunted location, they usually experienced more activity than most people normally encountered.

Case in point was the Victorian Mansion. They brought eight people to the house to investigate. They normally kept the group smaller, but word had traveled about the mansion, and everyone wanted to experience it.

The third floor proved to be trying for them. While they were in the Billiards Room, Terri felt as though the room was filled with men. She could sense as many as six of them gathered around. She wasn't fond of the feeling she got in Lillian's office. She had an uneasy sensation, one that made her feel as though the group was unwelcomed. Several photos snapped in the area revealed a strange mist. While they were on the third floor, they heard footsteps coming up the stairs towards them, but when they turned to look, the staircase was empty.

Mist in Lillian's office Photo courtesy of Conscious Spirit Paranormal

The group divided into teams and a group consisting of women headed to the basement. Like the others before them, the group became aware of a darker entity. At one point during the night, the walkie-talkie started behaving erratically. Even though no buttons were depressed, they could hear the men on the third floor very clearly. Once they left the mansion, the issue never presented itself again.

Terri also felt there was an irritated woman in the basement. Earlier, while Edwin was giving them a tour of the building, they spent some time in the Summer Kitchen. A later audio recording provided more information for the entity's concern.

"While Edwin was giving his tour, a woman kept trying to interrupt him. She was really angry because she felt he was telling the story incorrectly and was trying to set the record straight," Terri said with a smile.

The group also captured photos of dark shadows descending upon the group. Before each photo was taken, someone from the group felt as though someone was watching them, which prompted the photo. It was an investigation none of them would soon forget.

Shadows descending in the third floor cistern room

Massachusetts Ghost Hunters Paranormal Society (MGHPS) members: Marc Arvilla, Peter Lovasco, Lauren Sheridan, and Mike Galante

Chapter 31

Massachusetts Ghost Hunters Paranormal Society (MGHPS) investigated the Victorian Mansion four times. Each time provided more interesting than the last.

Founded by Marc Arvilla and Lauren Sheridan, the team is located out of Gloucester, Massachusetts. Mike Galante and Peter Lovasco are two other team members who have experienced paranormal phenomena at the house.

During one of their visits, they spent time in the master bedroom, attempting to communicate with Eino Saari. Some controversy surrounds Eino's death. While the police reports document it as an accidental mattress fire, others felt that it was due to careless smoking, coupled with consumption of alcohol. They asked a few questions of Eino, but received no responses. As soon as they got back downstairs to the Ladies Parlor, one of the team members pointed excitedly at the monitor.

A camera left in the master bedroom showed a very strange light anomaly. A figure 8 of light hovered in the middle of the room. As they watched, nearly holding their breath in surprise, the light bounced around the room for a few seconds before disappearing. Was it Eino Saari, responding to their difficult questions?

During another investigation, Peter Lovasco got more than he bargained for. Known as the group's "ghost magnet," Peter often experiences paranormal activity during investigations. Some members feel that if anything is going to happen, it will happen while Peter is nearby. His experience that night proved their point.

He came out of the Copper Room, on his way to the grand staircase when a full body apparition suddenly popped up on his face. What he saw will haunt him for the rest of his life.

"It was really tall, at least eight feet tall, with a black cape and a white skeleton face. The eyes were what got me. They were the size of billiard balls and they were solid black," he said with a shiver. The apparition rose into the air before disappearing into the ceiling, causing Peter to jolt backwards, nearly toppling over a floor candelabrum. While seeing an apparition was something most investigators dreams of seeing during an investigation, it was a terrifying experience nonetheless.

On another investigation, Edwin allowed them to sleep over. While Marc Arvilla slept in the Red Room, he became aware of something floating over the top of him as he rested in the bed. He opened his eyes, only to discover the entire ceiling was blacked out by something dark and heavy.

During the night, he heard a loud noise downstairs. When he went down to look, he found the front door wide open. Members of the team quickly joined him, professing that the door had been locked tight when they retired for bed.

Perhaps, their greatest discovery was a Spirit Box response they captured in the Billiards Room. They asked who was there with them and got the very distinct response of "Edward."

> *To watch the Youtube video, click on the link below or copy the link to your computer's browser.*
>
> *https://www.youtube.com/watch?v=BoArjphKbC8*

Like many others before and after them, they had unanswered questions. While the resident ghosts were willing to let their presence be known, they weren't always compliant about answering questions. The personal experiences they encountered made the mansion one of their favorite locations to investigate.

Peter in the spot where he saw the apparition.

MGHPS getting ready for the investigation in the kitchen

Bill Wallace

Chapter 32

Bill Wallace sat across the street at the South Gardner Hotel again, nursing a beer in the bar area.

The snow had all but melted, but it was still bitterly cold outside. He could see the Victorian mansion through the window. Lights flickered in several of the upstairs windows, which he imagined to be from flashlights.

He could feel the shifting energy in the house, and it didn't feel right to him. All the investigations were stirring up activity levels in the house, disturbing the dead who still resided there. He could imagine them, shrinking into corners as a group of strangers came into the room, armed with talking machines and bright, strange lights. The ghosts wanted it to stop. They wanted the house back to the way it had been before the new owners arrived.

Mattie wasn't happy about it either, and she wasn't shy about telling him about it. He didn't want to interfere with what the new owners were doing, but he couldn't just sit back and watch it all come tumbling down. He needed to do something. He just wasn't sure what to do.

Like the old owners, the new owners were allowing paranormal teams to investigate the house frequently and Mattie didn't like it. She liked Edwin well enough, mostly because her own father's name was also Edwin, but she despised all the people gallivanting through the house. Some of them were disrespectful, while others were just plain nosy. She chattered in his ear like an irate housekeeper, angry about all the mud on her floors. With a sigh, he finally pulled himself from his chair and walked across the street.

One of Bill's friends mentioned he was going to be at the Victorian investigation. Maybe he would walk over to say hello. It would also give him a chance to meet the new owners.

The driveway was filled with cars, some of them sporting paranormal team logos. As he stood at the end of the sidewalk, just beyond the giant "V" the former owners molded in the sidewalk, he stared up at the windows, watching the shadows pass by like apparitions.

The house had multiple layers of history. Like the other psychics before him, he knew that the ghosts from the Victorian era mingled with contemporary ghosts, blurring past with the present. The natural order that Mattie worked so hard to maintain was slowly being destroyed, as the new investigators brought in more and more ghosts with them.

Bill knew that most people weren't aware of the natural order that functioned inside a haunted house. There was usually an authority figure who kept the peace, acting almost like a dormitory monitor, ensuring that everyone behaved themselves. Mattie had served that role for more than a century with success, but it was all going to come toppling down if things continued.

Bill wasn't sure if the new owners even knew what was happening, but opening the house up for paranormal events was essentially turning the mansion into a ghost hotel.

Most people thought that ghosts were stuck in one place, but it wasn't always the case. Many times, ghosts followed the investigators, especially those who were sensitive to their presence. When a place was frequently investigated, it often became more haunted than before as the new ghosts decided to stay. He couldn't blame them. Who wouldn't want to live at the beautiful Victorian? Unfortunately, it was more than Mattie could handle. She had enough.

When he knocked at the door, Edwin answered.

It took Bill a moment to explain who he was and why he was there. After he was finished, he expected the new owner to toss him back out onto the sidewalk, but he didn't. Instead, Edwin invited him in.

He found his friend Derek and said hello, then he ended up spending the rest of the evening with Edwin. They sat in the kitchen well into the wee hours of the morning talking. Bill told him everything he knew about the house. Several times he got up to wander to an area that called to him, his hands moving together in front of him, like they did when he got impressions. By the time he left, a friendship was forged, and Edwin would invite him back to the house.

The house claimed him once again, finding a way to get him back inside.

As it would turn out, there was a reason for this.

Mattie needed him, but so did Edwin and Lillian.

He'd end up playing a very important role in their lives.

The Union Street entrance (servant's entrance)

Photo by Jason Baker

Chapter 33

As January slipped into February, the investigations dwindled and the house quieted down once more. The sounds of knocking and footsteps disappeared completely, making Edwin and Lillian wonder if the lost souls were finally getting used to them.

Edwin took Bill's advice to heart. They needed to slow down the investigations. He noticed that as the weeks went by, the house gradually came back to its normal rhythm. He could imagine Mattie Cornwell standing in the corner with a satisfied expression on her face.

As Edwin worked from his second floor office, he became less and less aware of the ghosts. The house started to finally feel like a home. He stopped worrying about the prospect of the apparition appearing in his face again, and he started worrying about more important issues, namely the lack of heat in the house.

It almost felt as though he and Lillian were living on separate islands. She stayed in the kitchen, which was heated by one pellet stove, and he remained in his office, where the second stove was located. The rest of the space surrounding them was frigid and brutal, far too cold to spend more than a few moments there. Even in the semi-warmth of his office, he still had to wear several layers of clothing to stay warm. It got to a point where they just holed themselves up in their heated zones and only came together late in the evening when Edwin finished his work.

They shared a quick dinner at the kitchen table, both usually so tired, they didn't have the energy to talk. Something about winter in the house seemed to drain their vitality. He wasn't sure if it was the constant battle to stay warm or the lack of human contact, but all he wanted to do after ten hours of working was to eat, watch a little television, and then fall into bed.

Was this how he wanted his life to be? He remembered the jubilance he felt as he stood in the foyer that first day they looked at the house, scarcely able to imagine owning something so grand. It was difficult to compare that feeling to the way he felt now. It seemed more like a burden than a luxury.

It was difficult living to a new town after leaving all of their friends and family behind. When they were in Dorchester, there wasn't a day that went by without people popping by to say hello. Their weekends and evenings were filled with conversations, food, and friends, and they never once had to worry about freezing to death in their own home.

Worst of all, they had no one to talk to. Although he used to have friends he could share his life experiences with, now that Edwin was going through one of the most challenging struggles ever, he didn't have anyone to talk to who would understand how it affected him personally. The combination of isolation and frustration was slowly turning him into a person he didn't recognize. He felt both restless and drained at the same time. He didn't know how much more he could take. The only thing he truly enjoyed was the tours. They gave him a small portion of what he was craving, some human interaction and a chance to talk about the horrifying events they lived through with people who wouldn't judge them.

He always was somewhat shy, but there was something fulfilling about leading people from room to room as he told them about the history of the house. He loved the enthusiastic look in their eyes as he regaled the stories of Mattie Cornwell, Eino Saari, and the little boy who wandered the hallways. It was his way of sharing the house with other people instead of keeping it to himself. It wasn't how he first imagined how life would be in the mansion, but at least it was something. It was one of the few pleasures he'd gotten since claiming ownership.

It also helped them make new friends. Slowly, through the connection with paranormal investigations, people started stopping by, wanting to spend time with him and Lillian in their haunted mansion. Unlike many of their former acquaintances, these people didn't frown when he told them about the doors slamming in the middle of the night. They didn't whisper to one another behind their hands when he talked about the little ghost boy who haunted their staircase. These people understood. They listened to his stories and even shared some of their own. It was a strange new world for them, but after nearly two years in the house, they now had people who appreciated their situation.

The collection of friends started with Bill Wallace and then quickly expanded. Soon after meeting Bill, they became friends with Derek Cormier and his friend, Bob Pfeiffer. The three of them spent many weekend evenings sitting at the kitchen table, talking. When they explored the house, they had many paranormal experiences they just couldn't explain.

As winter slowly gave way to spring, the investigations picked up again despite Edwin's better judgment. He had a hard time saying no to the requests. The groups were all so excited and enthusiastic at the prospect of seeing the house. They even provided him with some information that he found useful in understanding the hauntings.

In late spring, he had a group of investigators in from Connecticut.

While he was in the Ladies Parlor telling the group about the ornament that relocated itself to the middle of the room, a young woman named Kaleigh caught his attention. She seemed distracted by something in the hallway and kept turning her head to glance out into the hallway. Her head kept jerking to the side. He wasn't sure if she had seen something in the door that kept getting her attention, or if she was having some kind of nervous reaction. He caught Lillian's eye at the end of the presentation and she shrugged. She noticed the strange behavior as well.

The girl followed the group up to the second floor without further issue, but when they got to the Copper Room, she abruptly left in the middle of his story. Seconds later, she returned, looking as white as a sheet. She took Edwin aside to tell him what she saw.

"I just saw an apparition in the nursery doorway," she told him. She described the ghostly figure as a woman in her early twenties with dark hair that was pulled in a bun, wearing a blue dress with a white apron. The strangest thing was her eyes.

They were solid white.

Edwin pulled her aside, wanting to know what has happened to her in the Ladies Parlor.

"I saw you looking at the doorway. Were you seeing something there too?" he asked.

She seemed almost embarrassed by the question, but answered it anyway. "Yeah. I kept feeling like someone was standing in the doorway, but every time I looked no one was there. I thought if I kept looking, I might catch it off guard."

Kayleigh's experiences didn't end at the Victorian. Later, after returning home, she discovered something unnerving. Something had followed her home.

She pulled in her driveway and gasped at what she saw. A dark shape stood at the end of the pavement. It looked like a black cut-out of a person. Her heart began to race. It looked exactly like the figure Edwin described seeing on the second floor landing.

"What is that?" she whispered to herself. She stared at it, hoping she wasn't seeing what she thought she was seeing. Was it a shadow person?

Being an experienced paranormal investigator, she knew all too well how dangerous shadow people could be. She certainly wasn't eager to encounter one. As she sat there with the engine still running, the dark form raced across the driveway, before disappearing into the shadows.

The experience was unnerving and left her shaken. She came into the house, not feeling safe and warm like she usually did at home. The house was dark, and she was the only one at home. Every shadow became suspect and every noise felt threatening.

Something felt wrong. It felt like someone was watching her.

She wasn't sure if she was simply shaken from what she saw at the Victorian, and then again at the end of her driveway, or if there was a valid reason for the sensation of violation that overcame her. She turned all the lights on to chase away the shadows, but the feeling of being watched wouldn't leave her.

She somehow managed to fall asleep, but daylight wouldn't chase away the sense of paranoia. The feeling of being watched grew even stronger, following her through the rooms of her house. She turned around, feeling like someone crept up behind her, only to find the room as empty as it was before. She began hearing the distinctive sound of a person screaming, but when she went to look, no one was there.

The activity escalated over the course of a few weeks. One night, she woke up feeling as though she was pinned to her bed. When she finally was able to move, she found unexplained scratches on her body.

Not knowing what else to do, she reached out to her teammates for help. The group came over and did a cleansing of the house, but it didn't stop the activity. If anything, it felt as though it made the situation worse.

Maybe it's just my imagination.

She tried to believe her own words, but it was almost impossible. Every time she walked into a room, she felt eyes boring into her. After living with the sensation for nearly three months, she had enough.

She walked through the house with new determination. She sprayed holy water onto every wall, while carrying a stick of burning sage.

"I want you out of here!" she screamed.

The next morning, the house was once again quiet.

She wasn't sure why it worked this time after failing so many times before, but she was thankful to have her house back again. Not long after, she dropped out of the team and stopped investigating. Some things were best left untouched.

She was one of the lucky ones.

Not everyone else was as fortunate.

Lillian with Marion Luoma

Chapter 34

Marion Luoma felt a hypnotic pull every time she passed the Victorian mansion.

She wasn't a ghost hunter or even a paranormal enthusiast. She wasn't sure what she would do if she ever saw a ghost, but she was inexplicably drawn to the mansion on the corner.

When the previous owner opened the mansion up for a tour on Halloween, she and her son were the first in line. There was something about the house that called to her. She didn't know if it was the spectacular architecture, or just the resonance of history. All she knew was when she was inside of the house, she felt like she was supposed to be there.

As she drove past the mansion on her way to her husband's garage in nearby Westminster, she paused at the stop sign and stared up at the dark windows, wondering who was looking back at her. Life must have been so different back then. She tried to imagine what the house looked like in the late 1800's when it was in its prime. Would fancy ladies in long dresses sit on the porch sipping lemonade, or would they stay indoors to have tea in the parlor? Soon, she would discover more about the family who lived there.

The Pierce sons were a part of the gilded elite at the turn of the century, enjoying the opulence of the era. After their mother died in 1902, they became the newfound owners of a grand mansion and estate that was founded by a furniture empire. This included lavish parties in houses filled with priceless artwork and furniture. When Edward, the youngest son, opened the first Buick dealership in Gardner, his older brother Stuart wouldn't be outdone, so he launched the first Studebaker dealership in town, as well. It made her think of the book *The Great Gatsby*, because their lives were similar in many ways. They were wealthy and privileged. They were charter members of the local boat club and various social clubs in Gardner. By all accounts, they enjoyed everything life had to offer them.

When the Great Depression hit in 1929, Stuart was already long gone from the mansion, having moved to Georgia in 1923, and then to Wilton, New Hampshire in 1929. By this time, he was married and had a stepdaughter. By all accounts, he was sick of all the bickering and wanted to put some distance between him and the rest of his family.

After Stuart moved away, Edward and his wife, Bessie, became the masters of the mansion. They were well known around the city, being participants in various social clubs and activities. When they converted the mansion into a boarding house in 1926, they weren't prepared for the Great Depression of 1929.

With jobs scarce, less people were able to purchase automobiles or furniture, which gradually depleted the vast fortune. The Victorian began a slow and steady decline. By the time it found its way to the next owner in 1966, it was almost past the point of no return.

While Marion loved the history, she didn't give any thought to the reported hauntings. She heard the stories. Her own nephew Trevor had an encounter there when he was younger playing hide-and-seek, but she wasn't sure if she believed in ghosts. It just wasn't something that had ever touched her life. All that would change in a matter of months. She soon found herself in the middle of a paranormal drama that would alter her life forever.

Nothing would ever be the same once she stepped inside that doorway.

Having lived in Massachusetts all her life, Marion had a close network of friends and family and was active with the local Relay for Life group, helping them raise funds for cancer research. She worked at her husband's garage as a bookkeeper during the day when she wasn't babysitting the neighbor children. In the evenings, she spent family time with her husband and grown son. There was nothing paranormal about her life. She didn't even like watching scary movies, but something about the house spoke to her. It was as though she were hand selected like the others who were also lured inside the large, looming mansion.

She was outside her husband's garage when she considered visiting the Victorian again. The garage was getting an expansion, and soon they would need to dig up an area that was heavily planted with flowering perennials. She hated to throw the bulbs away, but she already transferred dozens of them to her home in Hubbardston and didn't have room for any more. Then the thought came to her.

Why not bring some to the Victorian mansion?

Then the flowers would go from one old house to another. It made perfect sense to her at the time. There was a slight historic connection between the two properties. The building her husband's garage occupied was built in the early 1900's. The house that sat beside it had once been the Westminster Café. With its close proximity to the train station, it was just a train stop away from the S.K. Pierce mansion. Passengers traveling along the route would often get off in Westminster for a bite to eat at the cafe before heading to the busy city of Gardner. Since the train stopped just in front of the Victorian, it was conceivable that some of S.K. Pierce's friends would stop in for a visit. It was enough to make her wonder.

Would they think she was crazy, or would they appreciate the gesture?

There was only one way to find out. She put a box of bulbs in the back of her SUV and headed towards Gardner. It seemed almost surreal pulling into the driveway and parking her vehicle, instead of just driving past, like she usually did.

As she walked up the stone steps to the Union Street entrance, she felt a sense of intrigue wash through her. *Was she really doing this?* With a deep breath for courage, she knocked on the door.

Edwin opened the door, his expression curious but cautious.

When she explained what she wanted to do, he seemed very touched by the gesture.

"Lillian is in the shower right now, but I know she'd like to talk to you. Can you come back later?" he asked.

Marion told him that she needed to get back to the garage but would be happy to stop by later that afternoon. She headed back to Westminster, to attend to some bookkeeping. While Edwin had been courteous, she still felt somewhat foolish. For all she knew, they thought she as just another ghost hunter hoping to get inside the house. She quickly absorbed herself in the shop ledger, hoping to get caught up for the day. The next thing she knew, there was a knock at the door. Lillian had tracked her down.

Lillian was unlike anyone she'd ever known. She was very stylish, with big silver earrings and jingling bracelets. She was dressed all in black, with her dark hair pulled into a high ponytail. She could have stepped out of a fashion magazine if it weren't for the sunny smile. She had an openness about her that made her instantly accessible. If you weren't already her friend, you wanted to be.

The two stood outside and talked for several hours, becoming fast friends.

Marion was the next one to join the group of carefully selected people. The house had taken hold of her soul.

She wouldn't realize how deep the connection went until she began having dreams about the house. It started for her in the same way it began with Edwin.

She had a prophetic dream.

An image similar to Marion's dream

Chapter 35

Marion had the first dream the night after she met Lillian. Others followed nightly, leaving her waking in a cold sweat, wondering what it all meant.

In the dreams, she was at the Victorian. She was walking around the rooms as if checking them to make sure they were okay. She saw herself looking up at the windows to make sure they weren't leaking and at the ceilings to inspect the cracks. She checked the floors in many of the rooms, looking for evidence of moisture from recent rainstorms. She was always alone in the dreams, but she wasn't concerned about her safety. Gone were the fears of ghosts. In its place was a resolute need to keep the house safe. She was a caretaker.

In one dream, she saw herself opening the massive Union Street side door with a key from her own key ring. She didn't know what the dreams meant, but they haunted her through her days, as well as her nights.

She would find herself at the Victorian frequently over the course of the next few months. As much as Lillian needed a friend, Marion didn't. Having grown up in the area, she had more friends than she had time to spend time with, but there was something irresistible about their connection. The minute the two met, she felt like it was meant to be.

They were supposed to be friends.

Sometimes she felt almost as if she were walking onto a movie set, the atmosphere was so perfectly Victorian. She loved everything about the place.

She loved the beautiful architecture. Standing inside the house was like traveling back in time to the 1800's. She marveled at the details that somehow survived the decades. She helped Lillian explore all the rooms, finding new clues to the history as they went along. Lillian showed her the maid's pantry, and how the flour and sugar bins were still mounted into the countertop. She showed her the hidden cabinet in the hallway between the kitchen and dining room where ice was placed to keep the perishable foods cold in the days before electricity. As Lillian began to fill the house with carefully selected antiques, Marion began joining her on her shopping ventures.

The Red Room became a showroom for the Victorian era. Lillian found an old vintage sewing machine that she displayed in a corner, adding a dress form fitted with a red satin dress that was representative of the time period. She fitted the ornate bed with a red satin bedspread, with curtains to match, and hung pictures on the walls depicting Victorian scenery.

Marion compared Lillian's decorating to the way S.K. Pierce must have built the house. No detail was overlooked. She was as precise in her selections as the man who chose the sixteen different types of wood for the interior. She would somehow find the perfect accessory and place it where it belonged.

The old nanny's room was outfitted with a twin bed and an antique baby carriage. She found a lifelike doll to place in the carriage, which Marion found to be creepy. Every time she walked past it, she would catch a glimpse of the doll out of the corner of her eye, fully expecting it to climb out of the carriage.

The friendship was also good for Lillian. Not having any friends in the area was wearing on her, something Marion could see in an instant. The two became very close. If they weren't out shopping or exploring the house, they would sit at the kitchen table drinking tea and talking.

Lillian seemed relieved to be able to share some of her experiences with someone, but Marion felt a tightening in her stomach with every new story. She wasn't crazy about the ghosts in the house. Frankly, they scared her. She didn't even like walking to the bathroom without having someone standing outside the door waiting for her. There was just something about the house that made her uneasy. She couldn't put her finger on it, but she didn't like being there alone.

Chapter 36

In August of 2011 the paranormal television show *My Ghost Story* flew Edwin and Lillian to California to film an episode about their haunted house. The experience created a whirlwind of emotions. It was the first time either of them was on national TV. As they looked around the studio at the pictures on the walls of the famous people who had been there, they had a hard time believing this was really happening to them.

It seemed surreal in so many ways. It felt as though everything they did in their lives up to now led up to this experience. As a young boy growing up in Boston, Edwin never dreamed he would one day end up on TV. It was a shining moment that would lead to even greater opportunities.

He felt as though everything was finally falling into place. With the increased publicity, more paranormal groups would be interested in investigating the mansion, which would lead to more money for the renovations the house so desperately needed. It was almost as though the house was helping them find the money to bring it back to its original grandeur.

> The activity in the mansion has increased dramatically. Edwin plans to have the house blessed. If the activity doesn't stop, he and his wife are going to move out.

In October Jeff Belanger, a national para-celebrity, filmed his popular web-based show *Thirty Odd Minutes* at the mansion. It would bring even more attention to the house and its resident ghosts. The sudden fame came with a huge price tag. Edwin found himself hounded by groups, all wanting to come in to investigate. People began stopping by unannounced, wanting a tour. He opened the door, not wanting anyone to feel slighted, but it was also beginning to wear on them both.

Any sense of privacy was now long gone. The house had become a paranormal hotspot, and everyone wanted to see it.

> *To watch the episode, click on the link below or copy the link to your computer's browser.*
>
> *http://www.30oddminutes.com/archive/tag/victorian-mansion/*

Lillian wasn't as thrilled with the changes as Edwin seemed to be. It felt like people were constantly tromping through her house. After each paranormal team left, she consistently found evidence of snooping. Closet doors would be left open, and the contents of her dresser drawers would get shuffled around as though someone was rifling through her personal belongings. Lillian placed signs on the beds, asking that no one sit on them, yet they would still find the imprints of bodies on the bedspreads. They found soda cans on the antique furniture, and trash left on the floors. It gave her a sense of being violated, almost as though a burglar was invited to meander through their home.

After one group left, she walked into the main floor bathroom and nearly had a meltdown. The toilet was clogged. She wouldn't find out until several hundred dollars later, that the clog was due to someone who attempted to flush a sanitary pad down the toilet. She had to take the money she had just collected from the event and hand it directly over to the plumber. Everything they put up with the night before was all in vain.

She got to the point where she dreaded the events. She and Edwin would be forced to seclude themselves in the kitchen and living room for the duration of the night, only to be interrupted frequently by a question or request. They struggled to stay awake until the group was ready to leave, not going to bed sometimes until the wee hours of the morning.

One night they both fell asleep on the sofa, when something woke Edwin suddenly.

Get up.

He felt as though someone shook his shoulder, jarring him awake. He looked around, taking in the room around him. The television was still on, and the credits were rolling at the end of the movie they were watching. He looked at Lillian, who had also fallen asleep. These late nights were getting harder and harder on them.

Go to the door.

He wasn't sure if he heard it or imagined it, but something told him to go check the door. He rose from the sofa, feeling his body protest. When he got to the door, he was just in time to prevent a paranormal team from walking out with a box filled with artifacts from the house.

"What are you doing?" he said, stopping the man.

The man gave him a guilty glance. "I was just going to borrow these. I didn't know you wanted them," he said.

Edwin pulled the box out of his hands. It was filled with Jay Stemmerman's records and paperwork. Of course he wanted it. He was so outraged that he told the group to leave immediately.

It was almost more than they could take. They were inviting people in to explore their home, giving them full access, only to regret it later in many cases.

They considered stopping the investigations altogether until they ran into the good groups that provided them with the information they needed. They were learning so much about the house and many of the findings were helpful instead of harmful.

Over and over, investigators and psychics alike would tell Edwin that S.K. Pierce wasn't happy with all the investigators roaming through his house. Eleanor was a firm believer in this, feeling that S.K. couldn't bear to see his home in its current condition, and he would never allow people of such a stature to have full access to it, either.

As Lillian had already figured out, doors were important back in the Victorian era. Guests and the wealthy elite would come through the front doors while the staff used the Union Street door. The doors were never propped open between the foyer and the hallway leading to the servant's door. They were always kept closed.

Another investigator who felt S.K. Pierce's snobbery was Christina Tregger Achilles, a member of New England Paranormal Observation Science Technology, a paranormal group located in Connecticut. Being a psychic medium, she sensed S.K. standing off to the side, watching them.

On one occasion, she was wearing a sundress. Although it wasn't considered scandalous by today's standards, S.K. took offense to it. He saw her as inappropriate and under-dressed, something he never allowed in his house back in his day. Could he be appeased with a simple conversation? Times were different now, something he might appreciate if it was explained to him.

Christina Tregger Achilles, with Chris Cox and Ceirra, the paranormal pug

CHAPTER 37

Paranormal teams traveled from everywhere to investigate at the Victorian mansion, but few came as far as Sara Christopher and her father, Mike Robishaw. They traveled from Alexandria, Virginia to take part in an investigation.

Michael Robishaw and Sara Christopher

Another team was filming a documentary and invited Alexandria Paranormal Investigations to join them. Although the location was intriguing, the investigation was different from what Sara and Mike were used to. Instead of setting up their own equipment and determining the schematics of the investigation, they were separated from one another into different groups, merging with the other team. It wouldn't be a night either would soon forget.

Sara describes herself as an empathic psychic, someone who could feel the emotions of others around her, including those from ghosts and spirits. She, too, experienced strong feelings in the Red Room.

Like many of the psychics before her, she agreed with the legend that a prostitute was killed in the mansion. She felt it involved a child in some form, as well. Psychic impressions are seldom crystal clear, and the mediums must sort out what's been revealed to them. In Sara's case, she felt that the woman was pregnant with the man's child, and the man wasn't happy about it. She saw him as someone who oversaw the mansion when it was a boarding house. She also suggested that the man was artistic, and he felt that the killing could advance his work to a new level. He was disturbed, but he became even more deranged after the murder.

Edwin was curious about this. Was she referring to Jay Stemmerman? He didn't know much about the man, but what he did know left him concerned. When they moved into the house, the walls were filled with strange paintings, signed by Jay Stemmerman himself. They were dark and broody, depicting naked women with centaur bodies. In the attic, they found dozens of shocking paintings, as well.

Eleanor suggested the energy of the house changed after Jay assumed ownership of the mansion. She wouldn't go into more detail, because she didn't like to speak ill of the dead, but it was enough to leave several lasting concerns in Edwin's mind. It made him feel glad that he removed all the sordid paintings from the house.

Edwin didn't know what to make of it. It was all speculation. For all he knew, Jay was an upstanding citizen who never did anything wrong beyond having an active imagination. It was easy to follow a false lead.

There was no denying there was a dark energy in the house, though. They saw it manifest many times over. How could they live with something like that in the house?

Unfortunately, the investigators and mediums that brought the issue to light couldn't do much to help them solve the problem. Edwin and Lillian needed to banish the negative entities, but nothing seemed to work. It made Edwin think about what

Kim Huertas told him. She said there were many advanced entities in the house, and getting rid of them wouldn't be an easy task.

The house was such a mixture of energy. While the dark energy was felt by many, others also connected with the lighter energy, namely the children. Many psychics and investigators felt there were two distinct children ghosts in the house. One was identified as the young boy, while the other was an even younger girl. Their voices were caught on audio recordings and they were often attributed to playful incidents that happened in the house.

While investigating with her team, empathic medium, Sara Christopher felt the presence of the little lost boy. He followed her around the house the entire time she was there, making her feel sad for him. He was too young to understand what happened to him, so it would be difficult to cross him over.

What he really wanted was his mother.

Being a mother herself, the boy stuck close to her, acknowledging her as a mother figure, something that he truly longed for, as would any small child. Sara said that he was cheerful and playful, someone who liked to play pranks on others, but his demeanor changed dramatically when he followed her to the basement. He became fearful and reclusive. He melted into the shadows and refused to come out.

She watched him linger in the shadows, a sense of sadness coming over him. A series of images sprang to her mind, one after another, almost bringing her to her knees. When it was all over, she felt like crying.

He drowned. She was certain of it, and his death wasn't accidental. She saw hands holding him down under the water, waiting until the last bubble of air left his lungs. Could this be linked to the stories surrounding the prostitute? Many other psychic mediums saw the two as being linked. They said that the little boy was her son, and after she was murdered, he quickly disappeared, too. Sara felt that his body was buried somewhere on the property.

This made Edwin uneasy. Did the boy drown in one of the cisterns? Was he the one who pulled Lillian into the basement to dig for the bones? Was he trying to tell her something?

Every answer only seemed to bring more questions.

Photo captured in the basement by Michael Robishaw of a shadow person. Taken with a full spectrum UV camera.

Michael Robishaw, Sara's father, also attended the investigation. As the founder of Alexandria Paranormal Investigations, Michael witnessed his share of hauntings over the course of the last twenty-five years. He avoided the tour that Edwin always gives so he wouldn't be influenced by the information. If he got psychic impressions, he wanted to know they came directly from the ghosts themselves.

While API is primarily a scientific-based paranormal team, Michael also has mediumistic abilities. He too felt the little boy, but like many others, was more concerned with the entity who haunted the basement. Early in the evening, they split up into separate groups, so he didn't see his daughter to compare notes until the end of the investigation.

His group started in the tunnel room. All the lights were off, leaving the basement lit only by the soft glow from the equipment they were using. They turned on their digital voice recorders and started asking questions.

"Is there anybody here who would like to communicate with us?" he asked.

There was no response.

They asked a number of other probing questions and received the same results. Whoever was down there with them clearly didn't want to talk.

Mike pulled out his Ovilus, an electronic speech synthesizer with a database preprogrammed with over two thousand words. The theory is that ghosts can access the database in order to speak through the device. When he turned it on, it started making random sounds, something it had never done before, so he turned it off and then on again. It spouted one word: "Frank."

That gave him a very bad feeling.

Whatever was down there wasn't good. He could feel the negative energy fill the room.

The minute they left the tunnel room, the entire team began seeing dark shadows race across the basement. Similar to Lillian's first experience, as soon as they saw the shadow, it would dart away.

Mike set up laser grids in various places, hoping the colored dots of light would help them see the shadow as it moved through them. As soon as the lights were on, he grabbed his full spectrum camera and began taking pictures. What he captured was enough to make him feel quite uneasy.

He captured several photos that clearly showed a dark figure moving throughout the room. They caught an arm and torso in one photo, and a leg in another photo just as it moved out of the frame.

Something wasn't right, though.

He began to feel overheated. His entire body broke out in a sweat, even though it was only fifty degrees in the basement. He walked to the doorway and stared out at the bank of dots from the laser grid.

Get out!

He began feeling a heavy sensation, as though the air was becoming thick and oily. He could see it filling the room with darkness, trying to push them out of his space.

Get out!

His spirit guides were all but screaming at him to leave. It was no longer safe down there, if it ever was in the first place. Regretfully, he turned and began packing up his equipment. As much as he didn't want to leave, he knew better than to go against the wishes of his spirit guides. They always knew when it was no longer safe.

They saved him more than once.

> *To review Alexandria Paranormal Investigation's evidence, please click on the link below or type the link into your computer's browser:*
>
> *http://alexandriaparanormalinvestigations.org/*

Edwin stood at the top of the basement stairs the next morning.

Something dark was in the basement.

It was clear that it didn't want people violating its space. Was this the same entity he saw darting across the doorway when he went to retrieve pellets for his stove? Was it trying to keep people away, so they wouldn't learn its secret?

This struck a chord with Edwin, making him remember what the other psychic medium told him.

Was Frank the dark entity who haunted the basement, not Edward?

He wasn't sure what to make of all the things the psychics told him. While many of them were similar, some of them conflicted. He was aware of the court battles Frank had with his stepmother, but he never heard anything that would lead him to believe that Frank was an evil person.

As far as he knew, Frank moved out of the house before his stepmother Ellen's death, settling two houses away on West Broadway with his wife and four daughters. He took over his father's furniture factory and continued to run it until 1937. The building burned to the ground the following year. Why would someone like Frank continue to hang around the basement in his father's old house? It didn't make any sense to him.

Others, like Eleanor, thought that the dark entity in the basement was something worse. They thought it was demonic.

Edwin didn't know who or what it was, but he gave the basement a wide berth anyway. He turned the light off and shut the basement door, feeling a rush of relief to have a closed door between him and the darkness.

What were they going to do?

They couldn't avoid the basement forever. All his tools were down there, along with the lawn mower and pellets for the stoves.

Some of the findings were scary, but others were intriguing. One that made him curious was the portals.

Several psychics pointed out a spot just beside the grand staircase where people often felt dizzy or faint. "Stand here," they told Edwin, and although he felt something, he wasn't sure it wasn't just his imagination.

"What am I supposed to be feeling?" he asked. He knew about the one on the third floor after hearing about it from the first psychic who visited the house, but he was unaware of another one.

A portal is a doorway to the other side, a place where spirits can come and go with ease. The thought wasn't exactly reassuring to him. It didn't sound like something most people would want in their house. Closing it wasn't an option, as he was told. It was an ancient and continuously used portal, so shutting it down would have tremendous ramifications.

A psychic medium named Barbara Williams investigated the mansion with Footsteps Paranormal. She too felt there were multiple portals in the house. Besides the commonly known portal near the grand staircase, she was also aware of one in the Billiards Room and another on a wall in the basement. She said that while there were eight ghosts who were tied to the house, a multitude of others came and went through the portals.

With the increase in investigations came the increase in activity. After months of relative quietness from the resident ghosts, it was a sudden shock to have it reappear so suddenly. Edwin and Lillian heard footsteps on the staircase so frequently that they no longer bothered to track them down. They knew from prior experience that no one would be there.

Edwin reached out to various self-professed paranormal experts only to have them make things worse. A psychic would do a cleansing, which would cause the activity to increase threefold. Investigators provoked the ghosts trying to get a reaction, despite Edwin's pleas for them to be respectful.

The activity grew to enormous proportions. There wasn't a single night when doors didn't slam or the dogs didn't growl. Bangs and thumps became common background noise. The house alarm would randomly start wailing, as would the doorbells.

And then it got worse.

Much worse.

Photo of a possible vortex or portal in the Copper Room Photo courtesy of Boston Paranormal

Chapter 38

None of it was what Lillian envisioned when she first saw the house.

She just wanted a normal life in a normal house. She wanted to fill it with friends and family while she happily restored it back to its former glory. Now, life was always a whirlwind of activity.

If there wasn't a paranormal group in the house, someone was knocking at the door, wanting a tour.

People roamed around the house as if no one lived there. After every event, they could count on some sort of damage. On the second floor landing, their one-hundred-and fifty-year-old credenza was badly scratched after investigators placed equipment on it, despite the signs. The tape the investigators used to secure their camera wires ripped the finish off the grand staircase handrail, as well as the hardwood floors.

Edwin had to nearly pull Lillian off the investigators when she discovered the damage.

"When is enough, *enough?*" she asked Edwin after an event.

He seemed to enjoy the investigations more than she did. She didn't get it. Nothing they did seemed to help. If anything, it was making things worse.

"How do we know what these people are doing?" she asked him. "Are you watching them to make sure they aren't just making the ghosts angrier?" she added. She knew enough about the paranormal world by now to know that investigators could cause the activity to increase. Instead of finding answers, they were stirring things up, and creating more questions.

Edwin wasn't convinced the investigations were causing harm until he found something one night. While cleaning up after a group of investigators left, he found a piece of paper with letters and numbers drawn on it and the words "yes," "no" and "goodbye" written at each edge. He showed it to Lillian, who confirmed what he thought he was seeing.

"That's a home-made Ouija board!" she said with a gasp.

They stared at each other, both wondering how it got there, and more importantly, if it caused any problems. They were warned by other teams to steer clear of Ouija boards. While some teams found them to be a useful tool, they could be dangerous in the wrong hands.

Ouija boards go back to the 1800's. For many decades, they were considered toys or novelties. During the spiritualist movement of the early 1900's, they were considered to be a faster method of receiving messages from the dead. It wasn't until later in the century that people began questioning the source. Some claimed it opened a portal to the other side, allowing in both good and bad entities.

When the next group came to investigate, Edwin showed it to one of the investigators, a man by the name of Michael Cram. He investigated at the house before, and Edwin was comfortable with his expertise and knowledge of the paranormal field. Michael raised his eyebrows when he saw it.

"You don't want to mess with those," he told Edwin. "If the wrong person is using it, they could open up more portals, and invite things that you don't want here. It's like leaving your front door wide open and allowing anyone to come in."

He went on to tell Edwin that the types of entities who communicate through Ouija boards were from a lower astral plane, the type you don't want to welcome into your home. Once you ask for a physical confirmation, such as a knock on the wall or a flicker of a candle, you are essentially opening a portal, allowing them in. Once they come through, they don't always leave. The fact that Edwin and Lillian didn't know who used the board was concerning, as well.

"If they didn't close down the session, they might have left the doorway open," Michael went on to say. The investigation hadn't started yet, so Michael didn't have a chance to scope out the house. He excused himself to walk around and see what he could find.

Michael's history in the paranormal started in childhood. His mother was considered an Irish witch, someone who often helped others with their problems. A talented medium himself, Michael spent over thirty years in the field investigating claims of hauntings. He was also studying with the Catholic Church, helping them investigate reports of demonic activity prior to requesting exorcisms.

If anyone could help them, it was Michael.

He found Edwin and Lillian in the living room a half hour later. His face was drawn tight. "You have a female here I'm not crazy about. She's not one of the Victorian-era spirits. She was brought here by someone," he said.

Edwin and Lillian exchanged glances.

"Was it from the Ouija board?" Lillian asked.

Mike shrugged one shoulder. "I'm not sure, but she was definitely brought in here. I tried to get her out, but she's very strong. She's not going to go without a fight." He went on to suggest that he could ward several rooms in the house to help prevent her from gaining access, but he needed to come back, because he didn't have everything he needed to do the job right.

Edwin and Lillian promised to call him to set something up. Unfortunately, they wouldn't do it before the entity had a chance to stage the next attack.

It had an agenda and it wasn't going to stop until it had what it needed.

Things quickly got rough.

It started with a visit from Derek and Bob, and then it rapidly spiraled out of control.

Lillian and Edwin

Chapter 39

Edwin opened the door, happy to see his friends Derek Cormier and Bob Pfeiffer on the doorstep.

Derek Cormier in the master bedroom during a tour

"Hey, come on in. Lillian just made a big pot of soup. Have you eaten yet?" he asked the two men, holding the door open for them. Even though he'd only known the two for a few months, it felt like they'd been friends for much longer. There was an ease about them. They could talk for hours, but it felt like minutes. After living in the house for several years, with most of his friends still in Boston, it was a nice change of pace to have people like Derek and Bob in their lives.

Edwin was intrigued by Derek's background in the paranormal. Besides being a paranormal investigator, Derek also once worked as a tour guide on the haunted war ship, the USS Salem, which was docked at the time in Quincy, Massachusetts.

Derek's friend, Bob, often joined him at the Victorian. Bob and Derek made an interesting pair. While Derek was stoutly built, with a shaved head and dark goatee, Bob was tall and thin, with a boyish demeanor. They brought a level of enthusiasm to the house that Edwin hadn't felt in a long time.

Bob Pheiffer

The four sat down at the kitchen table while Lillian served them big steaming bowls of soup. After a while, the conversation drifted towards the event Derek and Edwin were planning. The air churned with excitement as they went over their plans.

They wanted to have a haunted house event at the Victorian. They planned to stage each room with volunteers, all dressed in scary costumes. Bob was going to portray Freddy from the *Nightmare on Elm Street* series, while Edwin was going as a vampire. Derek was to manage the event, making sure everything went according to their carefully laid out plans.

Guides were going to lead tours through the mansion. The more they talked about it, the more excited they became.

"I can borrow decorations from the USS Salem," Derek said. "They have a big event there every year, but they have a bunch of stuff they won't be using this year."

The plan was quickly taking shape and Edwin was enthusiastic about the prospects. People from around town seemed interested in seeing the inside of the house. It would give them a chance to tour the mansion, while providing them with a chance to collect funds for renovations.

Lillian wasn't as thrilled by the idea.

"It's bad enough when we open the house up for investigations," she said, bringing a package of crackers to the table. "You really want all those people wandering through the house?"

Edwin knew she wouldn't be gung ho on the idea, but he didn't think it would be as bad as she considered it to be. "I'm sure it will be fine. We'll have volunteers here to walk them through. It's not like they'll have full access to the house," he said.

In his mind, he thought they'd just put away any breakables, and make sure all their personal possessions were safely locked away. If there was enough supervision, what could possibly go wrong? It would be a win-win for everybody. People who wanted to see the house would have an opportunity to tour it, and they might make some money in the process. Besides, why have a haunted Victorian mansion if you couldn't enjoy it?

"Let's just try it and see what happens. If we don't like it, we just won't do it again," he said.

Lillian looked at him skeptically, obviously still not sold on the concept.

After they finished eating, the three men walked upstairs to talk about the layout of the event. The cold air hit them like a wall as they left the warmth of the kitchen.

"I didn't realize it had gotten so cold," Edwin commented as they made their way up the grand staircase. He wasn't sure how they could have an event if the house was so cold. Surely people wouldn't want to spend much time there. He mulled it over as he walked, wondering how they would pull it off.

He dreaded the thought of another winter in the house. It was brutal living in an unheated house. Eventually they would have to figure out a better system for keeping the house warm, but he didn't know what it was right now. It needed so much work before they could even get to that point.

As they reached the second floor landing, Derek stopped short.

Edwin looked up in time to see what startled him. The decorative curtain hanging in the long hallway beside the bathroom moved. In the Victorian days, the curtain was used to block off the hallway, providing the family with privacy from the staff. Now, it was just a decorative curtain, pulled back against the wall with a fringed tie.

"Did you see that?" Derek asked.

Bob was quick to confirm it. "Yeah, the curtain just moved back as though someone was peeking out from behind it." Bob walked over to the curtain for a better look, and then nearly fell to his knees as if something had jolted him.

"Are you okay?" Edwin said, as Derek rushed to his friend's side.

Edwin wasn't sure what to make of it. Bob was pale and strangely lethargic. He wanted to get Bob downstairs to the heated area of the house. They helped him up, and then headed for the stairway. They made it nearly to the bottom when Bob collapsed on the stairs.

Hearing the commotion, Lillian came out of the kitchen.

"What's the matter? Is he okay?" she asked.

"Is he a diabetic?" she added.

Derek shook his head and told Lillian what they experienced.

"Come on, Bob. Let's get you into the kitchen where it's warm," Lillian said, reaching out to touch Bob's shoulder. The minute her hand made contact with his shoulder, she stopped short, her face growing as pale as Bob's was the moment he touched the curtain.

Edwin wasn't sure what happened, but it seemed as if whatever affected Bob transferred over to Lillian. She looked like she was struck by a shock of electricity. She pulled away from him, her eyes wide.

"Are you okay, Hon?" he asked, holding onto her as she nearly fell to the ground.

She had a strange look on her face that he didn't like. He knew Lillian for over twenty years and he never saw her overcome by something so quickly. It usually took her a full week of outright pain before she even acknowledged it. Being sick wasn't something she easily gave into, so this unnerved him.

"Yeah, I just need to go lie down," she said, walking into the living room to find the couch.

Edwin and Derek looked at each other. Edwin knew he had to let Lillian handle it the way she wanted to. He made a mental note to check on her before heading up to bed, and then turned to his friends.

While Bob was still pale, he was regaining some of the color back in his face. If nothing else, he just looked tired.

"Are you okay?" Edwin asked again, steading him as he started walking towards the door.

"Yeah. I just want to go home and rest. I don't feel so well," he said.

Since Bob was Derek's ride home, the two left, leaving Edwin and Lillian alone.

The next three days would unravel like a script from a horror movie. It would be the first of three negative things, one happening after another, finally pushing them over the edge.

By the end of the month, they would be forced to leave their home forever.

The hallway where Bob and Derek saw the curtain move (now removed)

Chapter 40

Lillian found her way to the couch and nearly collapsed into it. Her arms and legs felt heavy, as though they were made of lead. All she wanted to do was close her eyes and drift away. She almost felt as if she were drugged, her free will slipping away second by second. She barely remembered Edwin coming in to see if she was coming up to bed.

"No. I'll just stay here tonight," she told him, and then her world faded into a nothingness she never experienced before. She couldn't recall a specific moment when she felt the heaviness come over her. It seemed to gradually merge into her body, like a sunset fading on a horizon.

In some ways, it felt like a dream. She saw flashes, like images from a movie playing behind her eyelids. It was almost as if someone had taken over her body and was desperately trying to show her something.

She saw herself standing at the window just below the widow's walk, looking down at the "V" on the sidewalk below. The window was open and she could feel her sweaty palms press against the uneven wooden sill, splinters digging into her skin. It reminded her of what the psychic, Heather Anderson, experienced.

The cold wind brushed against her warm skin, chilling her in an instant, making her long black hair fly around her face as if it had a life of its own. Suddenly, the "V" on the sidewalk flew upwards towards her, but it was not as if she was falling. It was like the ground was racing up to get to her. The image ended, and she found herself in a thicket of woods.

She was unable to look around. It was as if someone else had control of her body. The feeling was very similar to what Edwin said he experienced on the night before they went to see the house, when he flitted through the room, like a ghost on the breeze.

She moved swiftly through the forest, darting around the narrow white birch trees in a speed she never could manage in real life. The thick organic scent of the swamp was heavy, and she felt the wind bite her skin as she spirited in and out of the slender white tree trunks.

Strangely, although she'd never been there before, she knew exactly where she was.

She was at the end of Union Street where it met Route 68. The area was never developed because of the swamp. It was a thicket of slender trees surrounded by thick, murky swampland. She never went there before, but this knowledge came to her as if she had been there many times. What was the woman trying to show her?

Every time she tried to swim to the surface of her consciousness, something would pull her back down. Flashes of coherence mingled with her dreams. In one of them, Edwin walked past her, saying something she couldn't quite grasp. Why wasn't he waking her up?

She reached for him, but something kept pulling her back into the world of murky dreams.

She didn't wake up for three days.

She never left the couch to eat, use the restroom, or even stretch. She was trapped inside her own body, held hostage there by an unseen force.

She wouldn't wake until Marion Luoma came for a visit.

Chapter 41

In early October, Marion asked Lillian for a favor.

She wanted to bring the Girl Scouts for a tour of the mansion.

Being the kind of person who always helps others, Marion was always looking for a chartable opportunity. If someone was having a yard sale, she helped organize it. If someone was having a bake sale, she showed up with a tray full of cookies. Since her neighbor's daughter was active with the Girl Scouts, she wanted to bring them on a tour of the mansion. Edwin and Lillian were quick to agree. They set a date, and the girls were ecstatic at the prospects of seeing the house.

The day of the event, the Girl Scouts and their chaperones showed up. Edwin happily took them on a tour of the mansion, telling them the history and some of the scary experiences they had there, toning it down for his younger audience. As a goodwill gesture, Marion asked each of the girls to donate a bag of pellets for the pellet stove, knowing how cold the house gets during the winter months.

The families dropped the pellets off at Marion's house during the week. When the last bag was delivered, she loaded them up in her SUV, planning to bring them over. She tried calling Lillian to set up a time, but the phone just rang and rang. After three days of calling, she grew worried.

She headed over to the Victorian.

A sense of trepidation washed over her as she pulled up to the house. Something bad happened. She could feel it in the pit of her stomach. In her mind, she saw them collapsed on the floor, overcome by carbon monoxide fumes, or worse. With the terrifying experiences they had, anything was possible.

She climbed the stairs to the Union Street entrance, like she did months before with the box of perennials, and then knocked on the door. After a few minutes, she heard the sound of movement inside the house. She let out a sigh.

"Thank God," she whispered under her breath. If they hadn't answered the door, she didn't know what she would have done. Called the police?

After a few minutes, Lillian came to the door.

Marion gasped at the sight of her. She'd never seen her this way before. Instead of the fashionable clothing and shiny silver jewelry, her hair was disheveled and she was dressed in rumpled clothing. She looked as though she'd been to bed for days. This was so unlike Lillian. Marion didn't know what to think.

"Are you okay?" she asked. She didn't want to say it, but Lillian looked like hell.

Lillian just stared at her for a moment, her eyes glassy as if she just woke up from a deep sleep.

"Yeah," she said, her words slurring heavily. "I haven't been feeling well."

Something stirred inside of Marion. Something wasn't right about her friend. It went deeper than a simple illness.

"I brought over the pellets for the pellet stove," she told her.

Lillian looked at her for a moment, as if she were having a hard time interpreting her words. Finally, she opened the door wider, inviting Marion inside.

"Let me go get Edwin," she said, walking towards the servant staircase that led to the second floor, just outside Edwin's office. Her movements were slow and arduous. She made it up one step, but had to use the railing to pull herself up the second step. She tried for a third, and then she collapsed on the railing.

"Edwin!" she called up the stairs, her voice barely audible.

Something was seriously wrong. Marion didn't know what it was, but she knew the house had something to do with it. She grabbed her arm and pulled her out of the doorway. She had to get her out of the house.

"Come with me. I want to show you something," she said, nearly dragging her friend off the wooden porch. By the time they made it to the side of the building where Marion had parked her SUV, Lillian had changed. Her color was better and the glassiness in her eyes had disappeared. Very slowly, she started to come back to herself. Gone were the sluggish movements and the slurred words. In its place was the vibrant personality her friend had always demonstrated.

Marion didn't know what had happened, but she knew it wasn't good.

Lillian began smiling and talking like she always did. The change was so abrupt, it was startling.

As they stood there chatting, Marion looked up at the second floor. Edwin was looking out at them, seemingly as surprised as she was at the sudden change in Lillian.

"Let me go get Edwin, so he can carry this in," Lillian offered.

The two made it in the door, but Lilian was too weak to even climb the stairs to the second floor as the house took a hold of her again.

She sat down on the bottom step hard, as if her legs had given out on her.

This wasn't good. Marion called for Edwin, and slowly the story began to unfold.

The Nanny's Room   Photo by Frank Grace (Trig Photography)

The piano in the first floor foyer   Photo by Frank Grace (Trig Photography)

Chapter 42

Those three days had been a living hell for Edwin, as well.

He couldn't remember much about them, because he was being influenced too, living through his own house of horrors. As he looked at Lillian, he felt like his world was crumbling to pieces.

Lillian meant the world to him. He loved her more than life itself, and he would do anything to make her happy. Knowingly leaving her on the couch for three days in a near vegetative state wasn't normal for him.

Why didn't he try to wake her up?

He had no idea.

He remembered walking upstairs that night after Derek and Bob left, leaving her on the couch. It should have struck him as strange, because it was something she never did before. In their twenty-four years together, they never spent a night apart in the same house. They had a routine they followed, a solemn promise they kept to one another. If they were in the same house, they would sleep in the same bed. It was unthinkable not to.

He fell into a dreamless slumber, as if tumbling into a black pit. When he woke the next morning, he heard the chanting woman again. The sound was beautiful, like a choir of angels singing a song with words he couldn't understand. When he opened his eyes, he was struck by a terrifying sight.

A woman was floating near the window, nearly four feet off the ground.

He gasped, unable to look away.

She had long dark hair that danced in the breeze and her face was frozen in sadness. She wore a long white gown that touched her bare ankles, something she may have worn to bed. The dress was old fashioned. It buttoned right up to the neck, like the sleeping dresses women wore in the early 1900's.

The worst part about her was her innate sadness.

Edwin could feel it filling the room with heart-wrenching misery. It was the sobbing people do when they've lost someone close to them. He's never been psychically inclined, but Edwin could feel her sorrow as though it was his own.

She was missing her child.

He stared at her for several long seconds, seeing her as though she were a physical being in the room. The only thing that was truly amiss was the fact that she was floating several feet off the floor. He felt horrified and mesmerized at the same time. He couldn't look away no matter how hard he tried. After a few seconds, she faded into the morning sunshine.

Fresh tears stained his face and he wiped them away, suddenly aware that he'd been crying. Her pain had been so real and intense. It felt like it had been his own. A part of him simply shut down. He couldn't handle it any longer. The bangs, the thumps, the slamming doors were nothing compared to the vision of someone who had long passed on, but was living in an eternal sorrow.

He didn't know why, but he thought she was the spirit of Bessie, Edward's wife, the last Pierce woman to reside in the house.

He could feel her profound pain over the loss of her daughter in the depths of his very soul.

He quickly fell into a deep depression. The feelings of sorrow just wouldn't leave him. He thought about the fading grandeur of the house, and the desperate need for repairs that he couldn't afford. He thought about the cold winters spent wrapped in blankets, trying to work with winter gloves on his frozen fingers. The bangs, knocks, shadows and phantom footsteps filled him with even more despair. He didn't know how he was going to survive.

What had they done?

He couldn't remember feeling this level of bone-deep fatigue and dismay since his father passed away. He wanted nothing more than to climb back into bed and pull the covers over his head, but he forced himself to get up and head to his office, where he spent the day working. When he finished working later in the evening, Lillian was still on the sofa.

He tried to wake her, but she just groaned, motioning him away. He couldn't remember why he didn't force the issue. Instead, he let her remain on the couch for three long days. Edwin barely remembers this time period. All he remembers was seeing the crying woman for three days straight at his window and resulting agony that filled his soul with darkness and sorrow.

By the third morning, her anguish reached a climax. Her cries spiked directly through him, leaving him weak and ravaged by her pain. It was all he could do to make it through the day, nearly sleepwalking through the hours until Marion arrived, waking them up from the nightmare they both could not escape.

After Marion left, he made sure Lilian had something to eat, and then helped her upstairs to the bedroom. She was so weak, it terrified him.

What happened to her?

And what happened to him that kept him from seeing what was going on with Lillian? Why did it take Marion's visit to snap them both out of the fugue they were caught up in? As he helped her Lillian the stairs, he thought about the way she came back to life as she stood outside talking with Marion. He watched her through the window, feeling a sense of wonder at the sight.

It must the house.

As Lillian climbed onto the bed, he began getting himself ready for bed. Absently, he could see her out of the corner of his eye, kneeling on the bed like she usually did, pulling the thick blankets around herself before easing down onto her stomach in her cocoon. The minute she sank down into the bed she began screaming.

"Get her off of me! Get her off!" she wailed.

She was completely motionless, as if paralyzed, but was screaming with all her might.

He rushed around to the side of the bed, not knowing what to do.

Should he try to pick her up? Move her?

Lillian answered the question for him. "Push me, Edwin. Get her off of me!"

He gave her a mighty shove and she rolled off the bed, hitting the floor with a thump.

Once she was off the bed, she was in motion. She stood up, her face filled with raw terror, tears streaming down her face. "I couldn't move," she told him. "I was completely paralyzed." With that, she broke down sobbing. Edwin rushed to her side and held her for what seemed to be hours, rocking her back and forth as her sobs grew heavier.

They had to get out of the house.

If they didn't, it might kill them both.

Bill Wallace

CHAPTER 43

Bill Wallace couldn't take it any longer. Something was wrong with Lillian. He could feel it so strongly, it consumed his thoughts. He wanted to go to them, but held himself back. He didn't want them to think he was crazy.

Finally, after three days, he had enough.

He drove to the Victorian and knocked on the door. It was the day after Lillian was pinned to the bed. When Edwin answered the door, Bill's fears were confirmed by the drawn expression on Edwin's face. He looked like he survived something horrific.

"Come on in," Edwin said, ushering Bill into the kitchen.

As soon as Bill walked in, he was thunderstruck by what he saw.

Lillian was sitting at the end of the table, her face ashen. Behind her, he could see the apparition of a woman with her hand on Lillian's shoulder. He just stood there staring, unable to form words.

The apparition was a woman several years older than Lillian. She had the same dark hair, but her features were sharper, her expression more malevolent. She looked like someone most people wouldn't want to mess with. Something about her made him very uncomfortable. As he stared, she smiled a very cold smile. A name formed in his mind.

Abigail.

"Are you okay, Lillian?" Bill asked. Before she could respond, he could see her face begin to change. It faded from her face to the face of the woman standing behind her. It was as if the woman was taking her over, claiming her body as her own. It was very similar to what had happened to Heather Anderson when she inadvertently channeled the woman from the Red Room.

"No, not really," she said, and then told him the story about the three days spent on the couch.

When she finished, Bill just stared at her, not sure how to proceed.

"She's still with you. She's standing behind you with her hand on your shoulder," he said as calmly as possible, hoping he didn't frighten her with the image. However, she needed to know how bad it was. Something had taken her over and was still very close to her. It would be hardly any effort at all for her to do it again. He was confused by the story, though. Why hadn't Edwin woken her up?

"Where were you when this all happened?" he asked Edwin.

Edwin didn't have a good answer. "I don't know," he started to say, when Lillian turned to glare at him. It was evident she was wondering the same thing.

"Why the hell didn't you come pull me off the couch?" she nearly screamed at him, using all her strength to utter the words. "I was there for three days. I didn't get up once. Why weren't you worried about me?"

"I don't know," he said, hanging his head. "I don't remember very much about it."

In the years Bill had known them, this was the first time he ever heard Lillian raise her voice at Edwin. He felt like he needed to intervene. He knew Edwin well enough to know that he would never do something like that to Lillian without a valid reason. The reality came to him in the same unexplained manner that many other things did. He just knew. He reached out and touched Lillian's hand.

"Edwin was being influenced as well," he told Lillian in his calmest voice. "That's how she did it. She knew that Edwin loves you so much that he wouldn't allow her to take you over, so she and the other spirits kept him at a distance from you."

Edwin sat down at the table, his eyes flooded with tears.

"I'm so sorry, Lil. I would have never done something like that. You know me. You mean the world to me. I just don't remember most of it." He put his face in his hands, his body shaking with sobs. After a moment, Lillian touched his hand.

"We'll work this out," she said softly.

Edwin looked up and watched her face. "We have to get out of this house," he told her.

Bill couldn't agree more. Someone in the house wanted to tell her story, and she was growing impatient with the two of them. She took over Lillian in an attempt to show her, but he feared it wouldn't stop there. Once the entity knew she could overpower Lillian, anything was possible.

"I think that's a very good idea. You need to get out. It's not good for either of you. They've been using you for a long time," Bill said. "You need to find your faith, find something powerful enough that you believe in, and fight this. No one else can do it but you."

Bill could see it on their faces. He could see what the house had done to them. If they didn't find some way of breaking free, he was afraid of what would happen next. If the apparition was strong enough to overpower Lillian for three days, what else was she capable of?

For all they knew, the next time might be even worse.

The thought was appropriately sobering.

Edwin looked up at him. The devastation on his face told the story of all the anxiety and hardships they both lived through. "We don't have anywhere else to go," he said.

They were trapped there until another option became available.

Bill just hoped they could survive long enough to find that option.

If they didn't escape quickly, he feared the house would claim them both, and soon.

Photo by Jason Baker

Chapter 44

Edwin made it through the next few days with a heavy heart.

He had come to hate the house. It stole his sense of security, bringing him back to the days when he was a boy, fighting for survival. There wasn't a safe place to be found within the walls. Every moment the danger lingered, growing stronger and threatening their very existence.

How could they go on living there after what had happened?

If Lillian was overcome so easily, what would stop them from doing it again?

What if they placed a butcher knife in her hands the next time?

He reached out to Michael Cram, asking if he could come to the house to do the cleansing he recommended.

Michael returned a few days later with his tools of the trade.

He did a Catholic Rite of Exorcism performed by a layman, and then sealed off the kitchen and master bedroom, protecting them from further attacks.

"This could last a month or a few years, depending on what you do. If you continue to have investigations, it's going to keep happening," he told them. The energy from the investigators coming in and out of the house were only serving to feed the entities, giving them the power to do the things they wanted to do, including inflicting harm on the homeowners.

"I'm going to give you both one of these," he said, handing them silver medals. "They're Saint Benedict medallions, and they've been blessed by a priest. Keep them with you at all times," he said. "I'm also going to place them at the corners of the master bedroom and Edwin's office, two places where you should feel safe."

After he was finished, the house definitely felt lighter. Edwin couldn't put his finger on what was different, but if nothing else, he felt more relaxed. It gave him peace of mind at that moment.

Edwin began watching Lillian closely, looking for signs that it was happening again. She seemed to be back to herself, but he took very little comfort in it. She was fine before and the ghosts had blindsided both of them anyway. They kept him out of the way the last time, and he knew they could do it again.

The cleansing Michael Cram seemed to help, but he knew there was even more that they needed to do. He had one more hope left. Months earlier, he had reached out to TAPS, the paranormal group that filmed the episode of *Ghost Hunters* there prior to them owning the house. They responded almost immediately, scheduling the week before Halloween as the week of filming, which was in two days.

The last thing he wanted was to be in the middle of another television show filming, but he the thought of them coming gave him a glimmer of hope.

Maybe they could help.

Ghost Hunters was one of the first paranormal television shows, bringing the concept of the paranormal world into people's living rooms well before it became an accepted field. Edwin had watched it religiously after purchasing his own haunted house. He truly respected the efficient scientific methods they used. While he had always been intrigued by psychics, he was beginning to wonder how accurate they were, especially considering that most of them told him greatly varying things. The fact that TAPS operated without a psychic was a comfort. He thought that if anyone could help them, it was a professional team like TAPS. If they couldn't find an answer, he hoped they would use their resources and provide him with someone who could. When the team descended on the mansion armed with full camera crews and production people, he began to rethink his decision.

The production crew spent several days filming. They put Edwin and Lillian up at a local hotel, so they could be close but out of the way. The crew bustled back and forth, carrying equipment and managing the production side of the filming.

The interviews were painful, coming so soon after Lillian's terrifying experience. As he spoke to the camera, Edwin found himself on the brink of tears. Lillian was his whole life and seeing her suffer had been devastating for him. As soon as the day was over, they were shuffled back to the hotel to spend the night.

It was a relief to be away from the mansion. For the first time in years, he felt like he could relax. In some ways, he wished he could just stay there forever. As they ate a quiet dinner at the hotel restaurant, they worried about their future.

"Maybe they'll be able to help," Lillian said.

She seemed much better, but a residue of her experience still lingered. The radiant woman he once knew was now a distant memory. In her place was a woman who hardly ever smiled, spending long moments staring into space, probably reliving the events that brought her to the brink of terror.

"What if they can't?" Edwin asked, not really expecting an answer.

"Then we need to move," she said, toying with her napkin. She looked up, her eyes dark and glistening, but still somewhat hopeful. "Iris is buying a house in Brockton. It's not a huge house, but she said we could live in their basement for a while if we needed to."

Edwin studied her, allowing the words to sink in.

Could he really abandon their dream house to go live in his sister-in-law's basement?

He sighed. "Let's take it one step at a time. Let's see what TAPS can do for us first."

If TAPS couldn't help, he didn't know if he had enough energy to continue fighting. Things were only going to get worse. Of that, he was certain.

By the time the investigation ended, they would know nothing more than they already knew. While most of the team was professional, it was evident they were there to film a television show.

Very little was found that they didn't already know, and the experience left them cold inside. Being the homeowner for a house featured on a paranormal show wasn't fun and games. It meant that your entire life would be disrupted before, during, and after the shoot. Once you signed the contract, they would have the right to tell your story any way they wanted. Edwin and Lillian quickly learned from their experiences with other shows that the truth wasn't always a priority. It became more about entertainment value and great ratings.

As the crew was leaving one member took Edwin aside for some advice. Grant, one of the founders of the group, seemed genuinely concerned. He spent a few minutes with Edwin, telling him what to look for and how to react to certain situations. It was the most helpful information he would receive.

After everything they experienced, it was another disappointment they suffered through.

If there was help, it would be difficult to find.

The disappointment and hopelessness felt like a bottomless pit of despair.

Photo of Edwin and Lillian in the kitchen with Ghost Hunters' members

Chapter 45

Edwin no longer slept at night.

He lay in bed, staring at the ceiling, trying to rationalize it all. What were they going to do? Everything they tried had failed, leaving them worse than before. In the back of his mind he knew it was going to just get worse.

What next?

He could handle the sounds of footsteps on the third floor, or the occasional clamor of the doorbell ringing, but the house had proven that it was capable of so much more.

How much else could they take?

Thoughts of Lillian being pinned to the bed mixed in with his own vision of the woman in white crying by the window. The images played in his mind, giving him little comfort. The house was quiet for now, but how long would that last?

What if the next time Lillian was taken over she did something horrific?

What if she hurt one of them?

The thoughts ran through his head over and over again.

They couldn't fight this. Nobody could. What they needed was to put some distance between them and the house, so they could build their strength. The two days at the hotel had been blissful, but they couldn't afford to stay there on their own. If they had a few weeks of distance, maybe they could muster the strength to continue, but right now they were nothing more than empty shells. They didn't have any energy left to fight it.

Where could they go?

They couldn't go back to the Dorchester house. They already rented out the apartment they lived in, and the other units were still occupied by her brother and mother. Lillian called Iris the day after TAPS left, but they had an issue with the new house. Someone broke in and stole all of the copper piping. They wouldn't be able to move in until they could replace it. They had to sit and wait it out.

The thought nearly killed him.

It was like Chinese water torture as they waited for the next drop to fall.

The next morning Derek Cormier called to remind him about the haunted house event. All the turbulence of the past few weeks had made him forgot about it.

"Yeah," he said faintly to his friend. "Come on over and we can start decorating," he told him.

After everything they experienced, everything they lived through, putting on a cheery smile and pretending everything was okay was the last thing he wanted to do. Unfortunately, there was no turning back. They had been planning the event for several months. All the pieces were in place. He would simply have to get through it.

Edwin is a people pleaser. It is both an asset and a liability. He has a hard time letting anyone down. Agreeing to the event was no different from agreeing to all the investigations. He hated to disappoint people. Since they already placed the advertisements, most of the town was aware of the event.

There was no backing out now.

The night before the event, Mother Nature had other plans for them. An unexpected snowstorm dumped over two feet of snow on the area. Edwin woke up the next morning with a sense of panic as he looked out the window. The snow was so deep, it was as though it swallowed the landscape, smoothing it out and erasing all the sharp edges.

It felt like it was always something. He spent the entire morning and afternoon alternating between snow blowing and shoveling the driveways and sidewalks. It would be the first time since they moved in that they opened the house up to the public in such a manner.

Derek and several of the volunteers showed up early to help get ready.

"This isn't good," Edwin told him, eyeing the mounds of snow outside. The piles in the yard were so tall, you could barely see out the first floor windows. He had no idea where people were going to park.

"Well, if we even have a dozen people show up, then it won't all be for nothing," Derek told him.

As it turned out, the event was more popular than anyone could have imagined.

People lined up down the street, waiting for their turn to see the magnificent mansion. Tours moved steadily through the house, starting in the library where Edwin would regale them with tales of his experiences, before they would be shuffled up the servant staircase to the second floor. A tour guide would meet them at the top of the stairs and bring them to each level of the house, including the basement.

When the last person filed out the door, the volunteers nearly collapsed. Six hours of tours was more than any of them were prepared to handle. Even so, everyone was ecstatic, because the tour was a wild success. Edwin felt good about the house for the first time in a long while. It gave him the smallest glimmer of home.

He would soon realize it all wasn't what it seemed.

It was always something.

"Hon, come here," he called to Lillian, as he noticed strange indented marks in the doorway of the library. As she came into the room, he knelt down to get a closer look. Dozens of small indents dotted the floor.

"Oh no," Lillian said as she noticed something else. The floor near the bookcases was marred with a long, deep trench. They'd find another similar one on the front porch, along with more puncture marks on the servant staircase and in the Red Room.

According to eyewitnesses, a man in a trench coat deliberately destroyed the hardwood flooring in many of the rooms. Witnesses came forward attesting to his actions. Some said they heard a strange sawing sound as the group stood in the library listening to Edwin's presentation, but hadn't been able to figure out where the sound was coming from. It was enough to turn a good thing into something horrid.

"Out of all those people who came, it only took one person to ruin it for everyone else," Lillian said, sadly.

If bad things come in threes, this was the final straw.

They couldn't take any more.

The next day they received a phone call that would change everything. Lillian's sister was finally able to move into her new home.

It was all over.

They would move out the next day, never to return.

Damage to the floors during the Halloween event

Chapter 46

The week following Thanksgiving, Marion Luoma went on her yearly shopping trip with her friends. She returned to find a message on her answering machine. It was Edwin telling her they weren't coming back.

They moved into her sister's basement, staying in a room that was smaller than any of the rooms inside their Victorian mansion. However, they were safe. She could hear the relief in his voice.

She felt a sinking in her stomach as she thought about everything they went through.

The house had finally won.

She didn't blame either of them for not wanting to return. They experienced so much, and the latest events had turned downright dangerous. Marion kept thinking about Lillian's face when she answered the door that day. What would have happened if she hadn't shown up? *Would it have gotten worse?*

During the month of December, Lillian began making quick day trips back to the mansion to retrieve her belongings. She called Marion on her way to ask her to meet her there. It was clear she didn't want to be in that house alone.

Marion wasn't surprised that Edwin never joined her.

He had enough. He couldn't stomach the thought of returning, not even for a second.

She would meet Lillian at the door, and the two of them would walk around the house, checking to make sure everything was okay. Then the two of them would carry out boxes and furniture, slowly emptying the house of their personal possessions. Later, they brought a moving truck to remove the heavier items, leaving only a few pieces of furniture.

The rooms became hollow. Footsteps carried throughout the house, echoing back in the silence.

The house felt lost.

As Marion walked around the rooms, she felt as though sad eyes were watching her. She wondered if they were aware of what they had done to Edwin and Lillian. Surely all the ghosts in the house weren't out to get them. Some of them, like the little boy who wandered the hallways, seemed to enjoy their company.

It wasn't until January that Lillian stopped going to the Victorian altogether.

It started with a break-in.

Someone noticed that a board covering one of the basement windows had been removed and the window was left open. Lillian met Marion at the house, and the two of them shored up the window, propping it closed with a board. They checked the house and nothing seemed amiss, but what would prevent people from breaking in again?

"What are you going to do?" Marion asked Lillian.

Lillian took a deep breath. "I'm going to give you a key. Can you look after the house?" she asked.

Marion was dumbfounded. She only knew them for eight months, and yet they trusted her enough to give her a key to their house? She didn't think about the mammoth task she was taking on, or the fact that she would have to walk around inside the house by herself. She just did what she always did when someone needed her help. She took the key.

Throughout the year, Marion visited the house at least once a week, just like she did in her dreams.

It was as if the house could foresee the future.

CHAPTER 47

The house sat empty for the next year. Marion checked on it several times a week, walking the rooms to look for water leaks or break-ins, packing up mail to send to Brockton for Edwin and Lillian, before locking the door behind her. There were no investigations, no people walking through the doors, except for Marion and the people who came along to help her, including her friends Heidi and Tina Aube.

In August of 2012, the television show *Paranormal Witness* portrayed Edwin and Lillian's experiences on their television show. The show aired on October 29th of that year, bringing more attention to the mansion.

Executive Producer Mark Lewis said in a blog article, "You could not imagine a house that could look more haunted than this one. It's absolutely beautiful, but looks like something out of *The Addams Family*. Inside it was pretty damned frightening. Lillian and Edwin can no longer live in the house – it is just too haunted – so we were there, in the basement, when it turned dark... and there are no lights. That final scene from *The Blair Witch Project* kept running through my head!"

> *Click below for a link for the article or copy the link to your computer's browser:*
>
> http://paranormalwitness.tumblr.com/post/52870791674/the-real-haunted-house-in-the-lost-boy

In April of 2013, the media attention continued when the popular television show *Ghost Adventures* contacted Edwin, asking if they could come in to film a show. Edwin and Lillian had five days to prepare the house, which involved fixing a panel in the master bedroom ceiling that fell down during the winter, as well as cleaning and staging all the rooms with furniture again.

The show was a tremendous success, and the owners felt much differently after filming was concluded. Even though they'd been down that road before with other shows, *Ghost Adventures* proved to be the most professional and most accurate of them all.

Click the link below for video clips from the show, courtesy of The Travel Channel, or copy the link address to your computer's browser.
<u>http://www.travelchannel.com/tv-shows/ghost-adventures/episodes/haunted-victorian-mansion</u>

As news of the filming circulated, paranormal groups began calling Edwin again, wanting to get in to investigate. He began to book groups during the summer, something that wouldn't end until the last day of November.

During this flurry of activity, he faced some adversity from a paranormal investigator from Connecticut, a man who has been known to attack other local haunted venues for a variety of unsubstantiated reasons. Because many of the paranormal shows displayed the information in a way that fitted their needs, he claimed that Edwin and Lillian were lying about many of the experiences they endured. He also felt that more of the funds from the events should have gone towards renovations to the house. He lodged numerous complaints with the city of Gardner.

Because of this, the town came in and shut them down for investigations.

The windows were once again dark.

The rooms were quiet.

If a door slammed, no one was there to hear it.

Cars still drove past slowly as the occupants stared up at the windows, wondering if anyone was looking back. Pigeons still roosted along the edges of the eaves, and snow still blanketed the sidewalks.

Be forewarned.

If the house starts to call for you, just keep on driving.

Photo by Jason Baker

Chapter 48

Life goes on, as it always does.

Edwin and Lillian never learned all the secrets of the house.

They never truly knew who haunted the basement, or what happened to the lonely little boy.

They never found out if a prostitute really died in the Red Room.

They wouldn't discover a lot of things, but what they knew was that they finally felt safe.

Edwin moved his home office from the Victorian mansion to Lillian's sister's basement. Lillian took a full-time job at a retail store, trying to help them stay current with the increased bills. Not only were they paying living expenses at Iris's house, they were also still paying the bills for a house they couldn't live in, but were having a hard time parting with.

It was evident that the house missed them. As Lillian was watching television one night, the screen became filled with static. She stopped and looked up, startled because televisions don't do that anymore. As she stared, a message was delivered that left her with cold chills.

"Come back," it said, before returning to the program.

Lillian turned off the television and went to bed.

Marion Luoma, Zach Menard, and Joni Mayhan investigating in the Tunnel Room. Photo courtesy of Tina Aube.

THE AFTERMATH
AUTHOR'S NOTES

I've always been drawn to the Victorian, as well.

It started in 2008 after I first discovered it looming on the corner of Union and West Broadway when I took a shortcut through Gardner. Like others who came before and after me, I was mesmerized by the sight of this massive, grand old Victorian.

It looked out of place in the modern world surrounding it, a grand dame years past her prime. When I saw the "for sale" sign in the front yard, I paused at the corner, my mind spinning.

With all my heart, I wanted to call the realtor and buy it.

The thought was thundering.

What would I do with an old rundown Victorian mansion?

Besides, I was already deep in debt with my own house.

I pulled my gaze from the dark windows and continued on, thoughts of the house never leaving me for long.

My story starts just before Edwin and Lillian moved out of the house.

Even though it sat vacant, it would never be totally abandoned.

It had us.

We began to laughingly call ourselves the Victorian Groupies, because we were there so frequently. As Marion Luoma went to check on the house several times a week, several of us went with her. While we were there, we always tried to get a reading on what was going on with the house. Throughout the course of the next two years, we collected many EVPs and we had even more experiences than I can fit in the body of this book.

I met Tina Aube years before on the social media giant, Facebook. She sent me a friend request after seeing some of my paranormal posts, and expressed an interest in investigating. At the time, I was the Massachusetts director of a national ghost hunting group, and we welcomed her aboard as a team member. Sometimes we just got together to stomp through the woods to explore abandoned buildings, and other times we investigated at public and local paranormal events. It was immediately clear to me that Tina had a true knack for collecting EVPs. Some of her findings totally blew me away. In time, I also discovered she was a phenomenal researcher, spending countless hours in front of the computer and at the library, digging for details. The combination of the two, as well as her sharp mind and keen senses, made her a great investigator. We teamed up time and time again to explore the hidden world around us.

Like myself, Tina was also entranced with the Victorian.

We came to realize that it wasn't just an accidental attraction. As we looked around at the others who were also drawn to the house, we started to see a pattern. All of the people who were drawn to the house would eventually play an essential role in the story. We were being collected.

Others who would join us were Sandy MacLeod, my paranormal sidekick, who ran the Meet up group, Footsteps Paranormal. She would go on to set up a website for Edwin and Lillian, and would participate in their events and fundraisers. Derek Cormier would also be one of the groupies, helping out with events, and eventually filming a B-grade horror movie inside the house, along with fellow film enthusiast, Bob Pfeiffer.

As we entered the house, we always felt welcomed for the most part. As we left one day, here is a response we received.

Click to listen to the audio recording or copy and paste onto your computer's browser:

https://soundcloud.com/jonimayhan/bye

The Victorian Groupies: (top) Edwin Gonzalez, Derek Cormier Eleanor Gavazzi, Joni Mayhan, Tina Aube, Marion Luoma, and Kayla Aube

When Edwin and Lillian opened the house up for investigations, I was one of the first people inside. Although I left my name out of the story, I was with Footsteps Paranormal and was there when the psychic medium began to pull her information, almost from thin air. I returned four more times before the Haunted House Tour in October 2011. During that period, I was going through paranormal issues of my own, which spawned my book, *The Soul Collector*. There is a chapter in the book about the tour at the Victorian, and what I had to face when I returned home afterwards.

The Soul Collector by Joni Mayhan
The true story of one paranormal investigator's worst nightmare.

I've been investigating the paranormal since 2009. Being a sensitive made the investigating more interesting for me. As a clairaudient, I am able to hear sounds as ghosts move into the room. They sound similar to an ear-ringing tone, the pitches varying according to the gender of the ghost. The minute I walked into the S.K. Pierce mansion for the first time, I could hear them swoop in to greet me.

When we investigate, we use various tools to capture evidence. My favorite tools are a standard digital voice recorder and the P-SB7 Spirit Box. The Spirit Box is a modified radio that scans rapidly through stations, landing on each station for just a quarter of a second. The theory behind it is that ghosts can use the white noise to speak to us in real time. While some people are quick to debunk the responses as stray radio voices, I beg to differ. After all, what are the odds of a stray radio voice answering a direct question correctly?

We like using the Spirit Box, because it provides us with instant responses. Instead of having to wait until we get home to review our recorded audio, we can hear the response right then, and respond accordingly.

Here is one of the first EVPs I captured at the Victorian. We were in the Summer Kitchen, sitting in a circle in the dark, trying to communicate with the ghosts in the house. There were six or seven people in my group, which is a bit large for a standard group. Typically, I like five or less. Two is even better. One person can ask the questions, while the other witnesses the responses.

When I start an EVP session, I always open it with a location tag to let myself know which room I'm in, so I know where it occurred later when I review my audio. I couldn't have been more shocked when I distinctly heard the sound of a woman telling me that she loved me.

> *Click to listen to the audio recording or copy and paste onto your computer's browser:*
>
> *https://soundcloud.com/jonimayhan/basement-opening-tag-and-2*

When my mother and her boyfriend came to Massachusetts to visit me, I brought them on a tour of the Victorian. While my mother was still on the fence about the entire paranormal world, her boyfriend was a definite skeptic. When I told the resident ghosts about this, here is their response.

I said "They don't believe you're really here, so you're going to have to help me here."

The response was candid, if not a little sarcastic. "Well, that's too bad," a male voice said.

> *Click to listen to the audio recording or copy and paste onto your computer's browser:*
>
> *https://soundcloud.com/jonimayhan/sb-dont-believe-youre-here*

Marion Luoma and Tina Aube were with me during this visit, so I asked the ghosts of the house if they wanted Marion to buy the house. Here is the response:

> *Click to listen to the audio recording or copy and paste onto your computer's browser:*
>
> https://soundcloud.com/jonimayhan/sb-would-you-like-marion-to

Over time, we learned that many of the ghosts weren't happy with where they were. They reached out to us for help numerous times. It was heart wrenching to hear. We wanted to help them, but we didn't know how. I told them about crossing over to the white light, but they either weren't able to or weren't willing to do so. Here is an EVP asking for help.

> *Click to listen to the audio recording or copy and paste onto your computer's browser:*
>
> https://soundcloud.com/jonimayhan/help-me-help-me-1

There was an intelligence there that we couldn't deny. They clearly knew what was going on around them. This washed away all the preconceived notions that ghosts were just living side by side with us in another dimension, unaware of our presence. During one session, I asked who owned the house and got the clear response of "Edwin."

> *Click to listen to the audio recording or copy and paste onto your computer's browser:*
>
> https://soundcloud.com/jonimayhan/red-room-sb-who-owns-this

Here are several other audio recordings of the ghosts saying Edwin's name.

> *Click to listen to the audio recording or copy and paste onto your computer's browser:*
>
> https://soundcloud.com/jonimayhan/get-your-story-right-edwin

> Click to listen to the audio recording or copy and paste onto your computer's browser:
>
> https://soundcloud.com/jonimayhan/red-room-remember-edwin-hi

The resident ghosts were also very familiar with Lillian. The feeling we got from the various responses we received was that they missed her greatly. While some of them chased her off, others were very sad to see her leave. When I asked if they wanted to pass on a message to her, they simply said her name.

> Click to listen to the audio recording or copy and paste onto your computer's browser:
>
> https://soundcloud.com/jonimayhan/red-room-say-something-to-her

They knew my name, as well. I always felt welcomed there. When I came to the door, I could feel and hear them swirl around me, like lonely people looking for a friendly face. When I asked if they remembered me, I actually capture two separate voices saying "Joni."

> Click to listen to the audio recording or copy and paste onto your computer's browser:
>
> https://soundcloud.com/jonimayhan/mbr-sb-joni-joni

Another time, I got a response that made me stop and think. When I asked if they knew my name, a male voice very clearly said, "Are you one of them?" Did he mean one of the ghost hunters, or one of the friends of the Victorian?

> Click to listen to the audio recording or copy and paste onto your computer's browser:
>
> https://soundcloud.com/jonimayhan/whats-my-name-are-you-one-of

They also knew what town we were in. I received clear responses on more than one occasion.

> *Click to listen to the audio recording or copy and paste onto your computer's browser:*
>
> https://soundcloud.com/jonimayhan/what-town-gardner

Here's another response to our inquiries about what town we were in:

> *Click to listen to the audio recording or copy and paste onto your computer's browser:*
>
> https://soundcloud.com/jonimayhan/stairs-she-lives-in-gardner

We often tried to learn more about the resident ghosts. When we asked if they were afraid of the entity in the basement, a male voice responded with "the devil."

> *Click to listen to the audio recording or copy and paste onto your computer's browser:*
>
> https://soundcloud.com/jonimayhan/billiards-room-ghost-box-1

When I asked the question again years later, I got a far different response. Someone told me there was "nothing threatening."

> *Click to listen to the audio recording or copy and paste onto your computer's browser:*
>
> https://soundcloud.com/jonimayhan/anyone-we-should-be-careful

We also wanted to know more about their personalities and determine if the ghosts in residence were familiar with the Pierce family. When we asked if they remembered S.K. Pierce, a woman responded with, "very friendly." We heard this same woman's voice many times over the course of just a few years. I came to wonder if this was the voice of Mattie Cornwell, the nanny.

Click to listen to the audio recording or copy and paste onto your computer's browser:

https://soundcloud.com/jonimayhan/billiards-room-ghost-box-2

Ellen Pierce was also a mystery. All I knew about her was what I could pull from the public records. I knew that she married S.K. when she was only 28, leaving me to believe that she was also very attractive. According to Eleanor Gavazzi, she was a trophy wife for an old, wealthy tycoon. She expected the world from the marriage, but didn't get it. She was left holding the bag after her wealthy husband died.

Ellen was active in her church and a member of the ladies' division of the Gardner Boat Club. She also had her own safe, one of the few remnants left from the Pierce family. It sits on the second floor landing with her name painted on the front. When I investigated with Footsteps Paranormal on the first event, the psychic medium kept picking up the name "Nellie." She said that someone in the house was named Nellie and she kept trying to talk to her. Through research, we later learned that Ellen's nickname was Nellie. I captured it once again at a later investigation.

Click to listen to the audio recording or copy and paste onto your computer's browser:

https://soundcloud.com/jonimayhan/second-floor-landing-gb-what

Marion, Tina, and I went to the Victorian to clean up after the Halloween event in October 2011. Lillian and Edwin were in Brockton and we wanted to take care of it for them, so they didn't have to make the long trip to Gardner.

The house was bitterly cold when we entered, a testament of what Lillian and Edwin had lived through at the house. Bundled up in many layers, we went through the house, packing decorations into tubs that we carried up to the third floor cistern room one by one. It was an exhausting process. The tubs were heavy and the steps were many, but we got through it over the course of several hours.

As usual, I brought my digital recorder along. I placed it on a small table near the grand staircase. I kept it running the entire time I was there, just to see if anyone wanted to tell us anything. We weren't ghost hunting, per say, but we always wanted to take the pulse of the house ghosts, just to see how they were faring.

When we were finished, we decided to move the dining room table back into the library room. I was already exhausted from all the trips up two flights of stairs with heavy totes, and my arms felt like spaghetti as I grabbed my end of the table. Without really talking it over, I took the end that would require me to walk backwards through the Ladies Parlor double doors, across the entry way, and into the library room. As I got to the doorway, I nearly bumped into the door frame. I later learn that the resident ghosts weren't happy about this.

The response I recorded on my digital recorder was "Be careful! Pay attention!"

Click to listen to the audio recording or copy and paste onto your computer's browser:

https://soundcloud.com/jonimayhan/watch-it-pay-attention

Like Lillian's experience when she visited the house for the second time, I discovered that the ghosts really enjoyed draining our batteries. Sometimes it would be through our digital recorders or other equipment, but most of the time it was our cameras and phones. Interestingly, many times when I got into my car, I discovered my batteries had miraculously regenerated. Here's an EVP of a ghost telling me he's sorry after I discovered that my camera battery was dead.

Click to listen to the audio recording or copy and paste onto your computer's browser:

https://soundcloud.com/jonimayhan/response-about-my-battery

Joni Mayhan, Marion Luoma, and Tina Aube during the Relay for Life Fundraising Tour in 2013

    Tina and Marion continued to have many more experiences at the Victorian during their weekly visits. Once when they were sitting on the chairs beside the grand staircase, they started hearing scratching noises coming from the basement door. Before either of them could get up, a dark grey mass shot out of the fourth stair, flew down the hallway and disappeared out the Union Street door.

    Both were so stunned when it happened, they couldn't even find words. Tina finally got up and opened the door, but nothing was there. The experience shook both of them to the core. Whatever was scratching at the door wasn't friendly, they could feel its anger radiating through the air.

Like Edwin and Lillian, the story that captivated us the most was the one about the little boy. As mothers ourselves, the thought that a small boy could be trapped inside a world he didn't understand made us sad. We talked to him often, encouraging him to find the white light and call out for his mother or father to come help him cross over into the light, but he never followed our advice.

Tina captured the following EVP in the room with all the shutters down in the basement. She was sweeping, but had her recorder running just in case one of them wanted to pass along a message.

A male voice says, "Who killed the boy?"

Click to listen to the audio recording or copy and paste onto your computer's browser: EVP courtesy of Tina Aube.

https://soundcloud.com/wait-till-you-hear-this/after-sweeping-just-before

This brings more validity to the claims of the little boy's existence, and also that he was killed, and didn't die of natural causes. Who was he and where did he come from? It's hard to say, since there wasn't a record of a little boy dying while living at the Victorian. Could it have been from the early years when deaths were much easier to sweep under the rug, or was he from another area and somehow managed to end up there?

I went right to the source again. I told them that I heard that the little boy never actually lived in the house. They told me, "They're wrong."

Click to listen to the audio recording or copy and paste onto your computer's browser:

https://soundcloud.com/jonimayhan/asking-about-little-boy-theyre

The same day, we asked if the little boy was there. A female, who sounds very much like the same voice we've come to attribute to Mattie says, "The door." Was she directing us to look at the door to find him? Or was she telling us to leave?

> *Click to listen to the audio recording or copy and paste onto your computer's browser:*
>
> *https://soundcloud.com/jonimayhan/little-boy-are-you-here-the*

No one knew his name, but I was sure the ghosts knew. When I asked, they responded very clearly with the name Franklin. I found it interesting that one of the Pierce son's was named Frank. Was there a correlation?

> *Click to listen to the audio recording or copy and paste onto your computer's browser:*
>
> *https://soundcloud.com/jonimayhan/sb-little-boys-name-franklin-1*

One thing we learned fairly quickly was that the little boy didn't like bubbles.

Often when we visited, we brought various toys that we left on the stairs for him to play with. This included tiny toy cars, coloring books, crayons, and balls. On one of our visits, I brought along a container of bubbles, thinking that he would enjoy them. Apparently he didn't. When we listened back to the audio that Tina captured, you can clearly hear him screaming "No!" in the background.

> *Click to listen to the audio recording or copy and paste onto your computer's browser: EVP courtesy of Tina Aube.*
>
> *https://soundcloud.com/wait-till-you-hear-this/4-1st-floor-landing-dont-think*

One of the most poignant audio recordings ever captured in the Victorian came when Tina and Marion were on one of their visits. Tina asks if the little boy is there and you can clearly hear him saying "Come and get me," on the audio in a sing-song, playful manner.

> *Click to listen to the audio recording or copy and paste onto your computer's browser: EVP courtesy of Tina Aube.*
>
> https://soundcloud.com/wait-till-you-hear-this/is-the-little-boy-here-just

We asked him his age and received a response of 11, although this seems strange, since we considered him to be much younger. Could there possibly be two little boys there?

> *Click to listen to the audio recording or copy and paste onto your computer's browser:*
>
> https://soundcloud.com/jonimayhan/basement-tunnel-room-gh-how

It's clear to us that the little boy is playful. Although the three of us have never seen him with our eyes, we've heard his voice many times. A part of me truly believes he's happy there in the house and has been there so long, he doesn't remember any other way. When we encourage him to cross over, we ask him to do something that is scarier than what he lives through each day.

We also believe that Rachel Pierce is also there to play with him. While the little boy prefers the grand staircase and the first floor rooms, guests in the house sense the little girl up on the third floor more than anywhere else.

Investigators have actually seen her on occasion, usually fleetingly and in shadow form. She was only two years old when she died, so her responses are usually very simple, something we'd expect from a toddler.

She likes to play with toys, so we would bring balls for her to move. She'd push them a few feet and then stop. Other times, we've watched her manipulate flashlights and laser lights.

One time, we set up a laser grid in the doorway of the Billiards Room, pointing it towards the doorway. As the four of us watched, a white light appeared at the edge of the door and began tracing the doorframe. This went on for several minutes as we all marveled at what we were seeing. We tried to debunk it, but there was no explanation for it. Was she moving the light or creating her own?

She's responded several times on our audio. In the following recording, I asked who just came into the room. You can hear a small girl's voice say, "I did." I then asked if it was the little girl, and the response was "yup."

> *Click to listen to the audio recording or copy and paste onto your computer's browser:*
>
> *https://soundcloud.com/jonimayhan/who-just-came-in-the-room-i-1*

On another visit, we captured another audio response with the same voice. When I asked, "Who is that?" the response was, "Come get me."

> *Click to listen to the audio recording or copy and paste onto your computer's browser:*
>
> *https://soundcloud.com/jonimayhan/who-is-that-come-get-me-1*

The voice of Maddie is heard time and time again on our audio. Here she is responding to Tina's request that they slam the door like they did with Edwin and Lillian. She responds, "Are you asking?"

> *Click to listen to the audio recording or copy and paste onto your computer's browser:*
>
> *https://soundcloud.com/jonimayhan/second-floor-landing-sb-slam*

We asked if Maddie was still there. Bill Wallace firmly felt that she was inadvertently removed during the house cleansing. When he went to the house, he could no longer feel her any longer. Knowing this, I kept asking about her, trying to either validate his claims or rest his mind.

Here is one response I received. It's the same voice from the previous audio recording, taking months apart. I asked if Maddie was still there and the response was quick. "Come talk to me. Come talk to me," she said.

> *Click to listen to the audio recording or copy and paste onto your computer's browser:*
>
> *https://soundcloud.com/jonimayhan/stairs-maddie-are-you-here*

Eino Saari was another interesting character. The legends stated that he died of spontaneous combustion, but we later learned that wasn't the case. Being a heavy drinker and smoker is a bad combination, often resulting in a mattress fire. It was fairly compelling, though. A fire in a very old house should have caused catastrophic results, but it didn't. Had one of the resident ghosts played a role in keeping the flames down to a minimum? Although we suspect this was the case, we never knew for sure.

One claim from another paranormal group had us intrigued. They suggested that Eino had actually committed suicide, dousing himself with alcohol and then lighting himself on fire. I couldn't imagine someone doing this to themselves, but I wanted to verify it. I asked Eino directly.

"Some people say he committed suicide," I said, telling the rest of the group.

You can hear a very soft whisper directly afterwards. He said, "No."

> *Click to listen to the audio recording or copy and paste onto your computer's browser:*
>
> *https://soundcloud.com/jonimayhan/master-bedroom-suicide*

I also was curious if we were using the correct pronunciation of his name. A friend who knew a bit of Finnish said that it would be pronounced differently than what we were saying. I asked for clarification and got the following response.

> *Click to listen to the audio recording or copy and paste onto your computer's browser:*
>
> *https://soundcloud.com/jonimayhan/mbr-sb-eino*

Marian King, a local researcher and friend, did a great deal of research for me as I wrote this book. She was able to pull more information about Eino. One of the things she learned was that he wasn't a Finnish immigrant, but his parents were. He was actually born in the United States. We learned that his mother's name was Seraphina and his father's name was Matti, something I later confirmed with him.

"And your father's name was Matti?" I asked.

"Matti," was the response on the Spirit Box.

Click to listen to the audio recording or copy and paste onto your computer's browser:

https://soundcloud.com/jonimayhan/einos-fathers-name-matti

Eino Saari's Death Certificate

The basement has a different feel to it compared to the rest of the house. While my first EVP was of the girl saying, "I love you," in the Summer Kitchen, the other rooms don't have the same friendly tone to them. The Tunnel Room, in particular, was a source of anxiety for most of us.

Many psychics have picked up on a negative entity who lingers down there. I've personally felt him many times. He comes in through the door near the furnace, in the place where they say Edward Pierce slept when he lived as a boarder in the house, and he strikes you with intimidation. The room suddenly grows very dark as he envelopes you in a black mist. It's so dark that it blots out the other lights in the room, leaving you feel as though someone threw a dark blanket over your head.

I encountered him over and over again during my visits at the house.

Many fundraisers would be held at the house for various functions. While Marion Luoma set up a tour to raise money for Relay for Life, another group set up a fundraiser to help replenish Gardner's local food pantry.

Chris Cox, the co-founder of New England Paranormal Observation Science Technology (NE POST), along with Christina Tregger Achilles, the other co-founder, wanted to help Edwin and Lillian do something that would help the local community. They visited the mansion many times before to investigate, and they became friends with the owners. In November of 2013, they set up an event at the house. They would give people a free tour of the house, providing they brought a bag or box of non-perishable food items with them. Many of us were eager to help, including me, Marion Luoma, and Tina Aube. The event was a tremendous success, and the community was delighted with the bounty we raised for them.

During the fundraisers, I always ended up giving tours of the basement, because most of the other volunteers weren't comfortable down there. Marion won't go down there unless she absolutely has to because she once was nearly pulled off her feet by a strong tug on her jacket. Since I knew the history and felt fairly comfortable there, the basement became my domain, for better or for worse.

It was okay in the beginning. I went down alone and I explained to them what we were doing. "Feel free to hide in the corners, if it makes you more comfortable. The groups will be coming through quickly, so they won't be here long," I'd tell them.

Everything was calm for a while, but after a few hours I could feel his impatience rising to the surface. I couldn't get through my spiel in the Tunnel Room as he came up behind me. All I wanted to do was to swivel around to make sure he wasn't about to give me a hearty push. If I did turn, all I'd see was darkness. Frequently, I would have brief chats with him.

"I'm sorry we're in your space, but I'm pretty much stuck down here until the event is over. Can you please just give us another hour?" I asked. It was usually enough to appease him and he'd back off again.

The other spirits in the basement weren't crazy about him, either. Here's an EVP I captured during one of my forays into the basement. The voice very clearly says "Scary." Was she talking about the dark entity? Or was she talking about us?

> *Click to listen to the audio recording or copy and paste onto your computer's browser:*
>
> *https://soundcloud.com/jonimayhan/basement-scary*

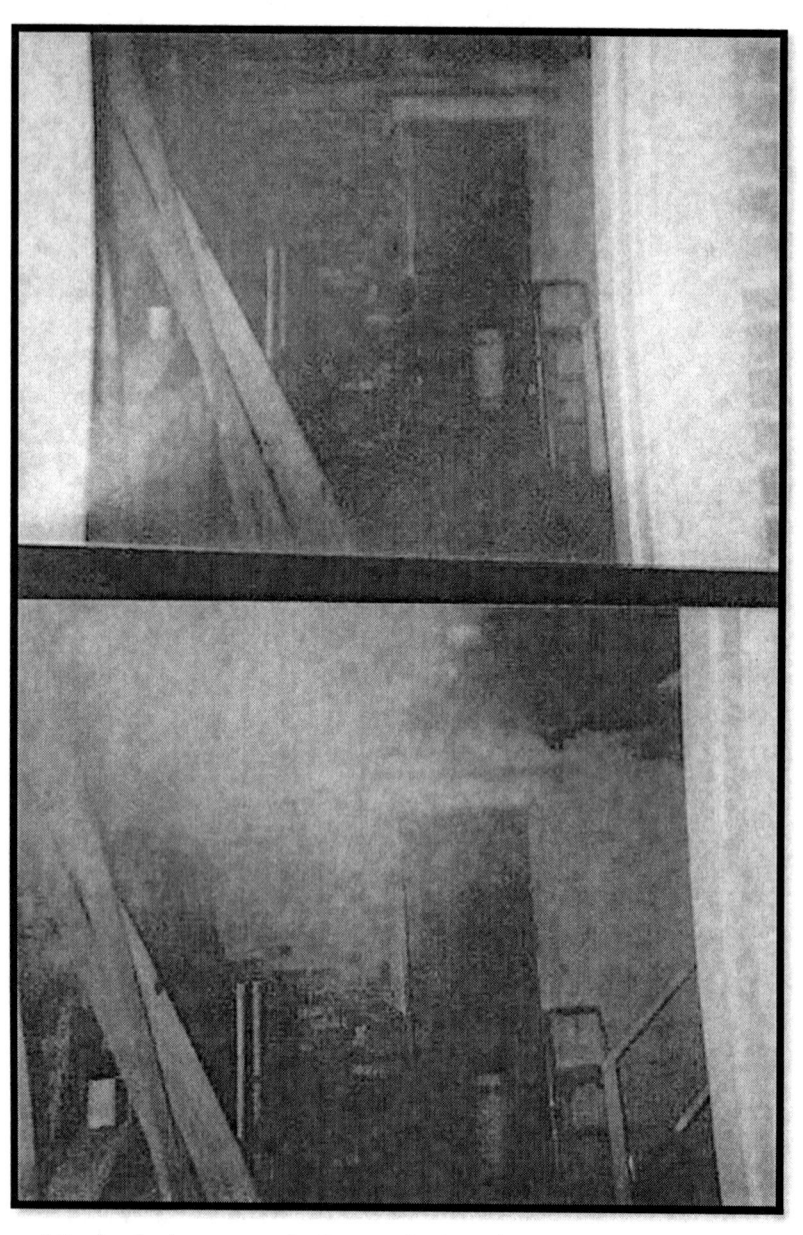

Mist in the basement (before and after photos)
Photos by Rodney Barr

Volunteers for the NE Post Food Drive Fundraiser.

(L-R) Christina Tregger Achilles (co-founder of NE POST, holding Ceirra), Rodney Barr, Joni Mayhan, Ozzie Andrade, Lillian and Edwin, Al Andrade Jr., Chris Cox (Founder of NE POST), and two Gardner fireman who were on duty for the event).

During my first investigation there as part of Footsteps Paranormal, the psychic medium was picking up on the prospect that children were used as labor in the furniture factory. She was saying, "They would sell their children into that kind of labor, because it provided them with the very small wages they needed." After she pauses, you can hear a whispered, "Thank you." Was this confirmation that children worked at the factory? We were never able to confirm this, but it was an interesting response.

    Child labor laws weren't established at that time, so it would stand to reason that they would be used to help support their families. The psychic medium suggested that S.K. would loan money to some of the local town people. When they couldn't pay him back, he would take their children to work in the factory. This wasn't something we could confirm, but then again it wasn't something they would have documented. While it was legal, it wasn't a situation that a proud family like the Pierces would promote.

> *Click to listen to the audio recording or copy and paste onto your computer's browser:*
>
> <https://soundcloud.com/jonimayhan/basement-thank-you>

This was something Eleanor Gavazzi would firmly deny. S.K. Pierce was very active in the community. When the high school needed a new location, he was on the board to make the decision.

"You can't be on the board for a new high school without being a trusted, upright member of the community. I've worked with school children and parents for years. They are very selective who they allow to be around their children and make decisions for them," she said.

I had a tendency to agree with her.

Like the basement, the third floor also had a mixture of ghosts. At times we would receive responses from a fairly friendly female, but other times an angry, sarcastic male would step in and silence everyone. Here's a recording of a friendly spirit, directing us to look, "Down here."

> *Click to listen to the audio recording or copy and paste onto your computer's browser:*
>
> <https://soundcloud.com/jonimayhan/third-floor-down-here>

When I asked what her favorite time of the year was, I got a very clear, intelligent response of "Autumn.

> *Click to listen to the audio recording or copy and paste onto your computer's browser:*
>
> <https://soundcloud.com/jonimayhan/whats-your-favorite-time-of>

But as time went on, the energy on the third floor seemed to change. Someone darker was stepping in, and he wasn't happy we were up there. Sometimes it would become so heavy, we couldn't stay for long. It felt as though someone was standing over us, screaming at us to leave. The audio supported this feeling.

I always wondered if Jay Stemmerman, the artist who supposedly won the house in a card game in 1966, was still there. I asked if he was there, and received a very angry response from someone who responded with profanities.

> *Click to listen to the audio recording or copy and paste onto your computer's browser: browser:*
>
> https://soundcloud.com/jonimayhan/jay-are-you-here-f-k-no

Hearing that response, I pushed a little further, telling him I knew who he was. The response was quick and to the point.

He responded with, "You've got no idea."

> *Click to listen to the audio recording or copy and paste onto your computer's browser:*
>
> *https://soundcloud.com/jonimayhan/i-know-who-you-are-youve-got*

He then followed it up with an insult. "You've got some weirdoes here," he said.

> *Click to listen to the audio recording or copy and paste onto your computer's browser:*
>
> *https://soundcloud.com/jonimayhan/billiards-room-sb-got-some*

There is someone there who controls the others. Sometimes I think he holds them back, preventing them from speaking. We've heard him step in several times, and the voice is always the same. Is this the same male we heard on the other audio? It certainly sounds the same. Here is a recording of us asking to say hello to Maddie. He asks us, "What's your point?"

> *Click to listen to the audio recording or copy and paste onto your computer's browser:*
>
> *https://soundcloud.com/jonimayhan/second-floor-landing-sb-say-hi*

During one of my final attempts to speak with the ghosts of the mansion, I got some direct messages. They were tired of talking to us, and they just wanted us to leave. After hearing that, I vowed to stop bothering them. If they had any secrets, they were no longer interested in sharing them. After everything they went through with the countless investigations, they made it clear that all they wanted was to be left alone.

"What can we help you with?" I asked.

"Getting you out," was the response. Clear and to the point.

> *Click to listen to the audio recording or copy and paste onto your computer's browser:*
>
> *https://soundcloud.com/jonimayhan/cistern-room-gb-getting-you*

Shortly afterwards, two more came forward, telling us to "Go away."

> *Click to listen to the audio recording or copy and paste onto your computer's browser:*
>
> *https://soundcloud.com/jonimayhan/gb-go-away-go-away*

During the writing of this book, Tina Aube and I discovered the real entrance to the tunnel in the basement. Others had mistakenly believed it to be on the left side of the room, but after we found old photos of the house left behind by the Veau family, we were able to locate the correct location. While the discovery didn't provide any more information to the haunted history of the house, it was interesting for us to finally solve one mystery.

I'm sure my story about the Victorian doesn't end here with the completion of this book, but I know this is where my part of the story ends.

It called to me, like it did with many others, and I responded.

Edwin and Lillian still don't live in the house. There are whispers of them possibly selling it. If that happens, I hope the next owners find some way to release the ghosts who linger there.

Everyone deserves to rest in peace.

Everyone.

The End

Links to our friends who investigated at the Victorian Mansion

Paranormal Unity Research Society' website:
http://www.nepurs.com/purs/investigations/the_victorian.htm

East Coast Paranormal Research Team's website:
http://www.ecprt.com/

Harvest Moon Paranormal's website:
http://www.harvestmoonparanormalinvestigations.com/default.html

Alexandria Paranormal's website:
http://alexandriaparanormalinvestigations.org/

Beyond The Veil Paranormal Research's website:
http://beyondtheveilparanormal.org

Massachusetts Ghost Hunters Paranormal Research Society's website: http://www.mghparanormal.com/

Photography Links
The author would like to thank the talented photographers who shared their photos for the book. Prints of these photos can be ordered by contacting the photographers directly.

Frank Grace's Photos: http://trigphotography.smugmug.com/
Jason Baker's Photos: JasonBakerPhotography@hotmail.com

Resources

Worcester County Deeds and Records
Gardner Weekly News
   Saturday, December 11 1875
   Saturday, January 8, 1876
   Monday, January 13, 1902
The Gardner News
   August 20, 1945
   December 13, 1951
   May 29, 1962
   April 9, 1963
   February 3, 1967
   February 6, 1967November 1, 2003
   July 28, 2006
   July 23, 2008
   October 29, 2010
   November 1, 2010
   October 28, 2011
Gardner, Massachusetts 1870 Census , courtesy of the Levi Heywood Memorial Library
Gardner, Massachusetts 1880 Census , courtesy of the Levi Heywood Memorial Library
Gardner, Massachusetts 1900 Census , courtesy of the Levi Heywood Memorial Library
Gardner, Massachusetts 1910 Census , courtesy of the Levi Heywood Memorial Library
Aaron Greenwood's Diary, Volume XXVII, courtesy of the Levi Heywood Memorial Library
City of Gardner Property Summary Report, courtesy of the Levi Heywood Memorial Library
City of Gardner Public Records, Section 2244, page 501-503, courtesy of the Levi Heywood Memorial Library
City of Gardner Public Records, Section 2503, page 549-550, courtesy of the Levi Heywood Memorial Library
Commonwealth of Massachusetts Certificate of Death #126 for Eino Saari

Gardner: A Portrait of its Past, 1978, courtesy of the Levi Heywood Memorial Library
Worcester County Archives Military Records List of Enlistees for World War II
Paranormal Witness Tumblr.com
Travelchannel.com

Interviews

The author would like to thank the following people for granting interviews and providing their personal accounts and research of the S.K. Pierce Mansion:

Edwin Gonzalez and Lillian Otero, owners of the S.K. Pierce Mansion
Eleanor Gavazzi, historian and researcher
Marian King, historian and researcher
Pam Meitzler, Librarian at the Levi Heywood Memorial Library
Mark Veau, former owner of the S.K. Pierce Mansion
Thomas D'Agastino, author and paranormal investigator
Heather Anderson, psychic medium and paranormal investigator
Michael Cram, psychic medium, demonologist, and paranormal investigator
Marion Luoma, caretaker of the Victorian mansion
Tina Aube, paranormal investigator and co-caretaker of the Victorian mansion
Derek Cormier, paranormal investigator
William Wallace, empathic medium
Sara Christopher, empathic medium and paranormal investigator
Michael Robishaw, empathic medium and paranormal investigator
Kimberly Huertas, psychic medium and paranormal investigator
Sandy MacLeod, empathic medium and paranormal investigator
Jeff Bartley, paranormal investigator
Lucky Belicamino, empathic medium and paranormal investigator
Kayle Boyce, paranormal investigator
Barbara Williams, psychic medium and paranormal investigator

Carl Johnson, demonologist and paranormal investigator
Andrew Lake, author and paranormal investigator
Terri Harlow, paranormal investigator
Members of MGHPS: Marc Arvilla, Lauren Sheridan, Mike Galante, and Peter Lovasco
Lily Colon, paranormal enthusiast

Face on the wall in Lillian's office   Photo by Ryan Jones

Photographs

The S.K. Pierce mansion today

S.K. Pierce's furniture factory that once sat across the street

Famous guests of the Victorian mansion (top, P.T. Barnum, President Calvin Coolidge, and Norman Rockwell)

Stuart Pierce

Stuart Pierce in a Buick from his dealership

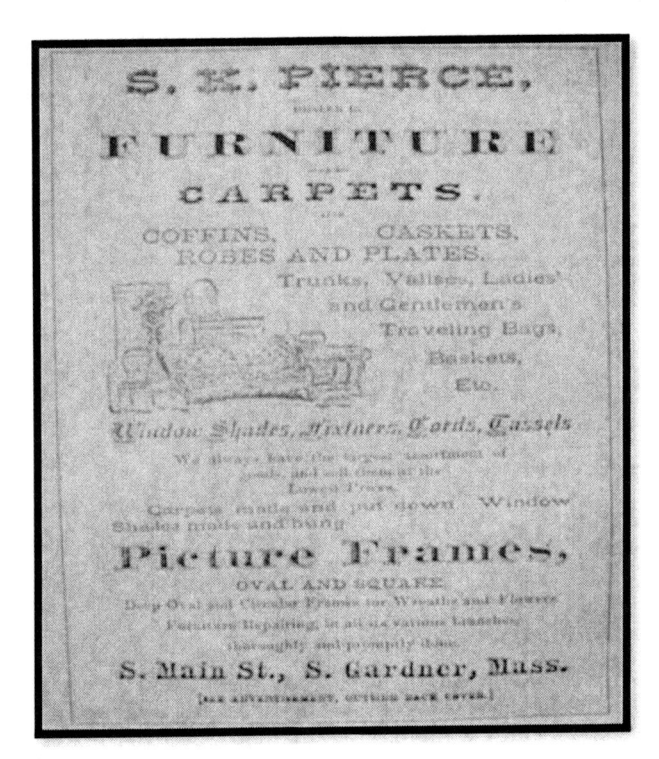

Ad for S.K. Pierce's furniture

Eino Saari's grave   Photo by Tina Aube

Woman ghost in the window. Photo courtesy of Conscious Spirit Paranormal

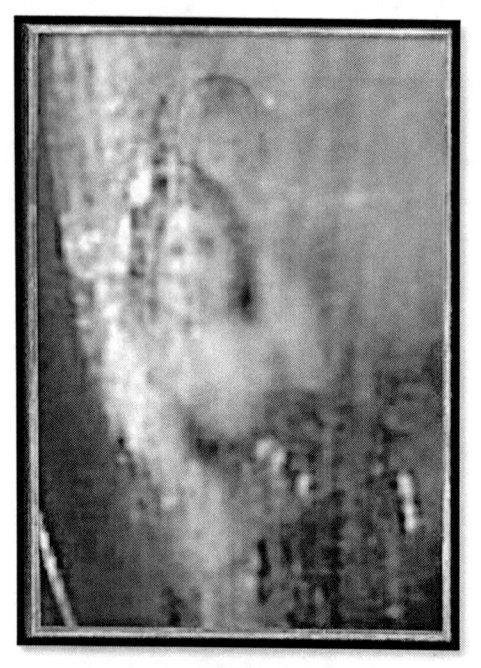

Woman and boy in the mirror. Photo courtesy of Boston Paranormal

Photo taken during the filming of the Ghost Adventures segment. Make-up being applied to the actor portraying Eino Saari.

Filming the ambulance scene at Broadway Pizza

Gardner Fire Department truck arriving for a recreation

Marion Luoma, Tina Aube, and Joni Mayhan, posing with Aaron Goodwin of the Ghost Adventures team prior to their lockdown investigation

Donna Landry, Joni, Marion, and Tina, with Ghost Adventures producer, Eric Paulen

Edwin with members of Ghost Adventures: Zak Bagans and Aaron Goodwin

Google Earth photos of the Victorian show a face looking out the library window, as well as a silhouette of a head in an upstairs window.

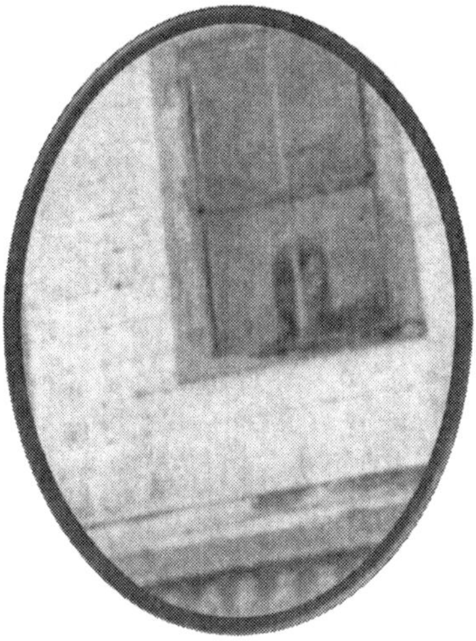

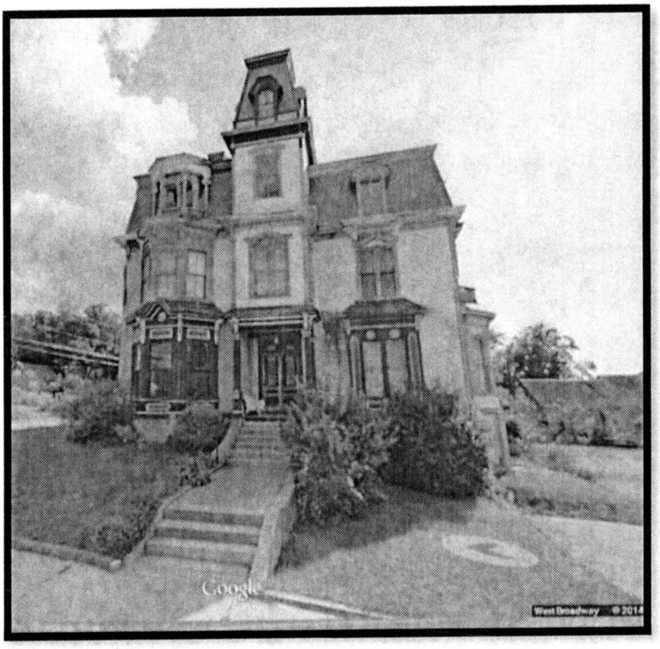
Google

About the author

Joni Mayhan is a paranormal investigator and author who lives in central Massachusetts. After surviving a horrific experience during a paranormal investigation, she went onto write *The Soul Collector*, which has become an Amazon.com top seller. Joni is currently working on her next book project. To learn more about the author, please check out her website: Jonimayhan.com or follow her paranormal blogs on Justjoniblog.com.

Please continue reading for a preview of Joni's paranormal true story The Soul Collector.

The Soul Collector

By

Joni Mayhan

Chapter 1

I was warned to never talk about him.

I was supposed to just walk away and forget the entire experience, totally erasing him from my memory. If I didn't, there was a very good chance he could come back to find me again. I held onto this story for several years, trying to follow their advice, but I just couldn't.

I needed to tell my story.

I wasn't in a very good place when he found me. I was at the end of a two-year relationship with someone I thought I would spend the rest of my life with, growing old together. When he walked away so suddenly, it left my whole life in shambles.

With my entire family living a thousand miles away, I didn't have anyone to turn to. I'm not the kind of person who cries to other people about her problems. I swallowed the pain whole, and then allowed it to consume me. It burrowed and spread, reaching into every cell of my being, leaving me nothing more than a shell.

I was forty-seven years old, living in a small house in the rural town of Barre, Massachusetts. I purchased the nine-hundred square foot ranch house after my divorce in 2005, hoping to find a place to rest before moving onto my happily-ever-after. Six years later, I was in the same place with no hope in sight.

After spending weeks locked inside my house with the curtains drawn, I finally decided to get out and do something.

People told me that staying busy was the best cure for a broken heart, so I tried.

A friend invited me to go ghost hunting. As it turns out, it was the worst thing I could have done. It brought me to the Soul Collector.

(Below: Joni investigating in the basement of one of her favorite haunted locations.

Chapter 2

I got into ghost hunting quite by accident.

I spent a solid three years after my divorce hiding out in my house. I didn't have any friends to speak of and had nowhere to go. Besides, people were hurtful and scary. I preferred spending the time with my pets or by myself, writing, reading, and watching movies.

Sometimes I feel like a hopeless cause. I've never been socially adept. Since grade school, I've had a difficult time interacting with my peers. Being small as a child, I was often picked on by schoolyard bullies. I didn't fare much better in high school. It seemed like every time I allowed myself to get close to someone, I ended up getting hurt. In the end, I decided it was better to just be alone and save myself the pain. It turned out to be a lonely decision that I would soon reconsider.

The one friend I retained into adulthood was actually an old high-school boyfriend who still lived in Indiana. Finding ourselves both single after years of marriage, we forged a long-distance friendship. John was the one who got me to come out of my shell. First, he talked me into setting up an online dating profile.

Initially, I was almost giddy with all the attention I was suddenly getting. After going for days without seeing another soul, I was being invited out onto dates with eligible men. John was doing the same thing back in Indiana and we started using one another as sounding boards.

"I need a woman's point of view," he'd say, then ask me a question. I'd offer my best advice, eventually helping him connect with his soon-to-be wife Melinda. I'd run situations and concerns past him for a man's point of view. We spent many long nights on the phone just chatting and helping each other through the hard times.

"You need to get out of your house," he told me one day. "Why don't you look into Meetup.com? Find something you like on there." He'd found a kayaking group there and enjoyed the occasional weekend outing with a group of people who shared his love of the water. He suggested I look into it to see if I could find a ghost hunting group, knowing how much I was into the paranormal.

While I had never investigated before, I was well versed on the subject. I'd spent the past few years amassing quite a collection of books on the paranormal. I read them from cover to cover, over and over again. I understood the difference between a residual haunting and an intelligent spirit. I was intrigued by the concept of EVPs, and even had my own digital recorder to record spirit voices. It was time to put my knowledge to work.

I took John's advice and quickly found a paranormal meet-up group. I signed up for their next event and waited eagerly for the day to arrive.

The first event was a wash out. The people who ran the event were a flaky bunch. They set up a meet-up at the Hoosic Tunnel in North Adams, Massachusetts.

Spanning over five miles, the tunnel snakes through the base of the Berkshire Mountains, cutting a path that was paved by bloodshed and death. People who dared enter it sometimes found themselves in the company of ghosts. Other people were smart enough not to walk several miles into a tunnel where an active train tunnel runs.

I had no doubt that the tunnel contained residual energy. The ground and stone have a tendency to absorb the vibrations from traumatic events in the past, replaying them like a movie, over and over again. A good example of this is Gettysburg. You can't walk out onto a battlefield without feeling the hair on the back of your neck prickle. It's as though Mother Earth is telling you, "Something happened here." People often see soldiers, or hear cannon fire, as history replays itself, but they seldom make contact with the apparitions.

While residual hauntings were interesting, making contact with an intelligent spirit was my overall goal. I had high hopes for the Hoosic Tunnel.

I brought my twenty-year-old daughter, Laura, with me to the event. We were both appropriately nervous about venturing inside. As we walked down the tracks leading to the tunnel, I could feel the anticipation rapidly turn to anxiety.

"What if a train comes?" I asked my daughter, eyeing the narrow space between the tracks and the stone walls. We might be able to press ourselves against the sides and hope for the best, but it sounded horrifically dangerous.

Laura shrugged. Suddenly, it didn't seem like such a great idea.

Several members of the meet-up group were gathered near the tunnel entrance. As we approached them, we could feel the air grow colder by several degrees.

"I'm glad to see you brought jackets," an older woman said to us. "It's quite a bit colder inside the tunnel," she said.

After quick introductions, we learned that she was the meet-up leader.

Something about her truly gave me the creeps. I wasn't sure if it was the way she looked, with her mop of unbrushed hair, or the way she was dressed in layers of skirts and shawls, accessorized by thick sandals with socks. It may have just been the wild look in her eyes that made me think of an escaped mental patient. Either way, she made me uncomfortable.

She had two other investigators with her. One was a younger woman who was the equipment expert. She walked around with an EMF meter in her hand. The other was a tall, thin man, who just stood back and watched.

"Are you getting anything?" I asked the younger woman.

"No. Nothing so far," she told me, showing me her EMF meter.

My daughter gave me a curious look, so I explained what an EMF meter does.

"It measures changes in the electro-magnetic field in an area. If a ghost comes close to us, we might see a spike in the reading," I told her. While I was anxious to have a paranormal experience, I hoped it would be a little more substantial than a blip on someone's meter.

I took my digital recorder out of my pocket and started recording, hoping for an EVP. I showed it to my daughter.

"When a ghost speaks to us, we usually can't hear them. But, if you are recording it with a digital recorder, you might record their response. It's called an EVP: electronic voice phenomena."

I asked a few questions, and then listened to the audio, hearing nothing but silence. I was disappointed, but was still hopeful. If we tried it again inside the tunnel, we might have better results.

We lingered near the entrance for several minutes. The others were milling around, talking. I was ready to go inside and get started. "Are we going in?" I finally asked.

The leader turned to look at me, her face frozen with fright. "No. I can't go in there. This place is sheer evil," she said, hopefully not noticing when I rolled my eyes.

"So, what are we going to do?" I asked, growing appropriately agitated. We paid ten dollars apiece for the experience, but we weren't going in?

"You can go in, if you want to," the leader said. "But, I'm staying right here." Her team members stuck to her side, refusing to budge as well.

I sighed and looked around, wondering what to do. It was a beautiful blue-sky day in early May. The leaves were just popping out on the trees, and the air was filled with the sweet scent of spring. We'd driven nearly two hours to be there. It seemed a shame to waste the trip only to just turn around and leave.

I turned to my daughter. "Wanna go in a little ways?" I asked.

"Might as well," she said, without much enthusiasm.

We'd spent thirteen years living in a haunted house. While we were both curious about the paranormal, we were both a little apprehensive. Sometimes opening a door to something brings you closer than you anticipated.

I'd read that ghosts often drained the batteries on your equipment, so I was well prepared for the walk. I'd put fresh batteries into four flashlights. I gave two to my daughter and kept the other two for myself. There was no way I was going to be submerged in the darkness with no light. It just wasn't going to happen.

As we were getting ready to walk in, three men joined us at the mouth of the tunnel. The oldest man was obviously the father of one of the younger men. They wanted to check out the tunnel but didn't have a flashlight. Not really thinking, I offered to let them follow us.

I should preface this with the fact that I am a little too trusting of others, at least at first. Sometimes my common sense takes a backseat to my willingness to please. It's a fault I will find myself making over and over in my life.

I walked in first, with my daughter behind me, and the three men trailing along behind us.

The tunnel was eerie. The minute we walked inside, the darkness quickly enveloped us with cold, damp fingers. I shined my light around, trying to get a feel for the place.

The tall, curved ceilings were lined with bricks. Many of the bricks had fallen, which was evident from the broken shards at our feet. Graffiti graced nearly every wall like strange artwork.

The tracks were difficult to walk on and water dripped from the ceilings, creating echoes through the tunnel. After walking for ten minutes, we were deep in the heart of the mountain. I turned around, surprised to find the tunnel opening no more than a tiny circle, floating in the darkness behind us.

It suddenly occurred to me what I was doing. I willingly led my beautiful daughter into a dark tunnel with three men I didn't know. While they seemed normal, I had no idea of their intent. My active imagination went into overdrive. What if they were bad men? I didn't think that serial killers usually hunted in packs, but who really knew?

"Ummm....you guys aren't serial killers," I said, trying to make it sound like a joke.

There was a long silence before one of the men finally spoke.

"I guess it's a little late to be asking that question, isn't it?" one of them said. He had a smile in his voice when he said it, but my discomfort level was already rising into the red zone.

"Let's turn around," I suggested, praying they wouldn't take that moment to reveal some evil personalities.

Forgetting all about my desire to do another EVP session, we turned around and made our way out of the tunnel in record time. Thankfully, the men were nothing more than true gentlemen and we parted ways at the mouth of the tunnel. I just stood there as they walked back towards the parking lot, feeling very foolish.

"What a stupid thing to do," I whispered to my daughter. I was so angry with myself for putting her in possible danger. If a train didn't run us over, the strangers could have turned out to be something other than just nice, ordinary men. What kind of mother was I?

I didn't have long to berate myself, because the meet-up leader was quickly approaching.

"Did you feel anything?" she asked, wide-eyed.

I was embarrassed she was even asking me. Admitting that I *did* or *didn't* feel something felt like social suicide. What if someone heard us? They'd think I was just as crazy as she was.

Honestly, the only thing I felt was the sense of intrigue followed by the rush of overwhelming fear. I wasn't afraid of ghosts. I was afraid of the men walking behind us and the situation I'd put us in. We nearly ran back to the car.

It would be several years later before I'd try it again.

The Soul Collector is available on Amazon.com and on Barnesandnoble.com in paperback and E-book format.